MARK WAID · DAMIAN COUCEIRO

INCORRUPTIBLE

VOLUME 7

ROSS RICHIE Chief Executive Officer • MATT GAGNON Editor-in-Chief • WES HARRIS VP-Publishing • LANCE KREITER VP-Licensing & Merchandising • PHIL BARBARO Director of Finance
BRYCE CARLSON Managing Editor • DAFNA PLEBAN Editor • SHANNON WATTERS Editor • ERIC HARBURN Assistant Editor • ADAM STAFFARONI Assistant Editor • CHRIS ROSA Assistant Editor
STEPHANIE GONZAGA Graphic Designer • CAROL THOMPSON Production Designer • JASMINE AMIRI Operations Coordinator • DEVIN FUNCHES Marketing & Sales Assistant

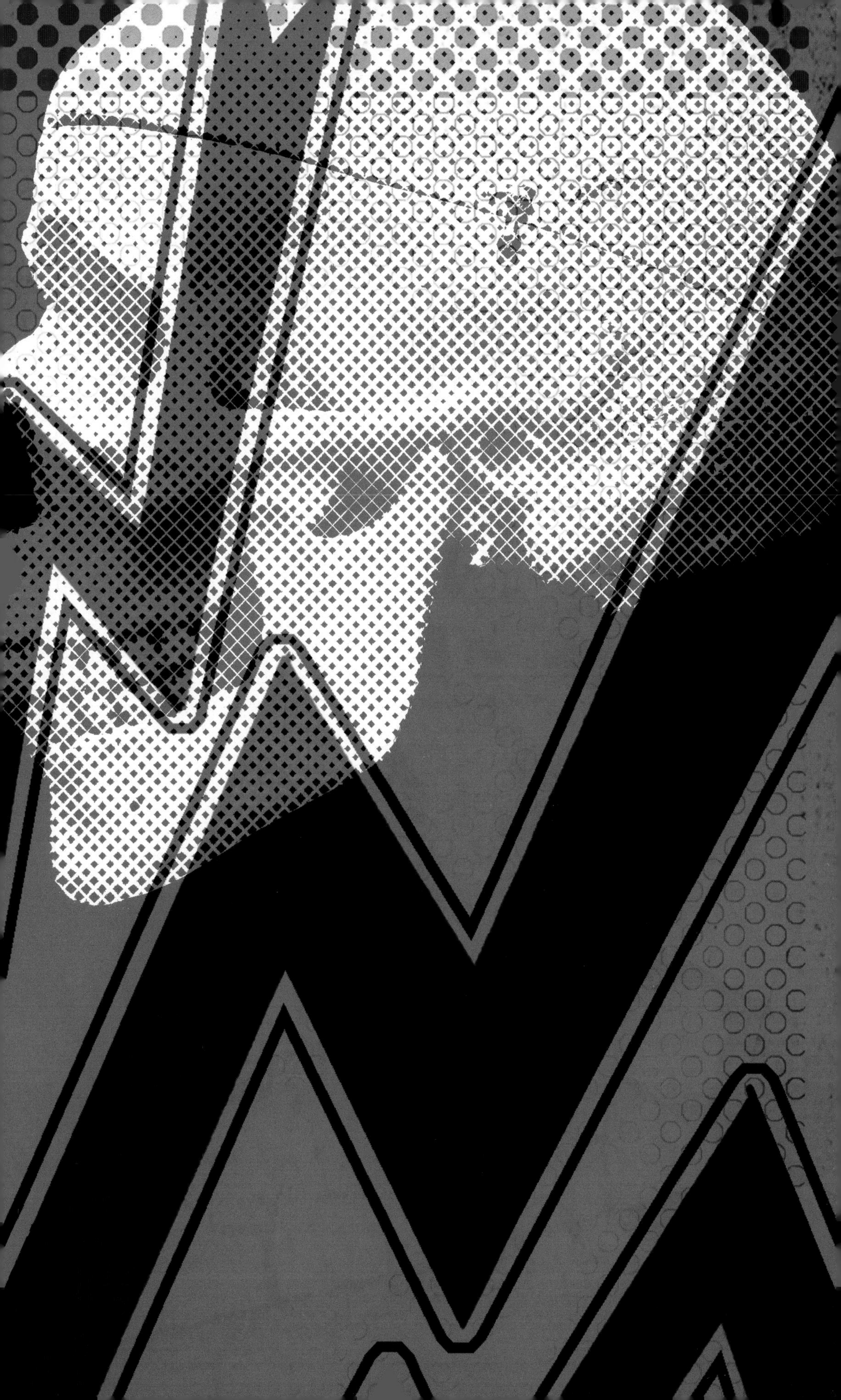

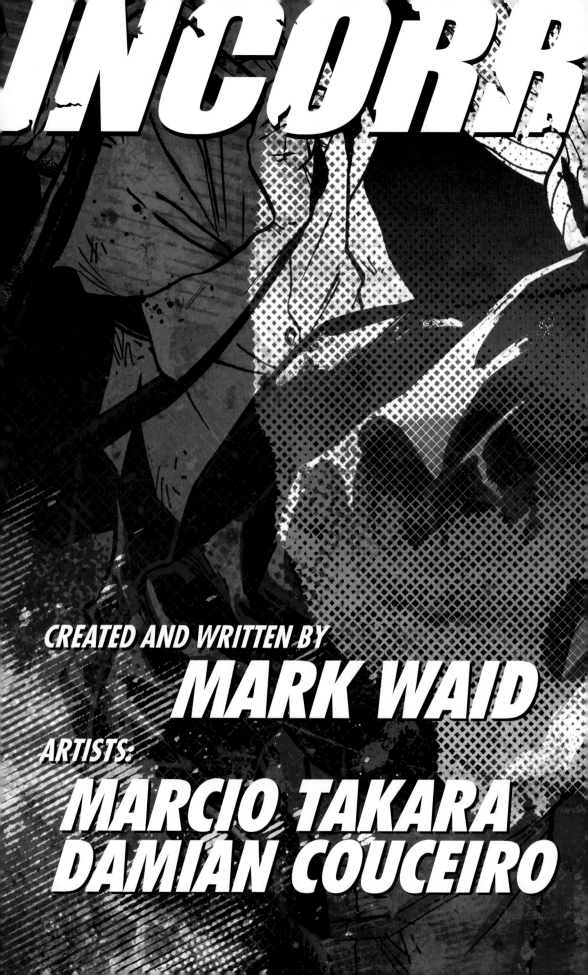

INCORR

CREATED AND WRITTEN BY

MARK WAID

ARTISTS:

MARCIO TAKARA
DAMIAN COUCEIRO

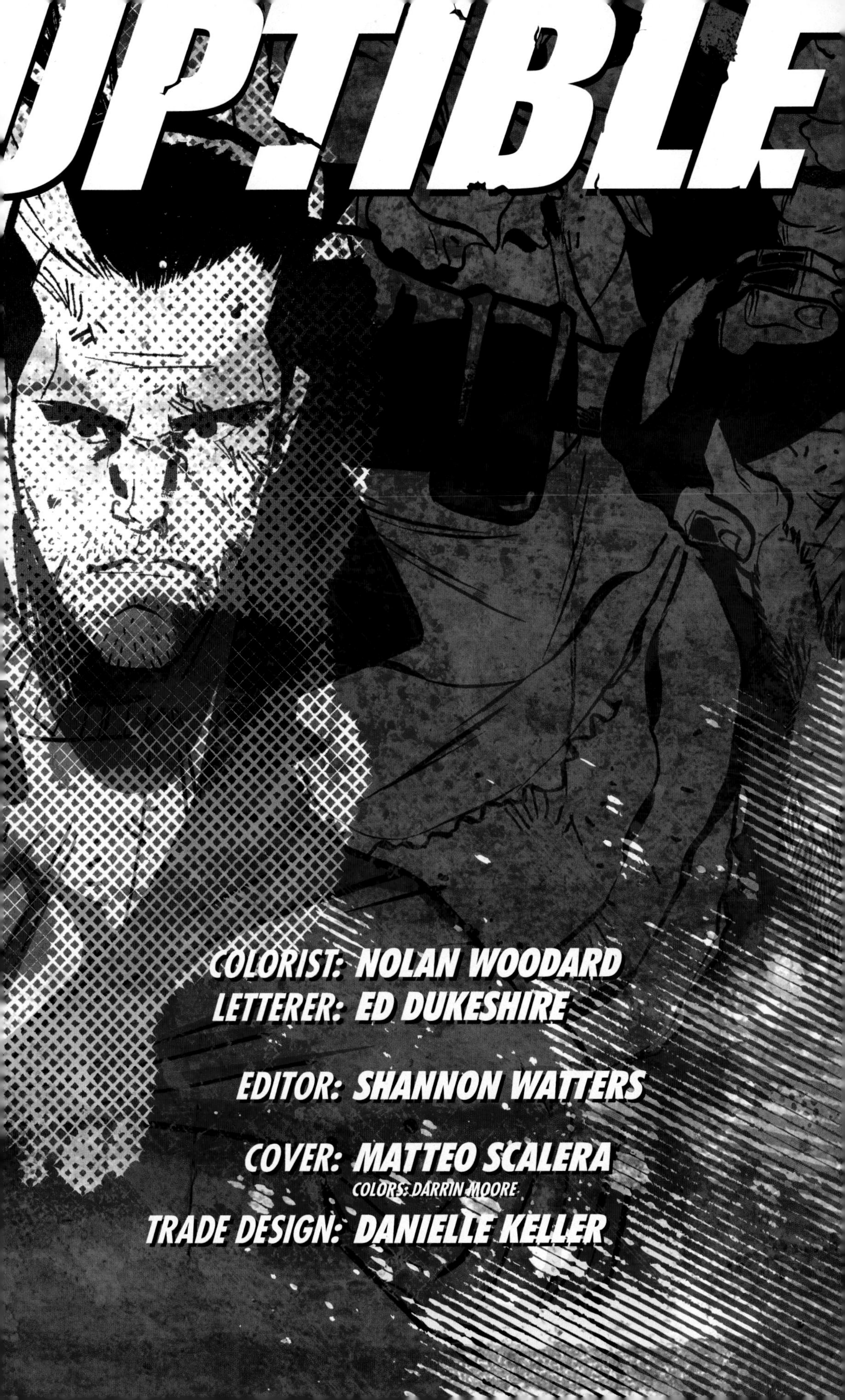

COLORIST: NOLAN WOODARD
LETTERER: ED DUKESHIRE

EDITOR: SHANNON WATTERS

COVER: MATTEO SCALERA
COLORS: DARRIN MOORE
TRADE DESIGN: DANIELLE KELLER

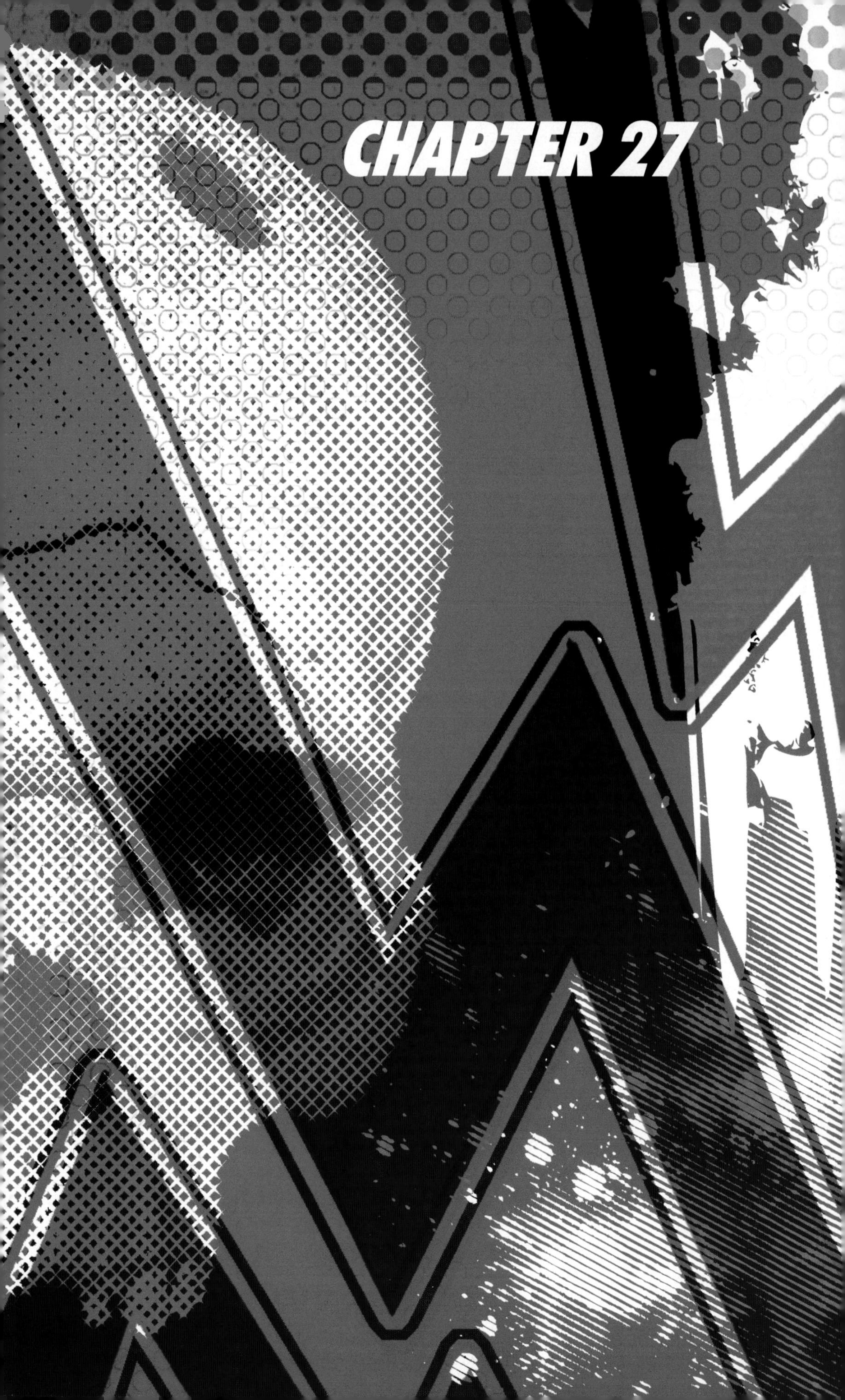
CHAPTER 27

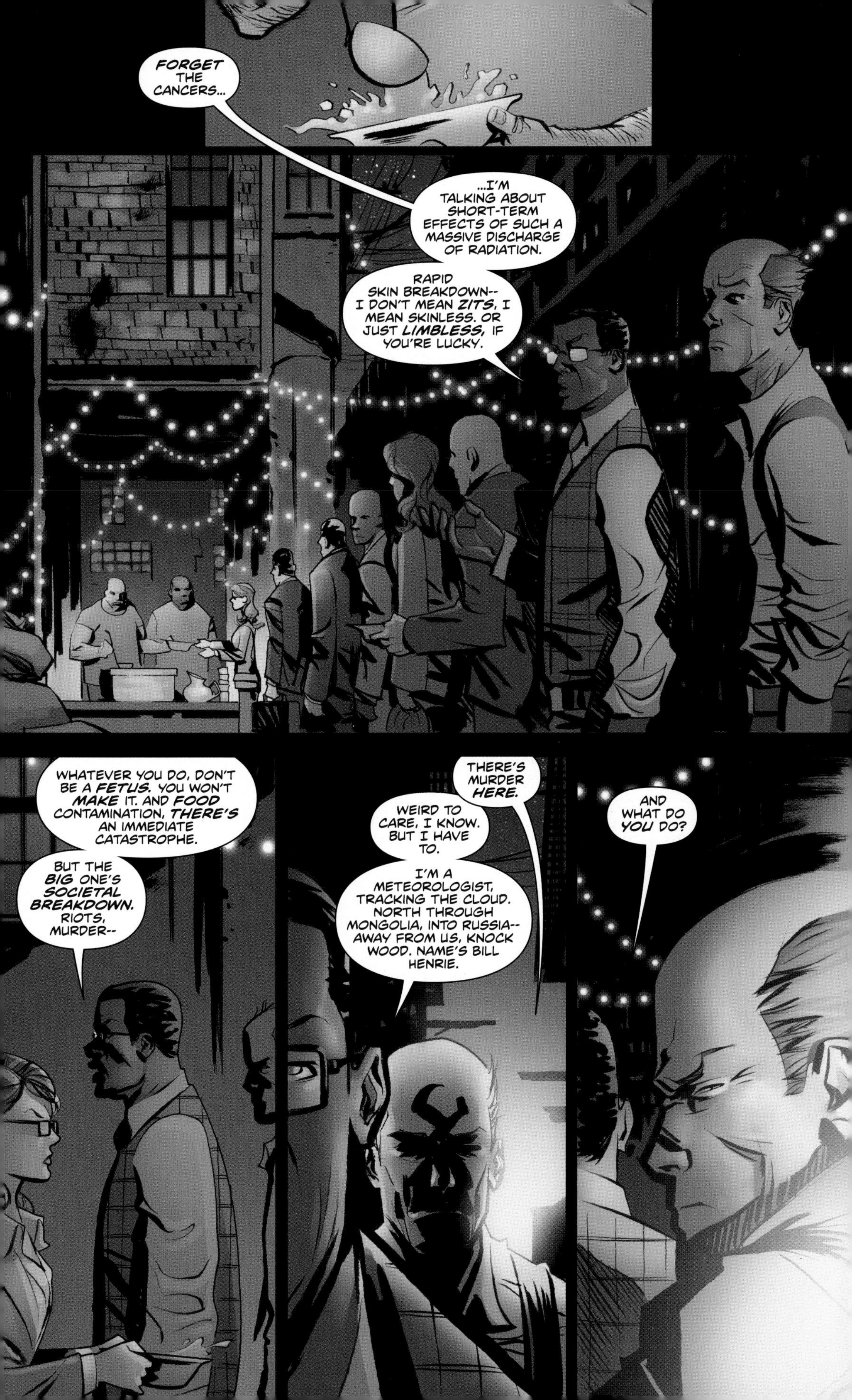
FORGET THE CANCERS...
...I'M TALKING ABOUT SHORT-TERM EFFECTS OF SUCH A MASSIVE DISCHARGE OF RADIATION.
RAPID SKIN BREAKDOWN-- I DON'T MEAN ZITS, I MEAN SKINLESS. OR JUST LIMBLESS, IF YOU'RE LUCKY.
WHATEVER YOU DO, DON'T BE A FETUS. YOU WON'T MAKE IT. AND FOOD CONTAMINATION, THERE'S AN IMMEDIATE CATASTROPHE.
BUT THE BIG ONE'S SOCIETAL BREAKDOWN. RIOTS, MURDER--
THERE'S MURDER HERE.
WEIRD TO CARE, I KNOW. BUT I HAVE TO.
I'M A METEOROLOGIST, TRACKING THE CLOUD. NORTH THROUGH MONGOLIA, INTO RUSSIA-- AWAY FROM US, KNOCK WOOD. NAME'S BILL HENRIE.
AND WHAT DO YOU DO?

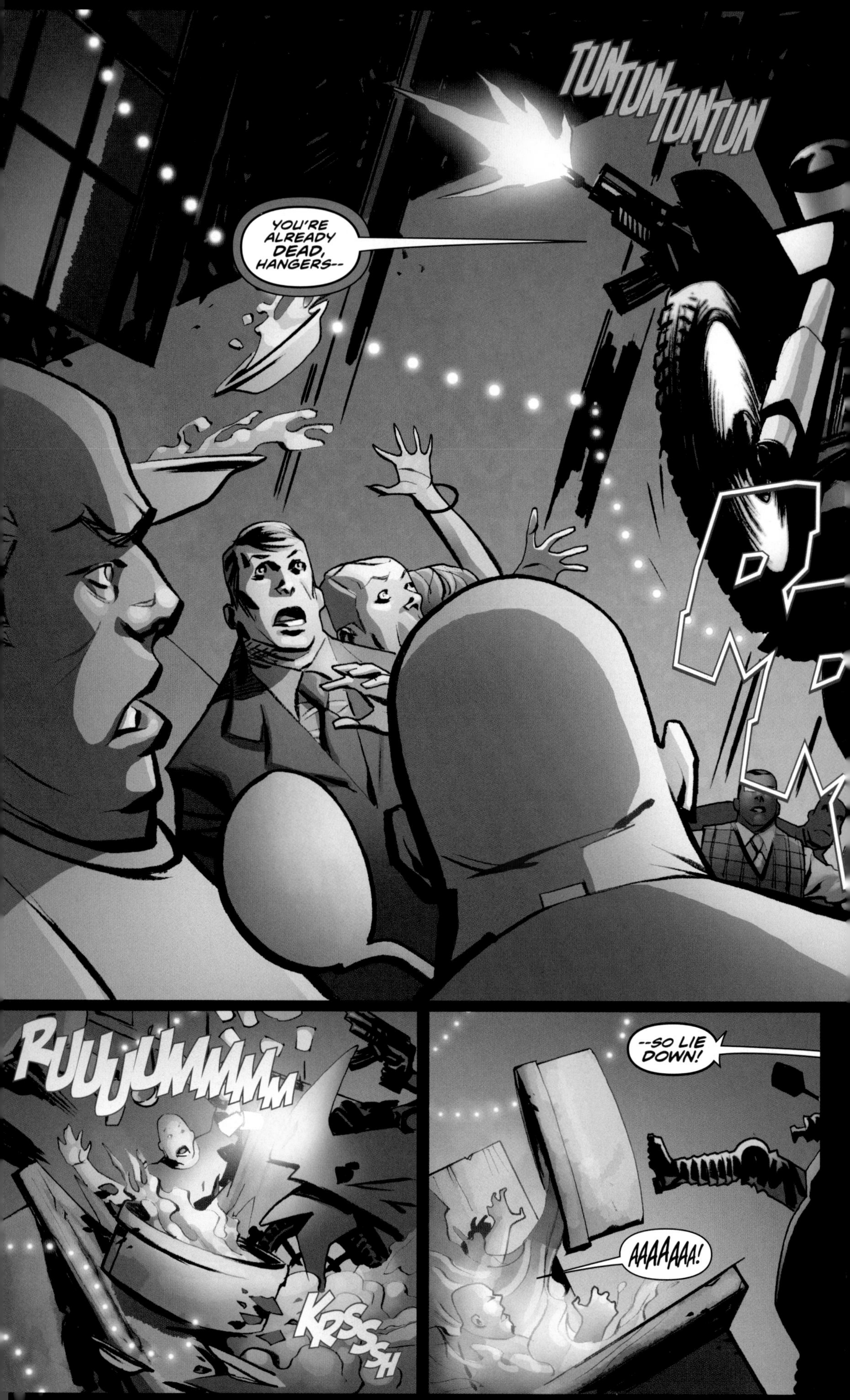
TUNTUNTUNTUN
YOU'RE ALREADY DEAD, HANGERS--
RUUUUMMMMM
KRSSSH
--SO LIE DOWN!
AAAAAAA!

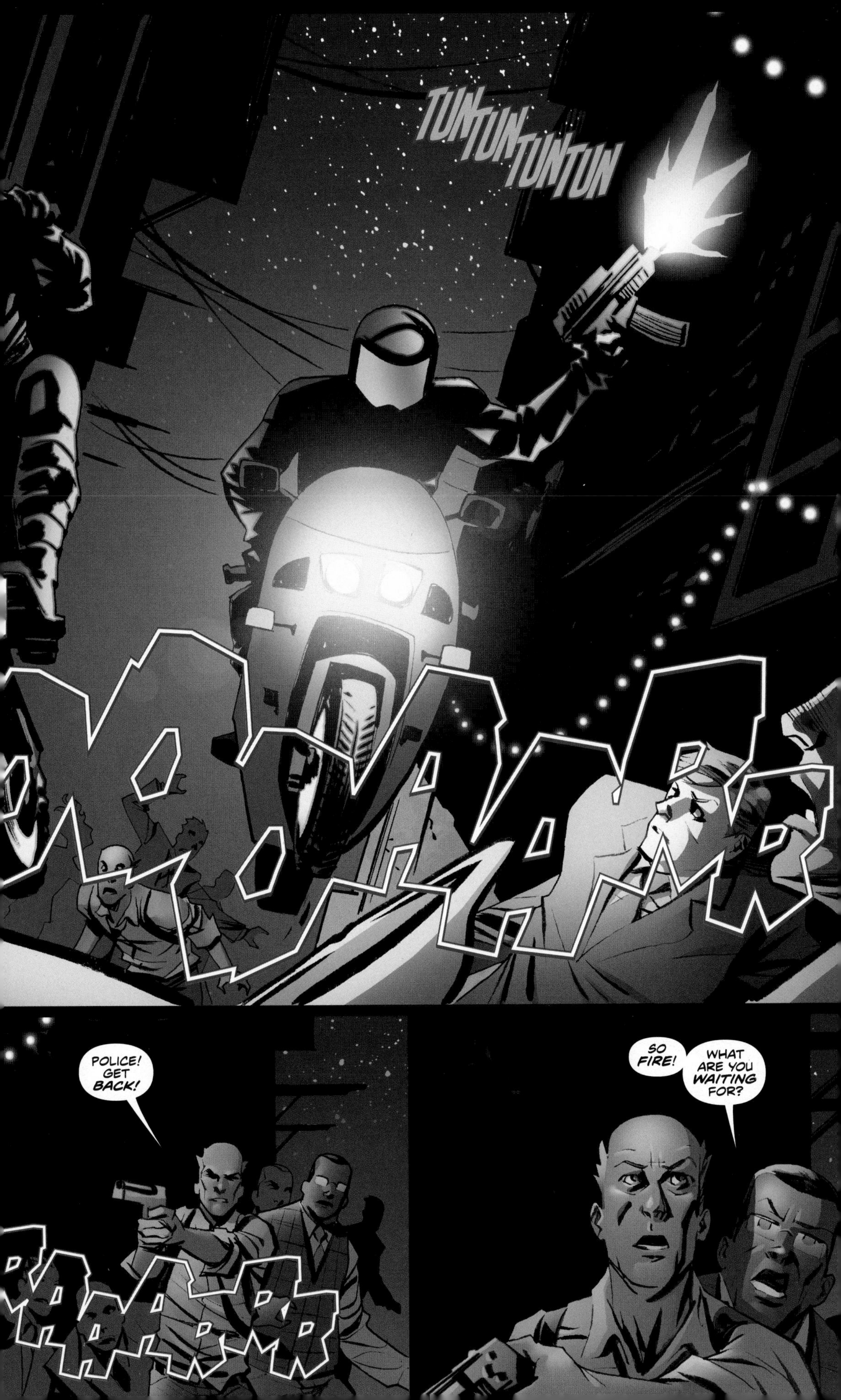
TUNTUNTUNTUN
POLICE! GET BACK!
SO FIRE!
WHAT ARE YOU WAITING FOR?

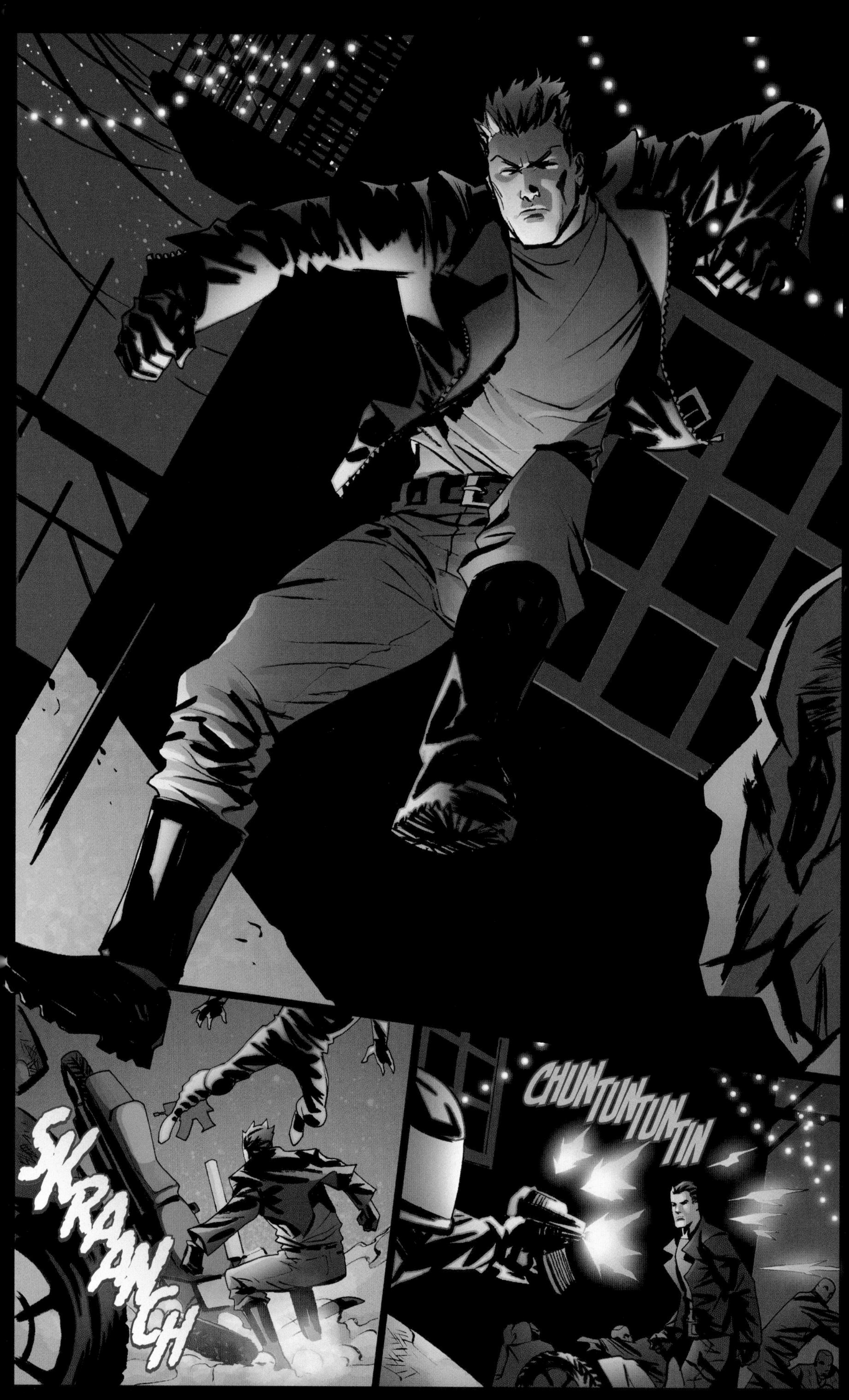
SKRANCH
CHUN TUN TUN TUN TIN

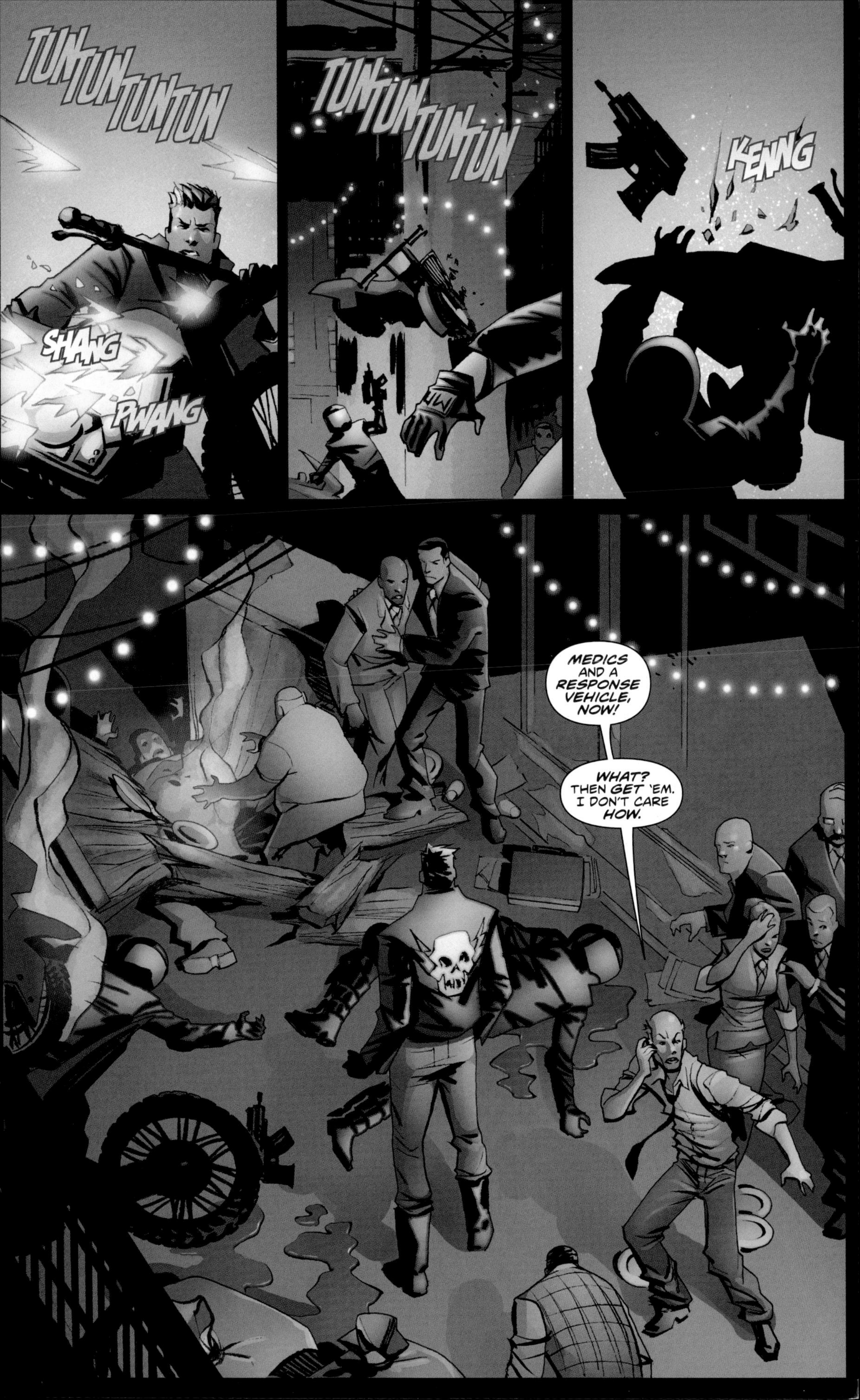
TUNTUNTUNTUN
SHANG
PWANG
TUNTUNTUNTUN
KENNG
MEDICS AND A RESPONSE VEHICLE, NOW!
WHAT? THEN GET 'EM. I DON'T CARE HOW.

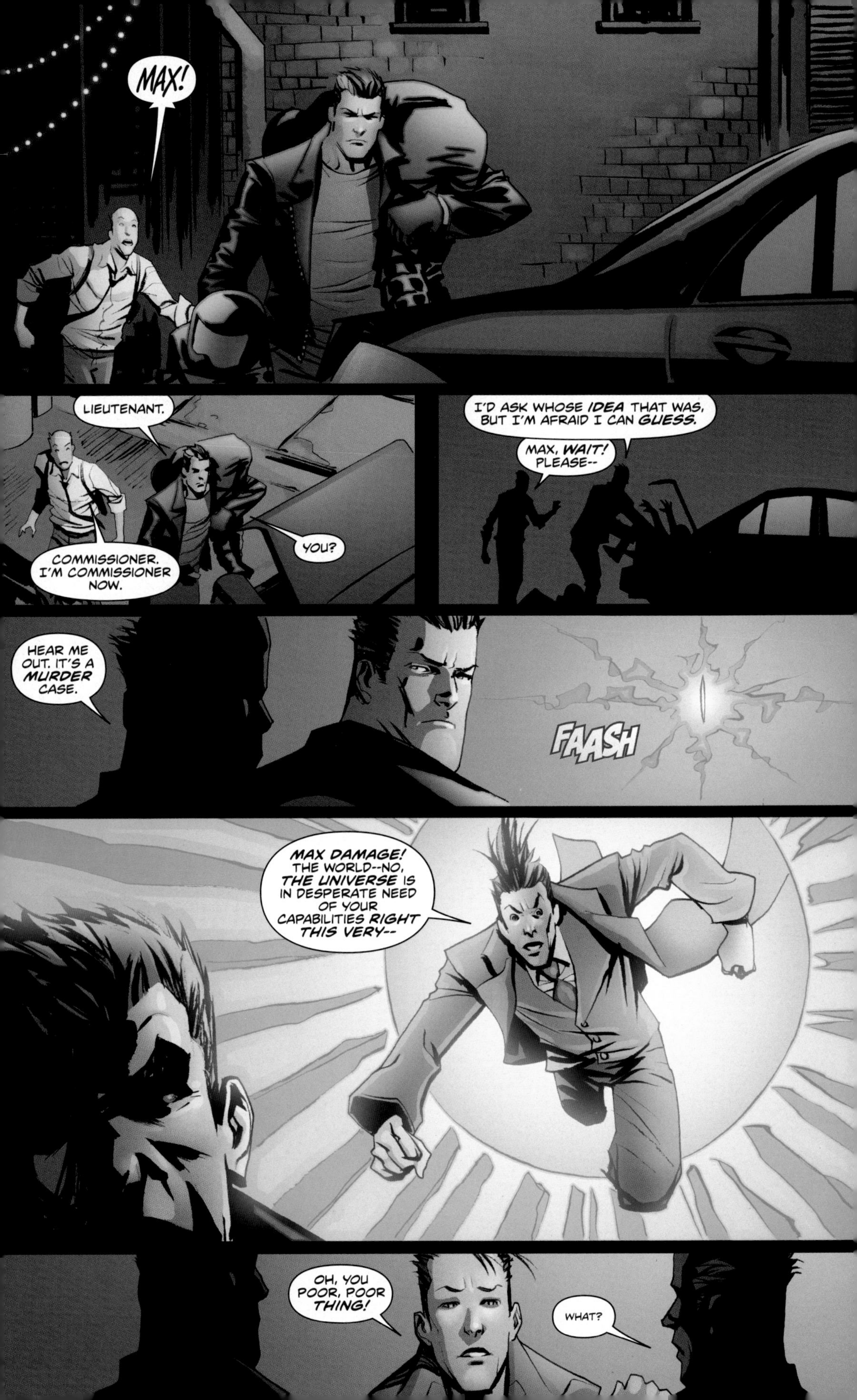
MAX!
LIEUTENANT.
COMMISSIONER. I'M COMMISSIONER NOW.
YOU?
I'D ASK WHOSE IDEA THAT WAS, BUT I'M AFRAID I CAN GUESS.
MAX, WAIT! PLEASE--
HEAR ME OUT. IT'S A MURDER CASE.
FAASH
MAX DAMAGE! THE WORLD--NO, THE UNIVERSE IS IN DESPERATE NEED OF YOUR CAPABILITIES RIGHT THIS VERY--
OH, YOU POOR, POOR THING!
WHAT?

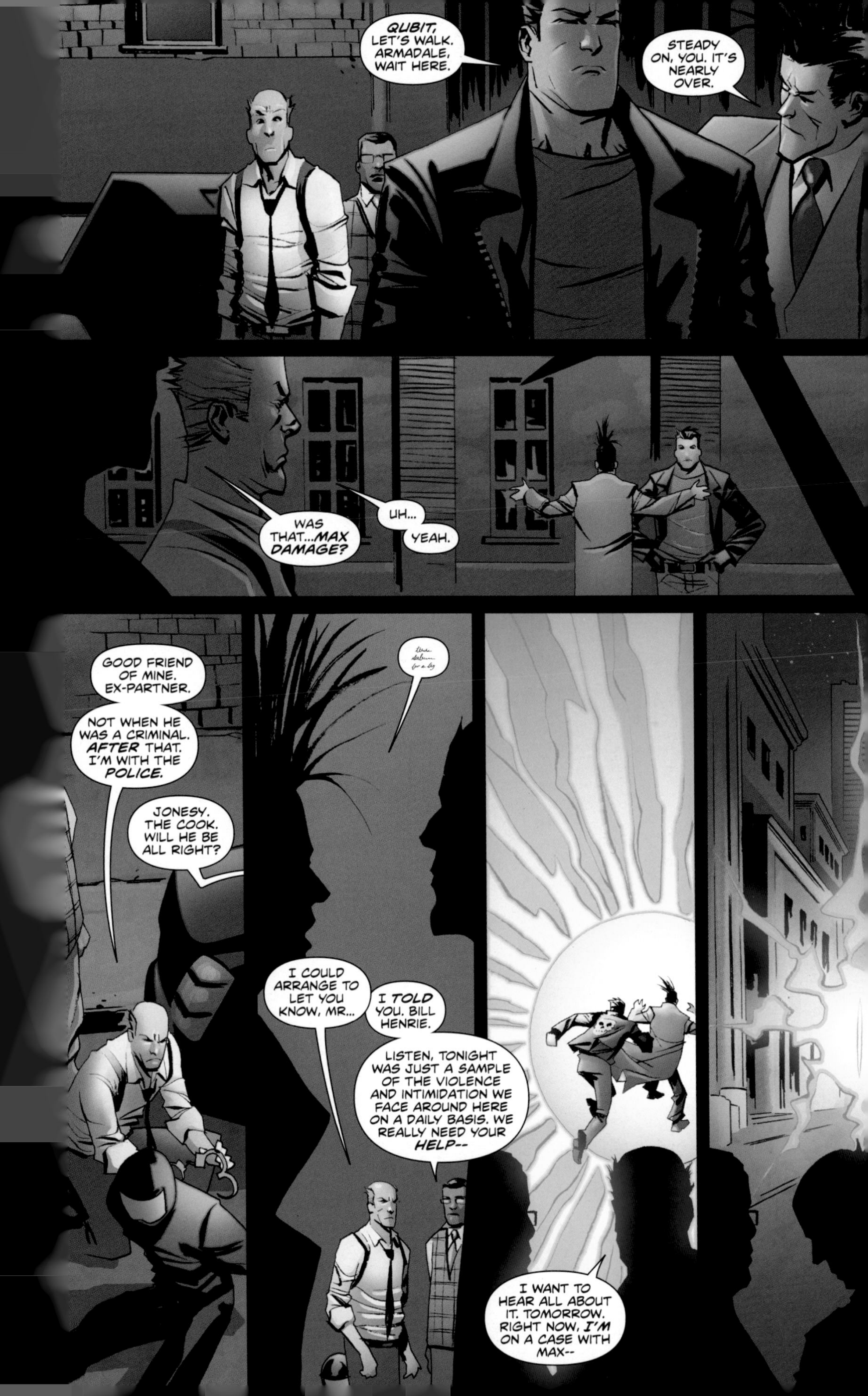
QUBIT, LET'S WALK. ARMADALE, WAIT HERE.
STEADY ON, YOU. IT'S NEARLY OVER.
WAS THAT...MAX DAMAGE?
UH...
YEAH.
GOOD FRIEND OF MINE. EX-PARTNER.
NOT WHEN HE WAS A CRIMINAL. AFTER THAT. I'M WITH THE POLICE.
JONESY. THE COOK. WILL HE BE ALL RIGHT?
I COULD ARRANGE TO LET YOU KNOW, MR...
I TOLD YOU. BILL HENRIE.
LISTEN, TONIGHT WAS JUST A SAMPLE OF THE VIOLENCE AND INTIMIDATION WE FACE AROUND HERE ON A DAILY BASIS. WE REALLY NEED YOUR HELP--
I WANT TO HEAR ALL ABOUT IT. TOMORROW. RIGHT NOW, I'M ON A CASE WITH MAX--

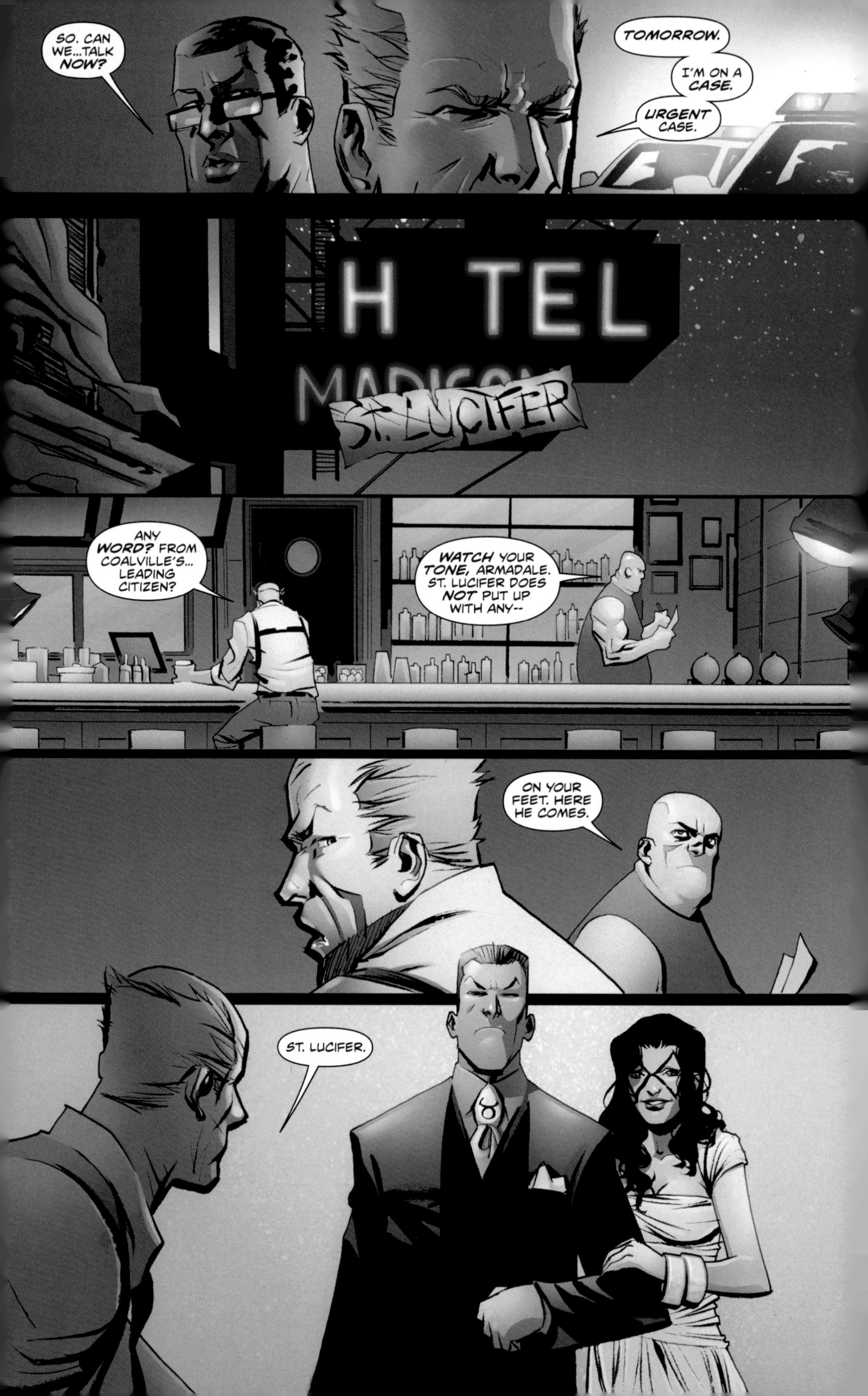
SO. CAN WE...TALK NOW?
TOMORROW.
I'M ON A CASE.
URGENT CASE.
H TEL
ST. LUCIFER
ANY WORD? FROM COALVILLE'S... LEADING CITIZEN?
WATCH YOUR TONE, ARMADALE. ST. LUCIFER DOES NOT PUT UP WITH ANY--
ON YOUR FEET. HERE HE COMES.
ST. LUCIFER.

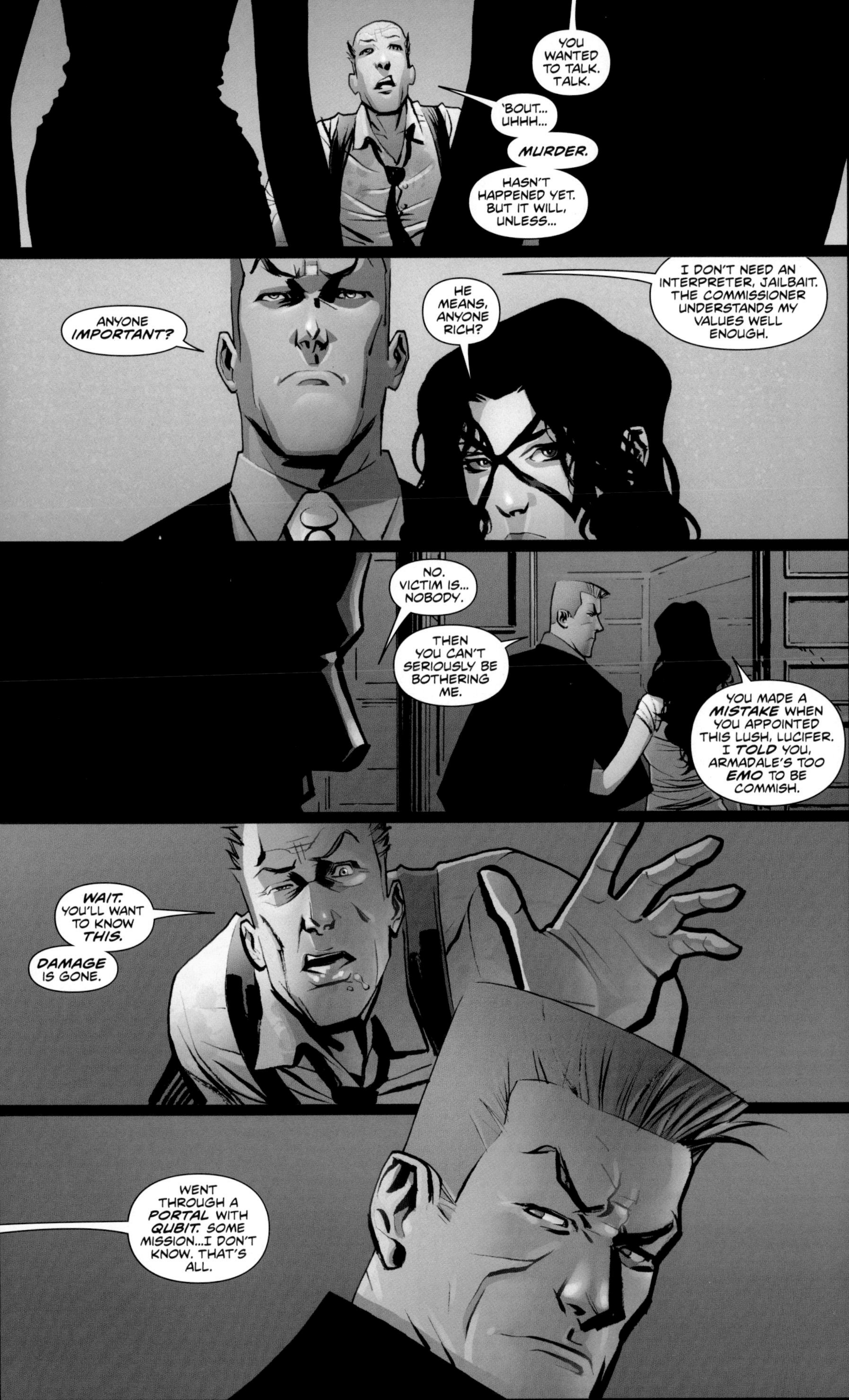
YOU WANTED TO TALK. TALK.
'BOUT... UHHH...
MURDER.
HASN'T HAPPENED YET. BUT IT WILL, UNLESS...
ANYONE IMPORTANT?
HE MEANS, ANYONE RICH?
I DON'T NEED AN INTERPRETER, JAILBAIT. THE COMMISSIONER UNDERSTANDS MY VALUES WELL ENOUGH.
NO. VICTIM IS... NOBODY.
THEN YOU CAN'T SERIOUSLY BE BOTHERING ME.
YOU MADE A MISTAKE WHEN YOU APPOINTED THIS LUSH, LUCIFER. I TOLD YOU, ARMADALE'S TOO EMO TO BE COMMISH.
WAIT. YOU'LL WANT TO KNOW THIS.
DAMAGE IS GONE.
WENT THROUGH A PORTAL WITH QUBIT. SOME MISSION...I DON'T KNOW. THAT'S ALL.

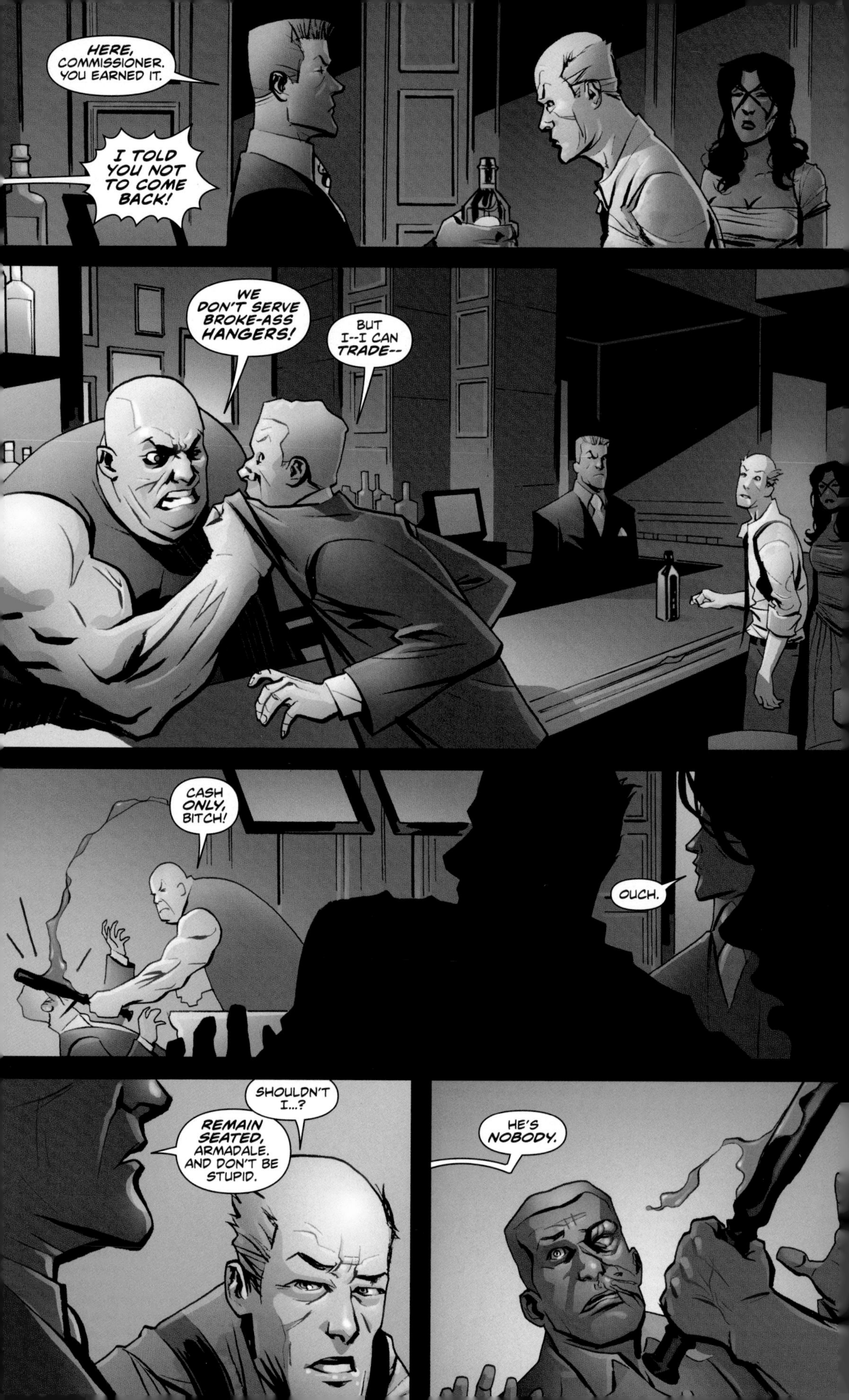
HERE, COMMISSIONER. YOU EARNED IT.
I TOLD YOU NOT TO COME BACK!
WE DON'T SERVE BROKE-ASS HANGERS!
BUT I--I CAN TRADE--
CASH ONLY, BITCH!
OUCH.
SHOULDN'T I...?
REMAIN SEATED, ARMADALE. AND DON'T BE STUPID.
HE'S NOBODY.

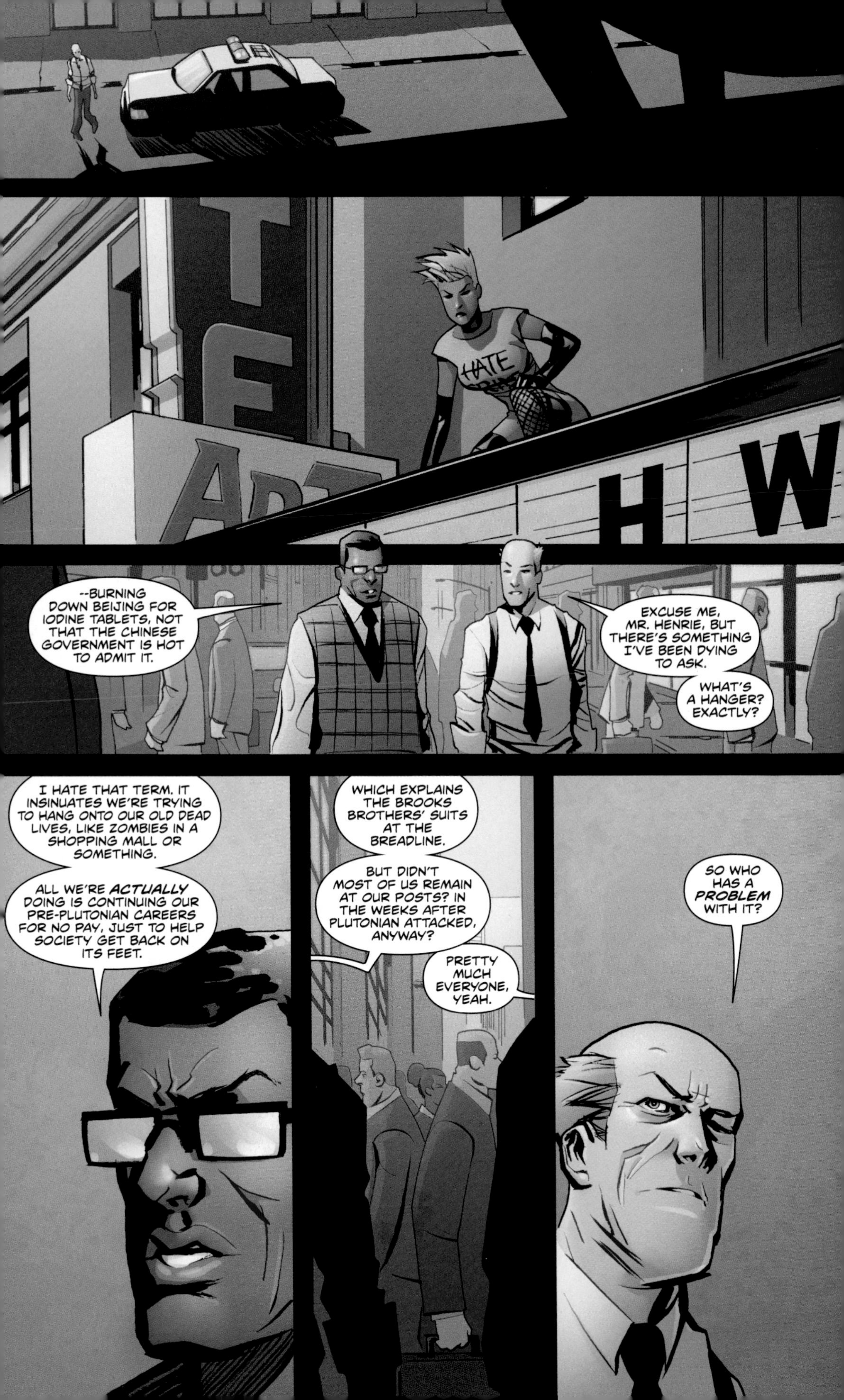
--BURNING DOWN BEIJING FOR IODINE TABLETS, NOT THAT THE CHINESE GOVERNMENT IS HOT TO ADMIT IT.
EXCUSE ME, MR. HENRIE, BUT THERE'S SOMETHING I'VE BEEN DYING TO ASK.
WHAT'S A HANGER? EXACTLY?
I HATE THAT TERM. IT INSINUATES WE'RE TRYING TO HANG ONTO OUR OLD DEAD LIVES, LIKE ZOMBIES IN A SHOPPING MALL OR SOMETHING.
ALL WE'RE *ACTUALLY* DOING IS CONTINUING OUR PRE-PLUTONIAN CAREERS FOR NO PAY, JUST TO HELP SOCIETY GET BACK ON ITS FEET.
WHICH EXPLAINS THE BROOKS BROTHERS' SUITS AT THE BREADLINE.
BUT DIDN'T MOST OF US REMAIN AT OUR POSTS? IN THE WEEKS AFTER PLUTONIAN ATTACKED, ANYWAY?
PRETTY MUCH EVERYONE, YEAH.
SO WHO HAS A *PROBLEM* WITH IT?

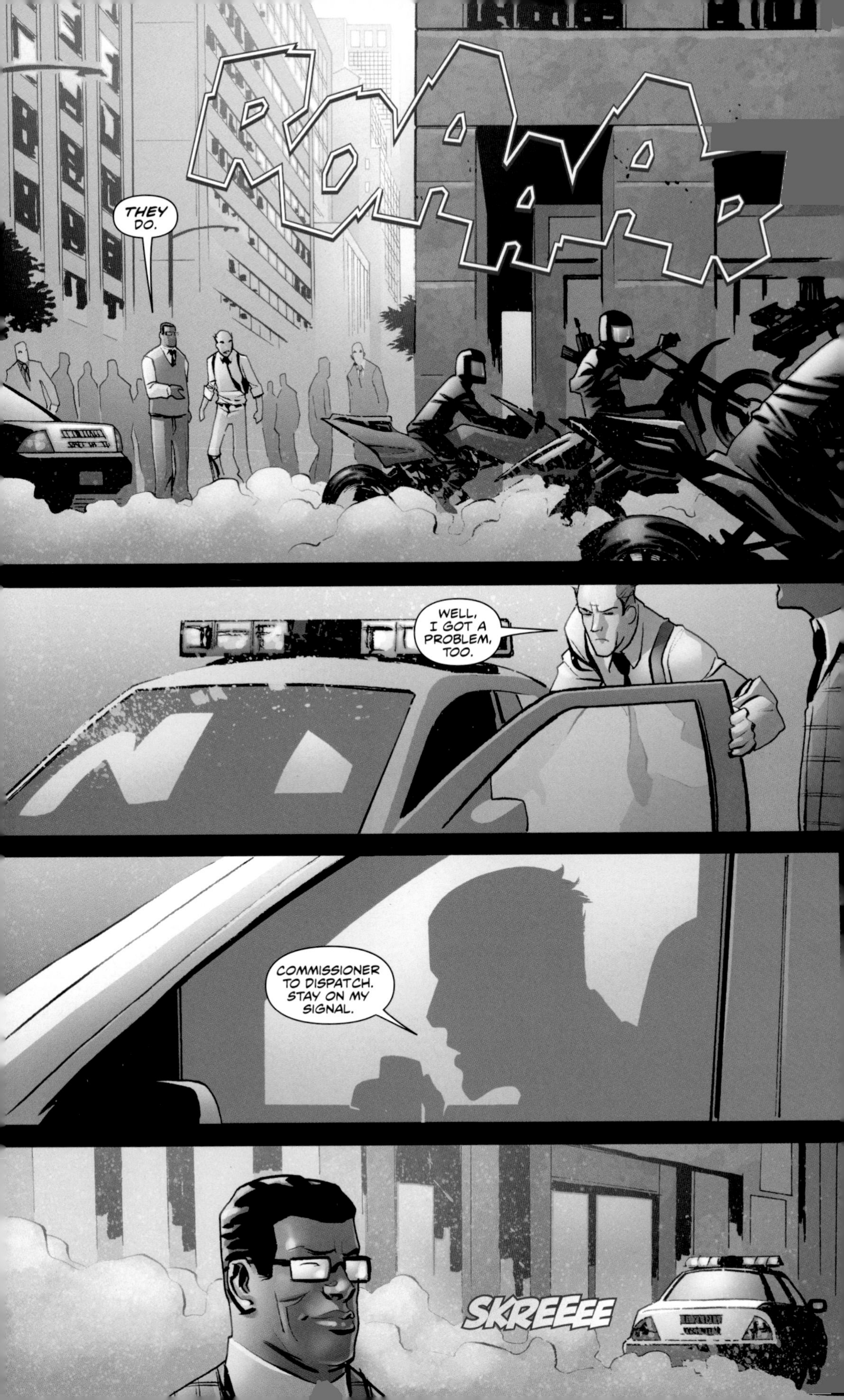
ROOAAAR
THEY DO.
WELL, I GOT A PROBLEM, TOO.
COMMISSIONER TO DISPATCH. STAY ON MY SIGNAL.
SKREEEEE

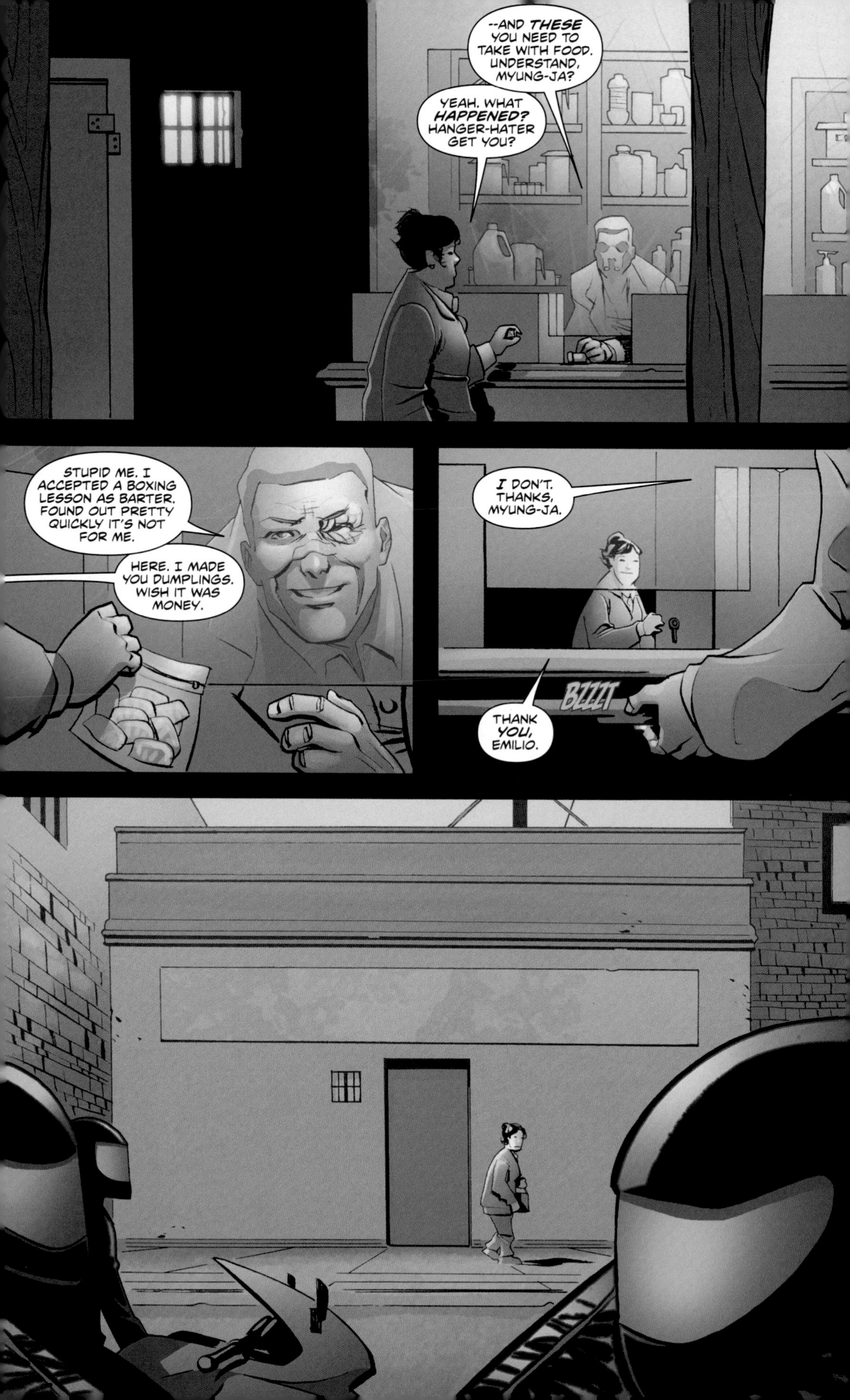

--AND THESE YOU NEED TO TAKE WITH FOOD. UNDERSTAND, MYUNG-JA?
YEAH. WHAT HAPPENED? HANGER-HATER GET YOU?
STUPID ME. I ACCEPTED A BOXING LESSON AS BARTER. FOUND OUT PRETTY QUICKLY IT'S NOT FOR ME.
HERE. I MADE YOU DUMPLINGS. WISH IT WAS MONEY.
I DON'T. THANKS, MYUNG-JA.
BZZZT
THANK YOU, EMILIO.

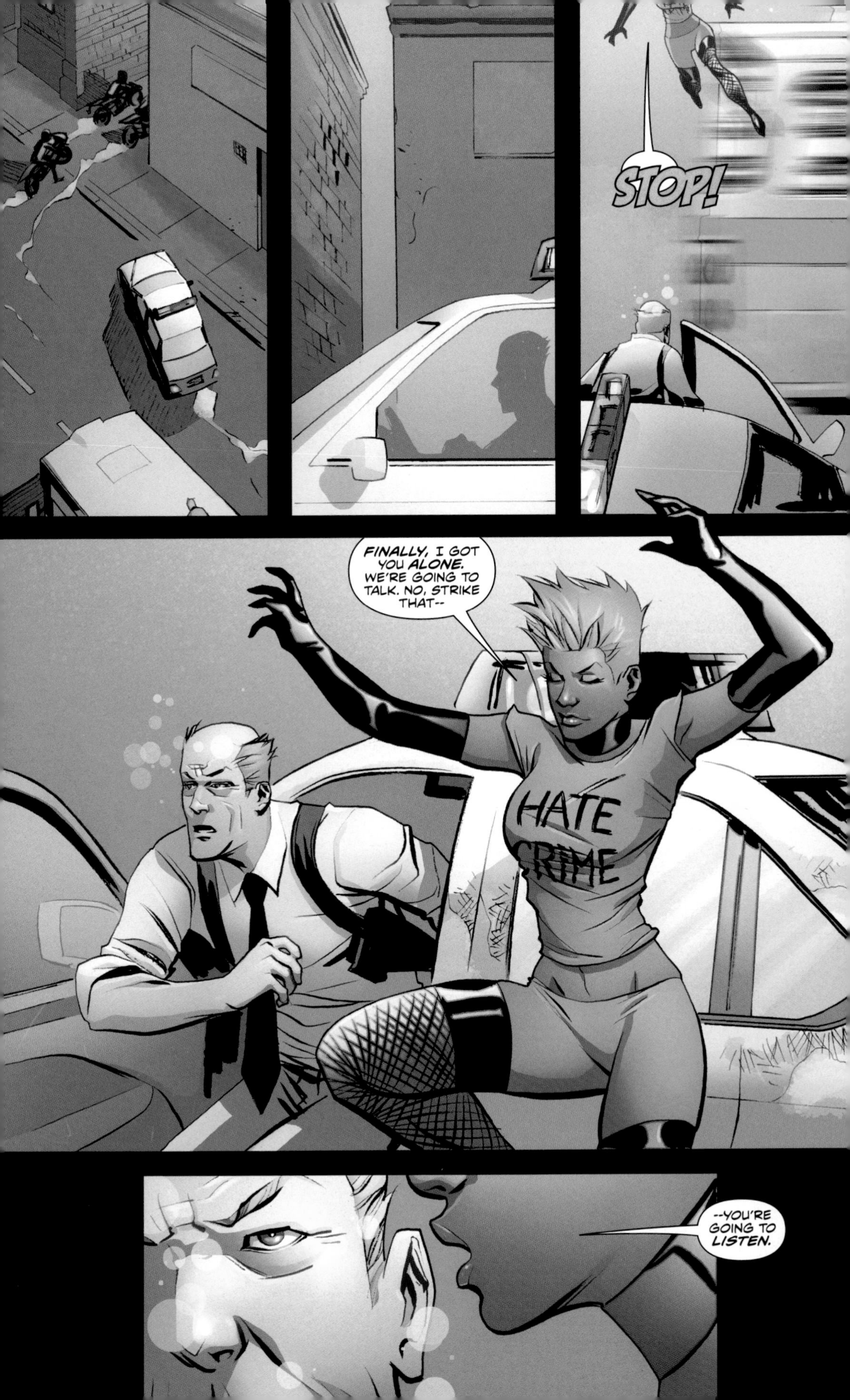
STOP!
FINALLY, I GOT YOU ALONE. WE'RE GOING TO TALK. NO, STRIKE THAT--
HATE CRIME
--YOU'RE GOING TO LISTEN.

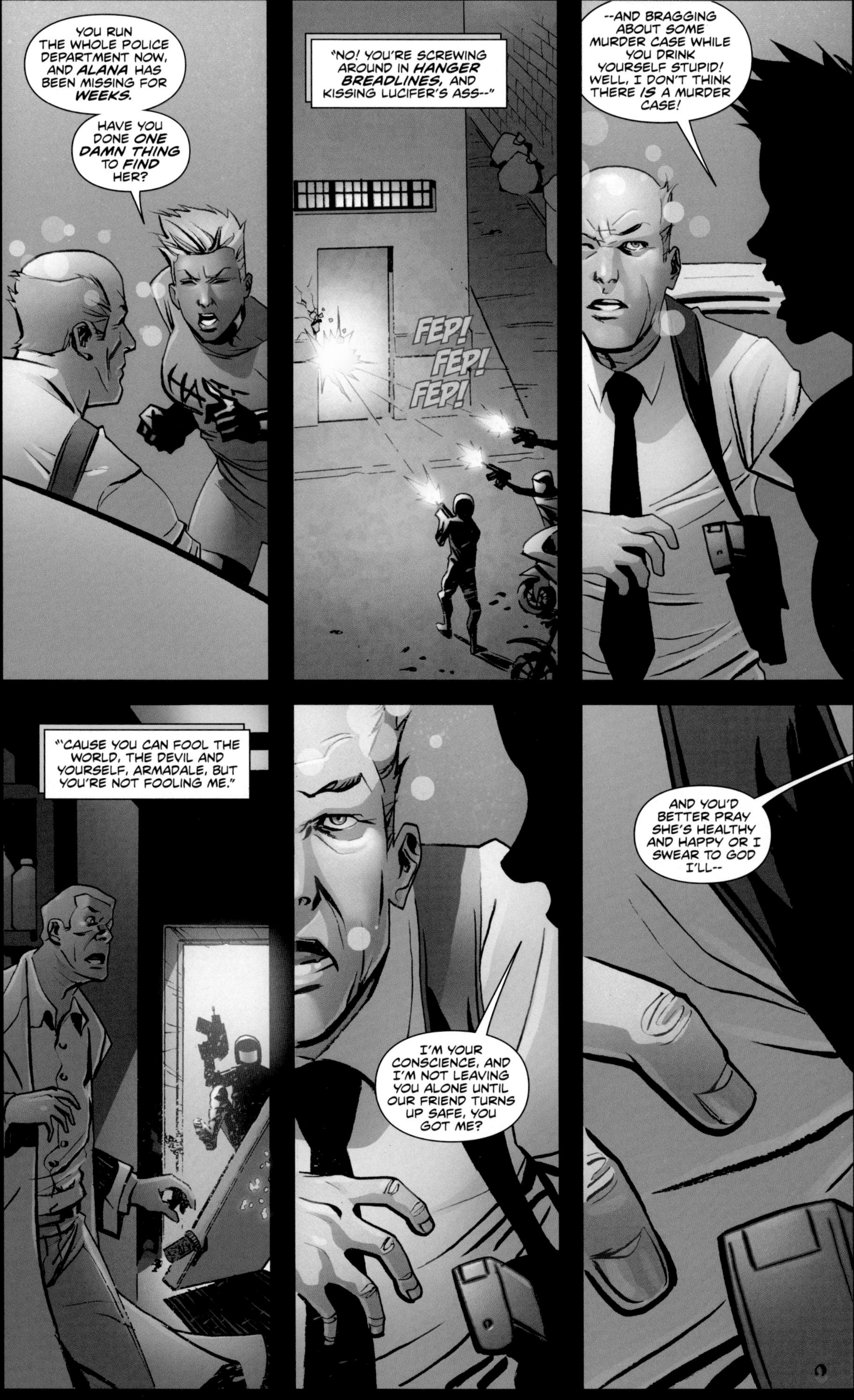
YOU RUN THE WHOLE POLICE DEPARTMENT NOW, AND ALANA HAS BEEN MISSING FOR WEEKS.
HAVE YOU DONE ONE DAMN THING TO FIND HER?
"NO! YOU'RE SCREWING AROUND IN HANGER BREADLINES, AND KISSING LUCIFER'S ASS--"
FEP! FEP! FEP!
--AND BRAGGING ABOUT SOME MURDER CASE WHILE YOU DRINK YOURSELF STUPID! WELL, I DON'T THINK THERE IS A MURDER CASE!
"'CAUSE YOU CAN FOOL THE WORLD, THE DEVIL AND YOURSELF, ARMADALE, BUT YOU'RE NOT FOOLING ME."
I'M YOUR CONSCIENCE, AND I'M NOT LEAVING YOU ALONE UNTIL OUR FRIEND TURNS UP SAFE, YOU GOT ME?
AND YOU'D BETTER PRAY SHE'S HEALTHY AND HAPPY OR I SWEAR TO GOD I'LL--

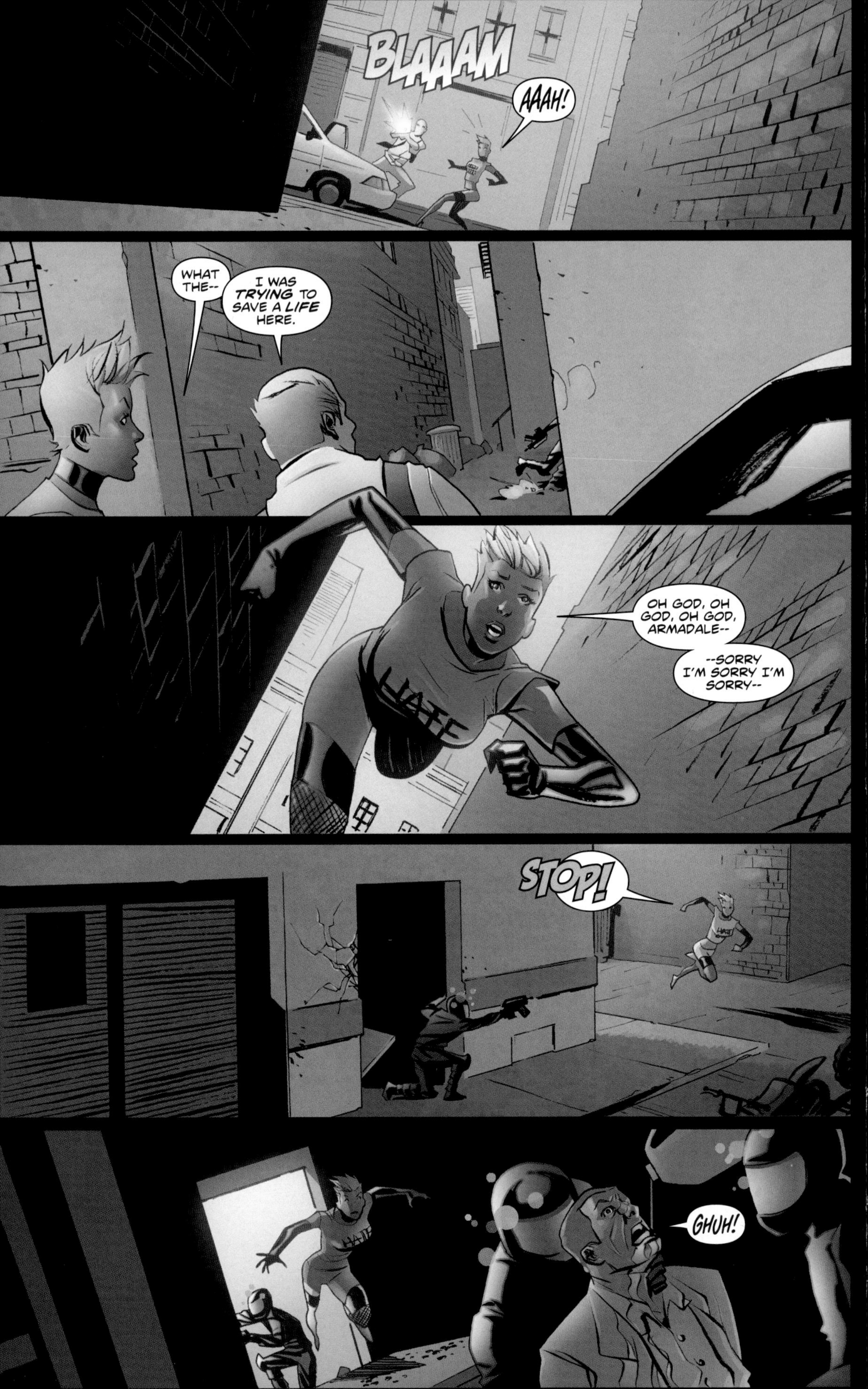
BLAAAM
AAAH!
WHAT THE--
I WAS TRYING TO SAVE A LIFE HERE.
OH GOD, OH GOD, OH GOD, ARMADALE--
--SORRY I'M SORRY I'M SORRY--
STOP!
GHUH!

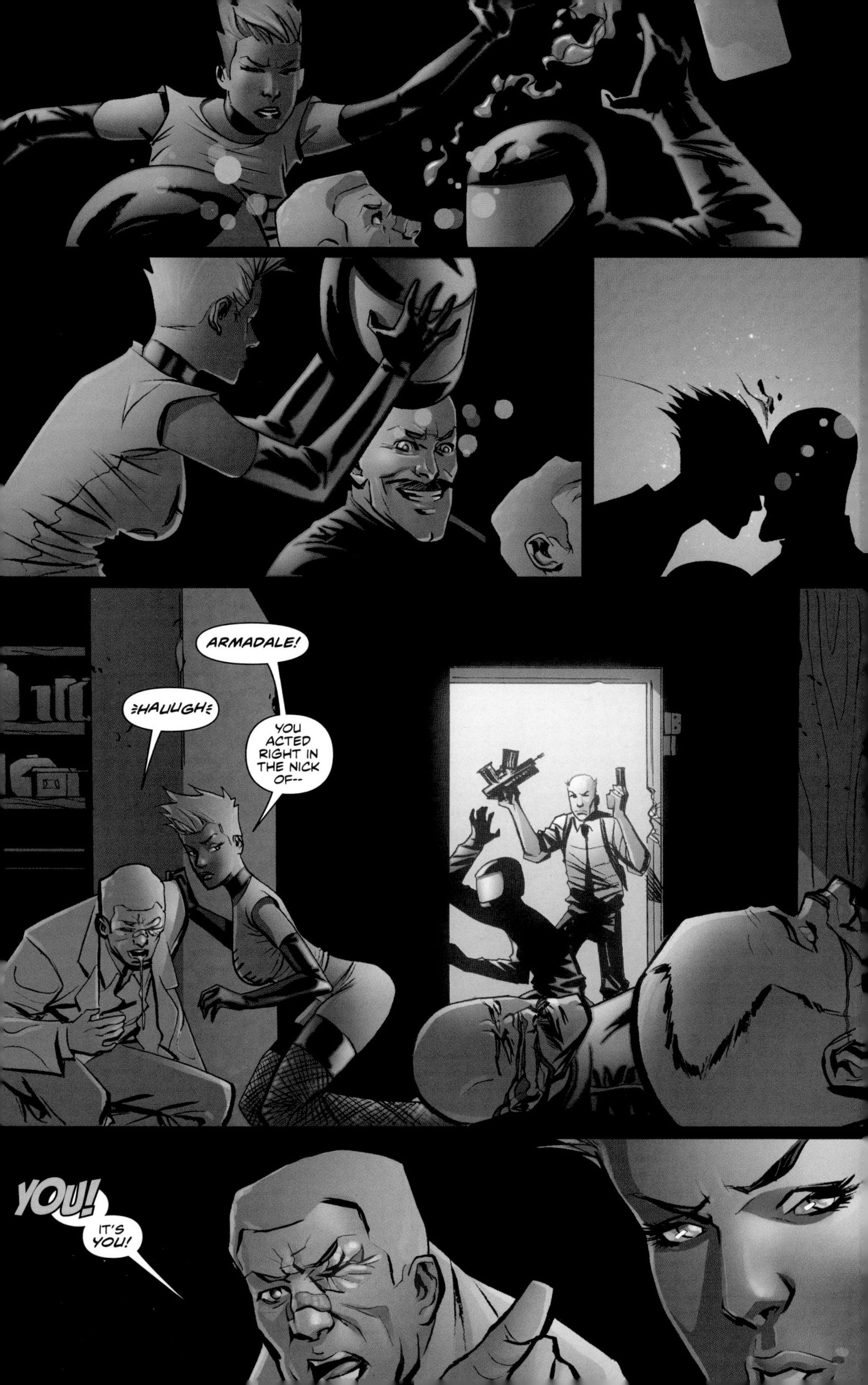
HAUUGH
ARMADALE!
YOU ACTED RIGHT IN THE NICK OF--
YOU!
IT'S YOU!

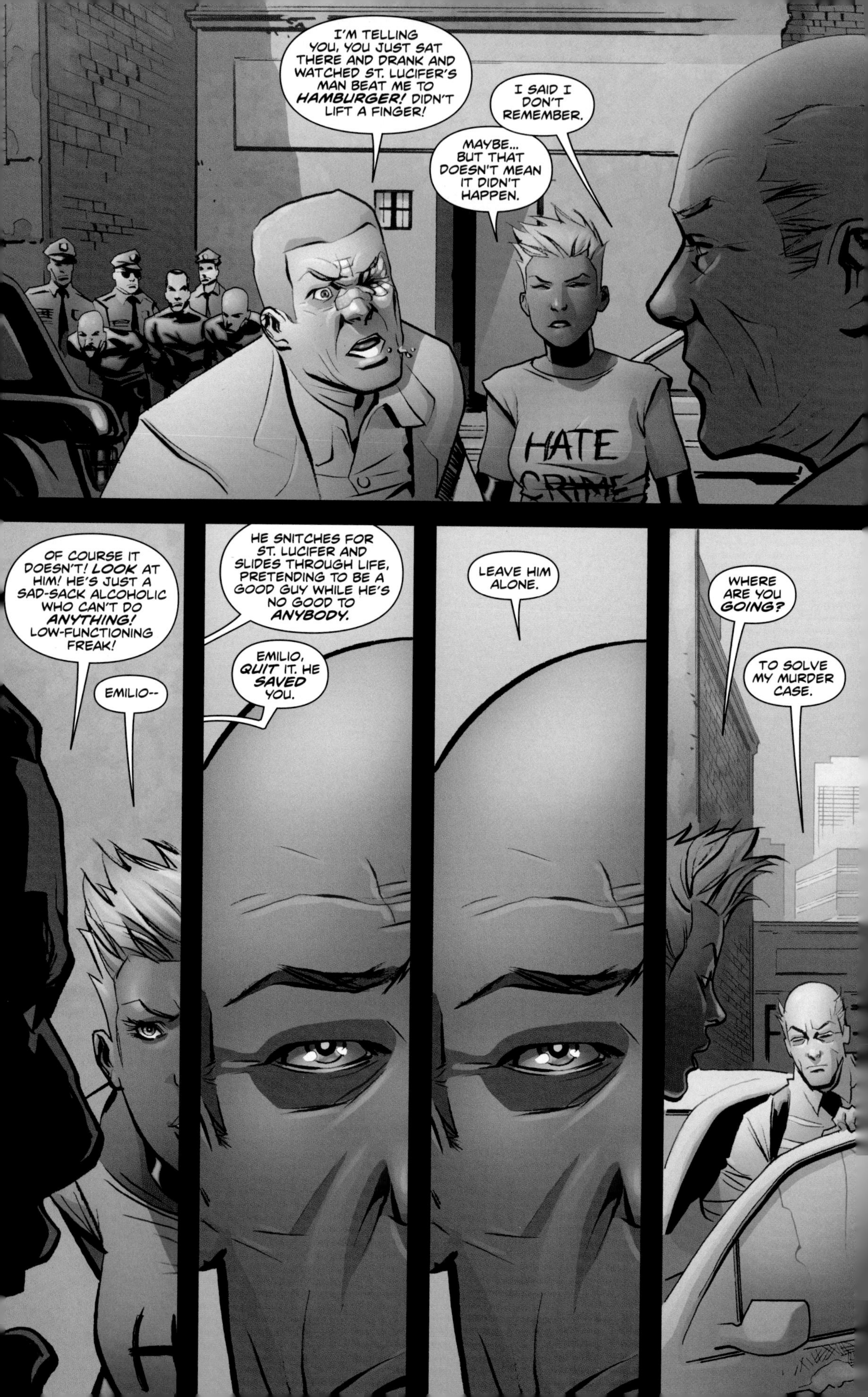
I'M TELLING YOU, YOU JUST SAT THERE AND DRANK AND WATCHED ST. LUCIFER'S MAN BEAT ME TO HAMBURGER! DIDN'T LIFT A FINGER!
I SAID I DON'T REMEMBER.
MAYBE... BUT THAT DOESN'T MEAN IT DIDN'T HAPPEN.
HATE CRIME
OF COURSE IT DOESN'T! LOOK AT HIM! HE'S JUST A SAD-SACK ALCOHOLIC WHO CAN'T DO ANYTHING! LOW-FUNCTIONING FREAK!
EMILIO--
HE SNITCHES FOR ST. LUCIFER AND SLIDES THROUGH LIFE, PRETENDING TO BE A GOOD GUY WHILE HE'S NO GOOD TO ANYBODY.
EMILIO, QUIT IT. HE SAVED YOU.
LEAVE HIM ALONE.
WHERE ARE YOU GOING?
TO SOLVE MY MURDER CASE.

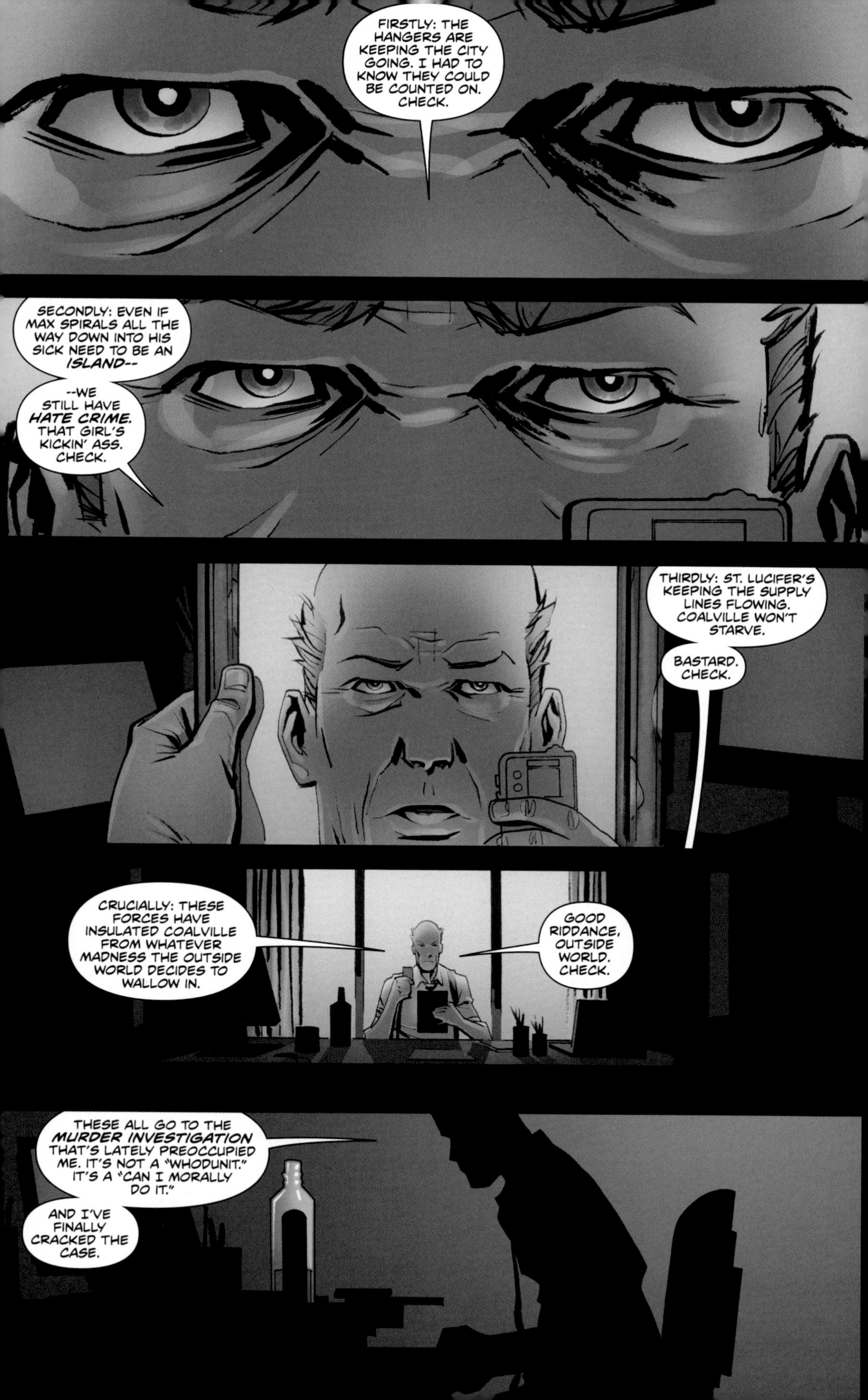
FIRSTLY: THE HANGERS ARE KEEPING THE CITY GOING. I HAD TO KNOW THEY COULD BE COUNTED ON. CHECK.
SECONDLY: EVEN IF MAX SPIRALS ALL THE WAY DOWN INTO HIS SICK NEED TO BE AN ISLAND--
--WE STILL HAVE HATE CRIME. THAT GIRL'S KICKIN' ASS. CHECK.
THIRDLY: ST. LUCIFER'S KEEPING THE SUPPLY LINES FLOWING. COALVILLE WON'T STARVE.
BASTARD. CHECK.
CRUCIALLY: THESE FORCES HAVE INSULATED COALVILLE FROM WHATEVER MADNESS THE OUTSIDE WORLD DECIDES TO WALLOW IN.
GOOD RIDDANCE, OUTSIDE WORLD. CHECK.
THESE ALL GO TO THE MURDER INVESTIGATION THAT'S LATELY PREOCCUPIED ME. IT'S NOT A "WHODUNIT." IT'S A "CAN I MORALLY DO IT."
AND I'VE FINALLY CRACKED THE CASE.

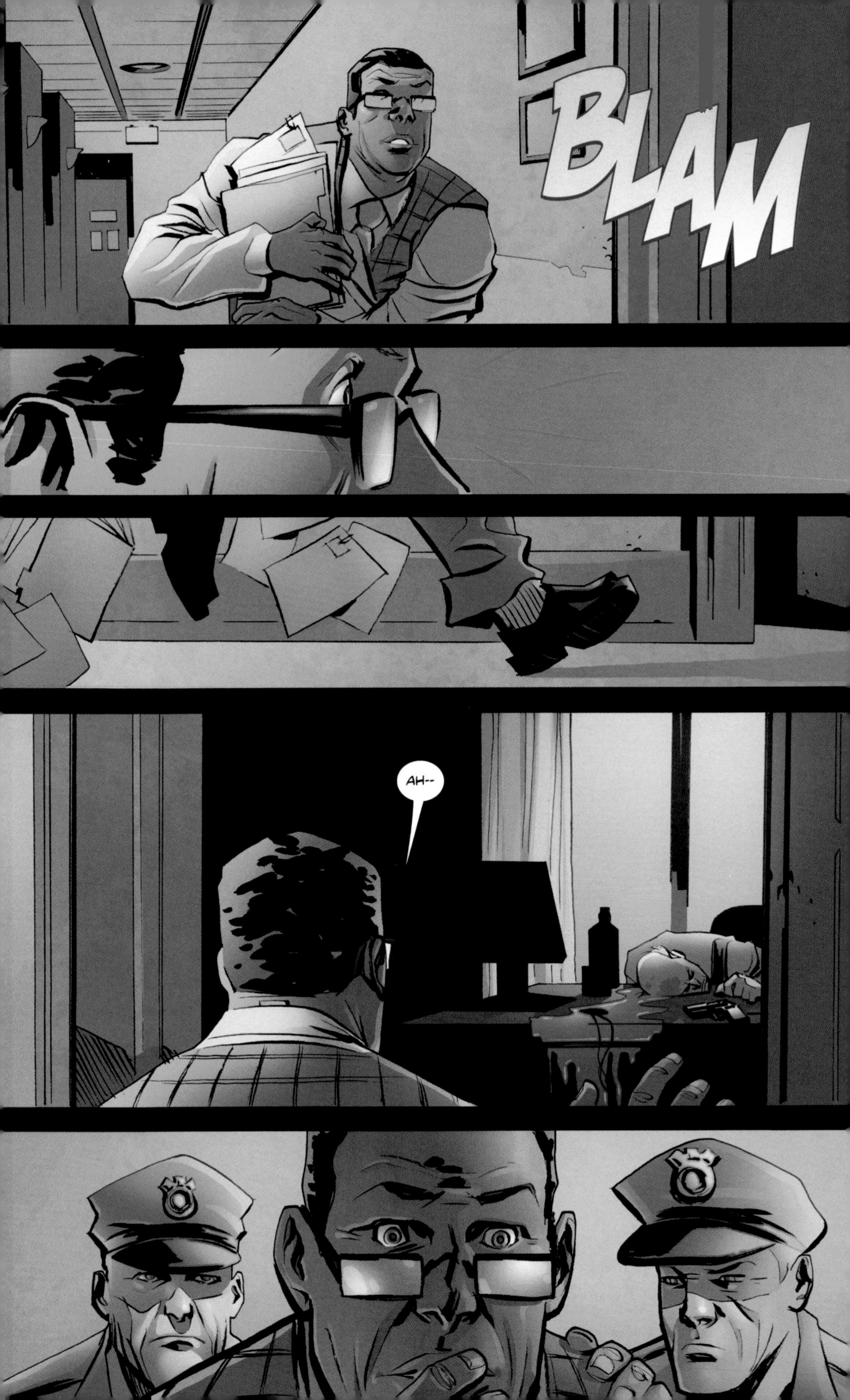
BLAM
AH--

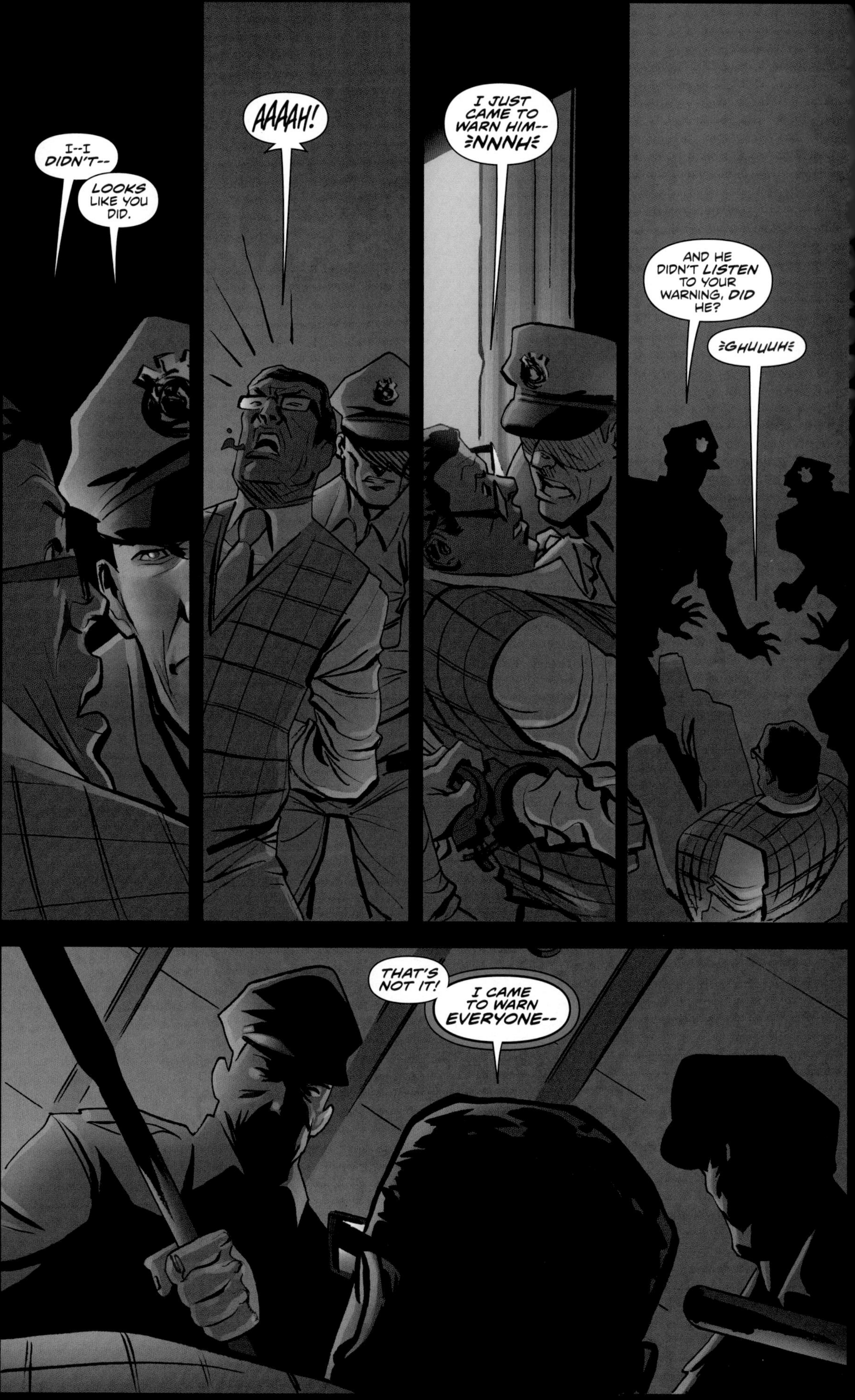
I--I DIDN'T--
LOOKS LIKE YOU DID.
AAAAH!
I JUST CAME TO WARN HIM--
NNNH
AND HE DIDN'T LISTEN TO YOUR WARNING, DID HE?
GHUUUH
THAT'S NOT IT!
I CAME TO WARN EVERYONE--

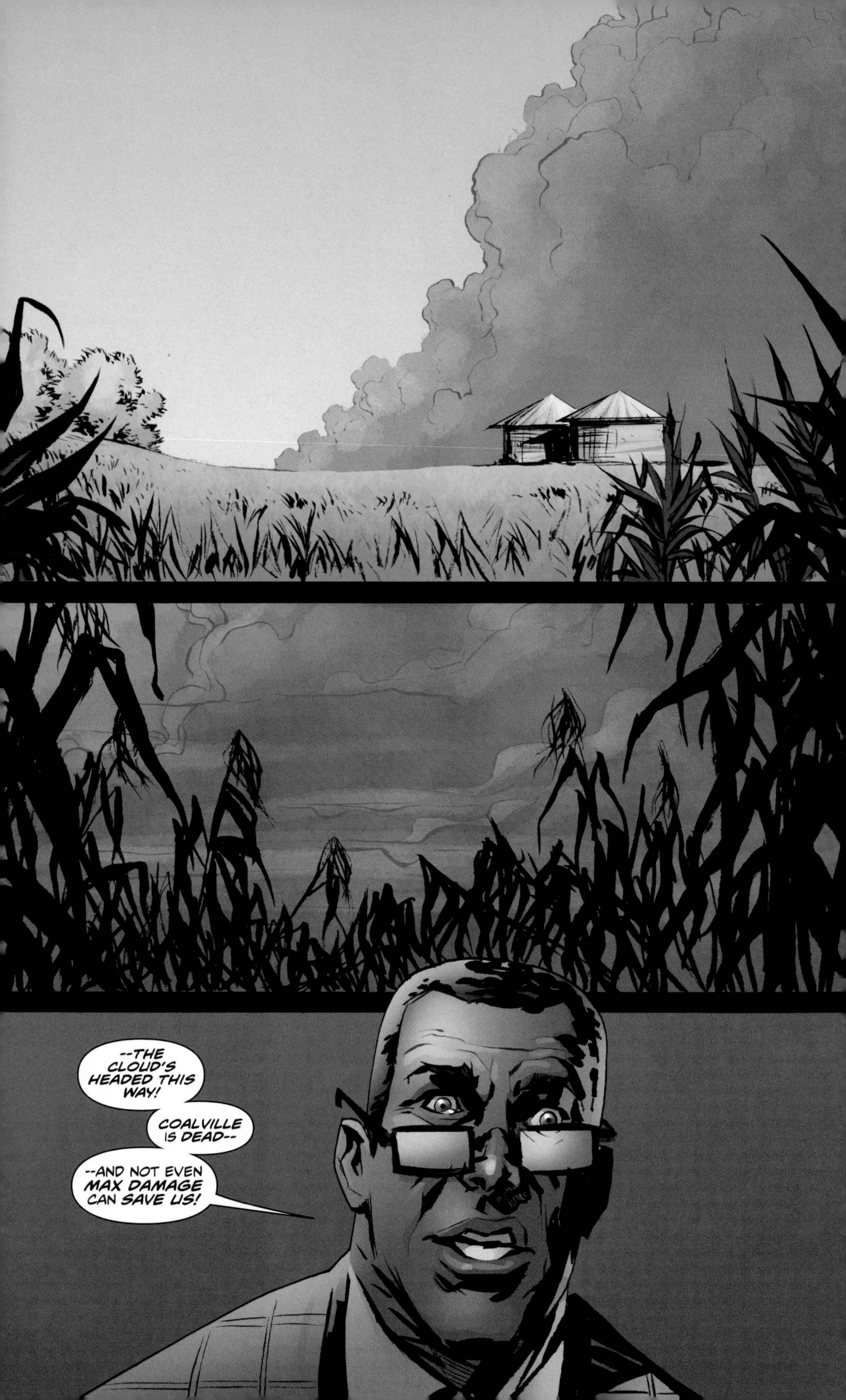

--THE CLOUD'S HEADED THIS WAY!
COALVILLE IS DEAD--
--AND NOT EVEN MAX DAMAGE CAN SAVE US!

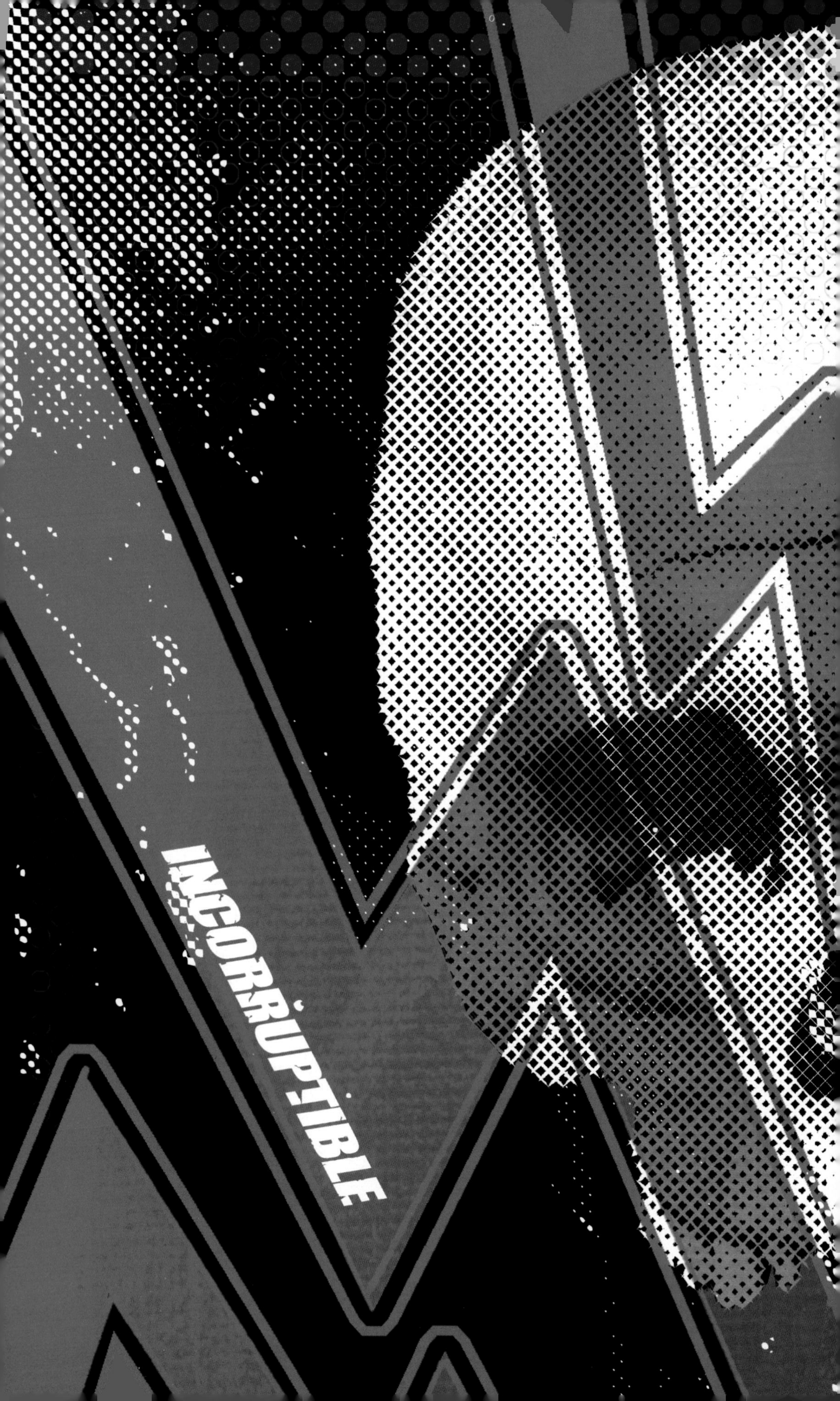
INCORRUPTIBLE

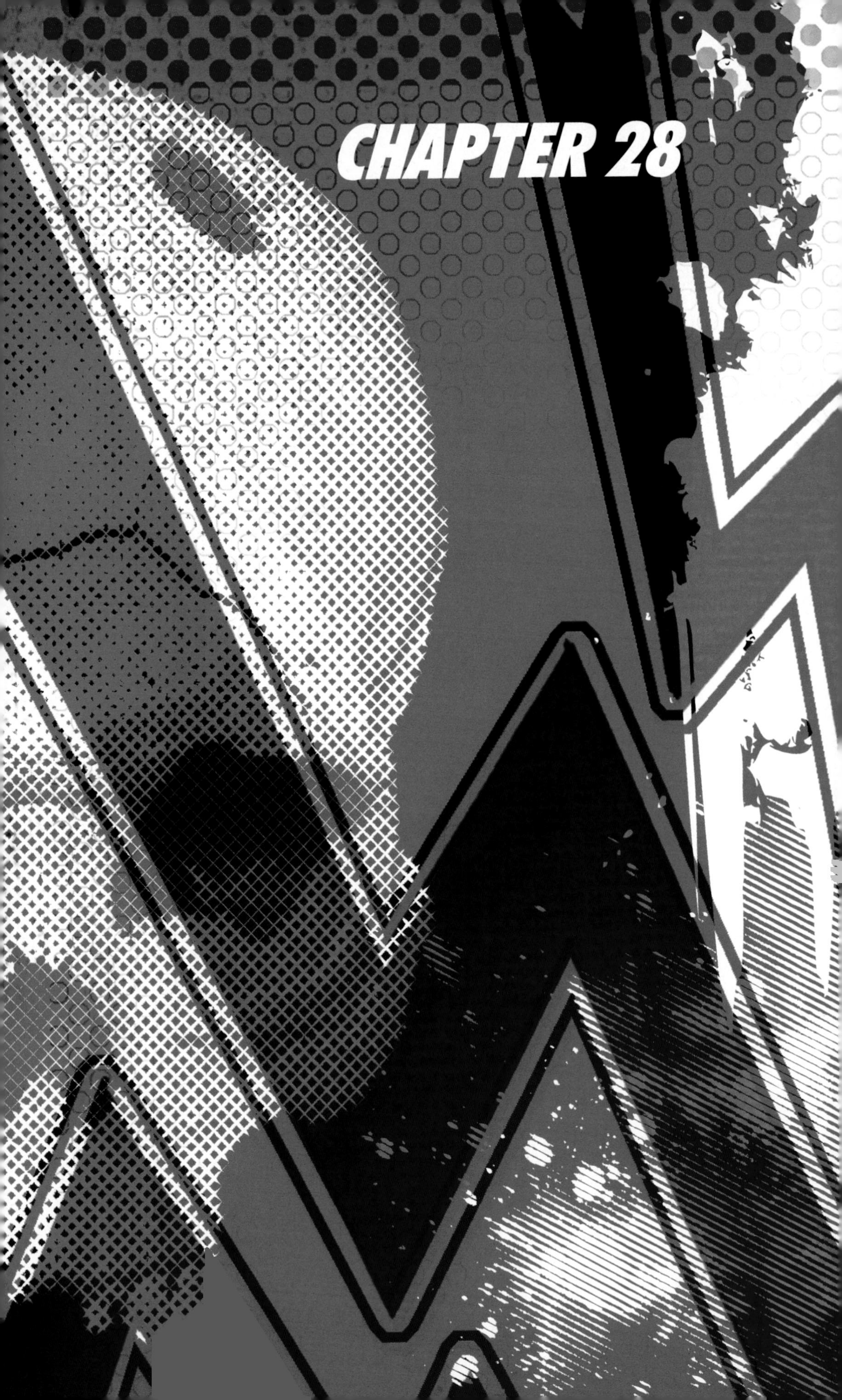
CHAPTER 28

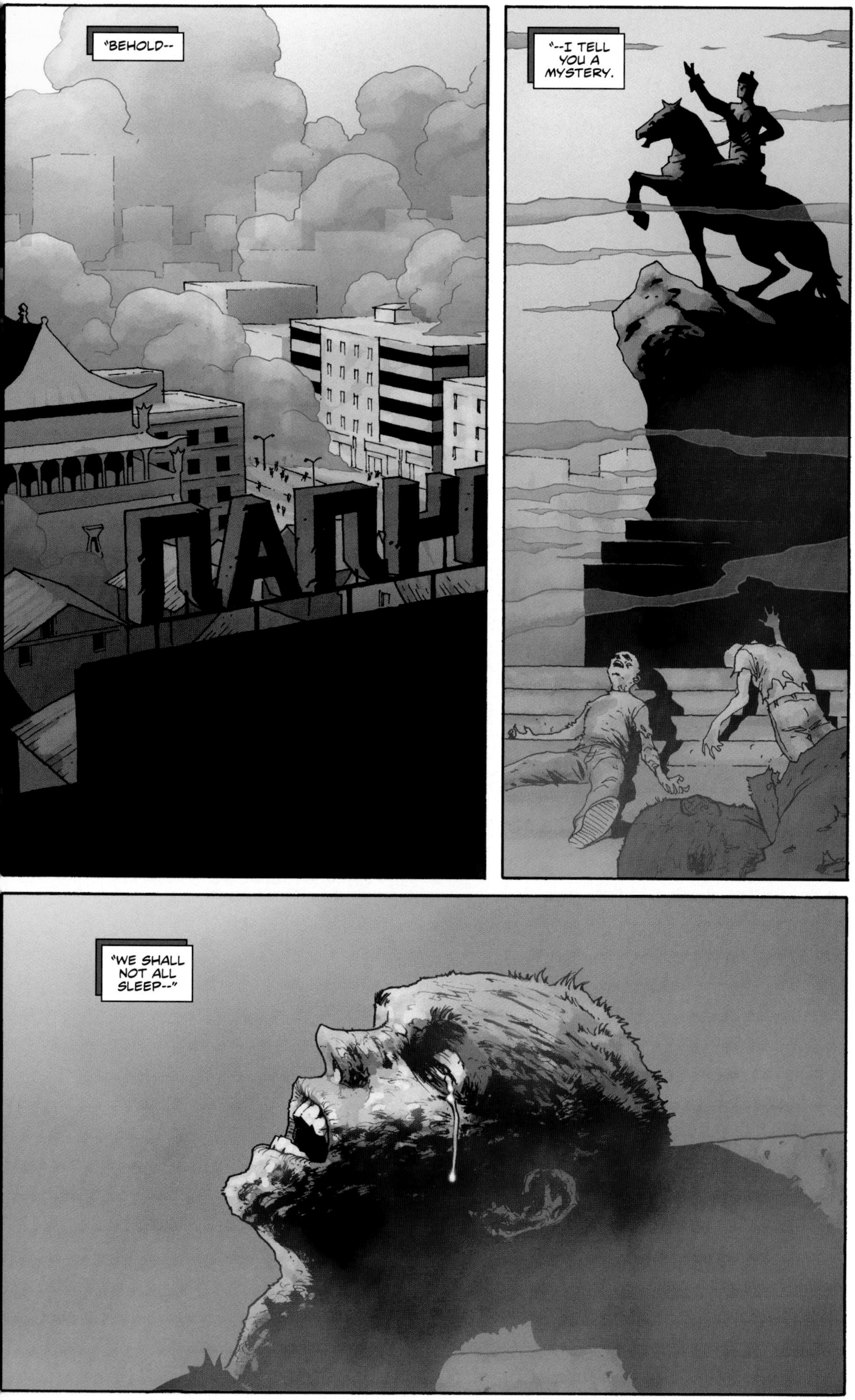
"BEHOLD--
"--I TELL YOU A MYSTERY.
"WE SHALL NOT ALL SLEEP--"

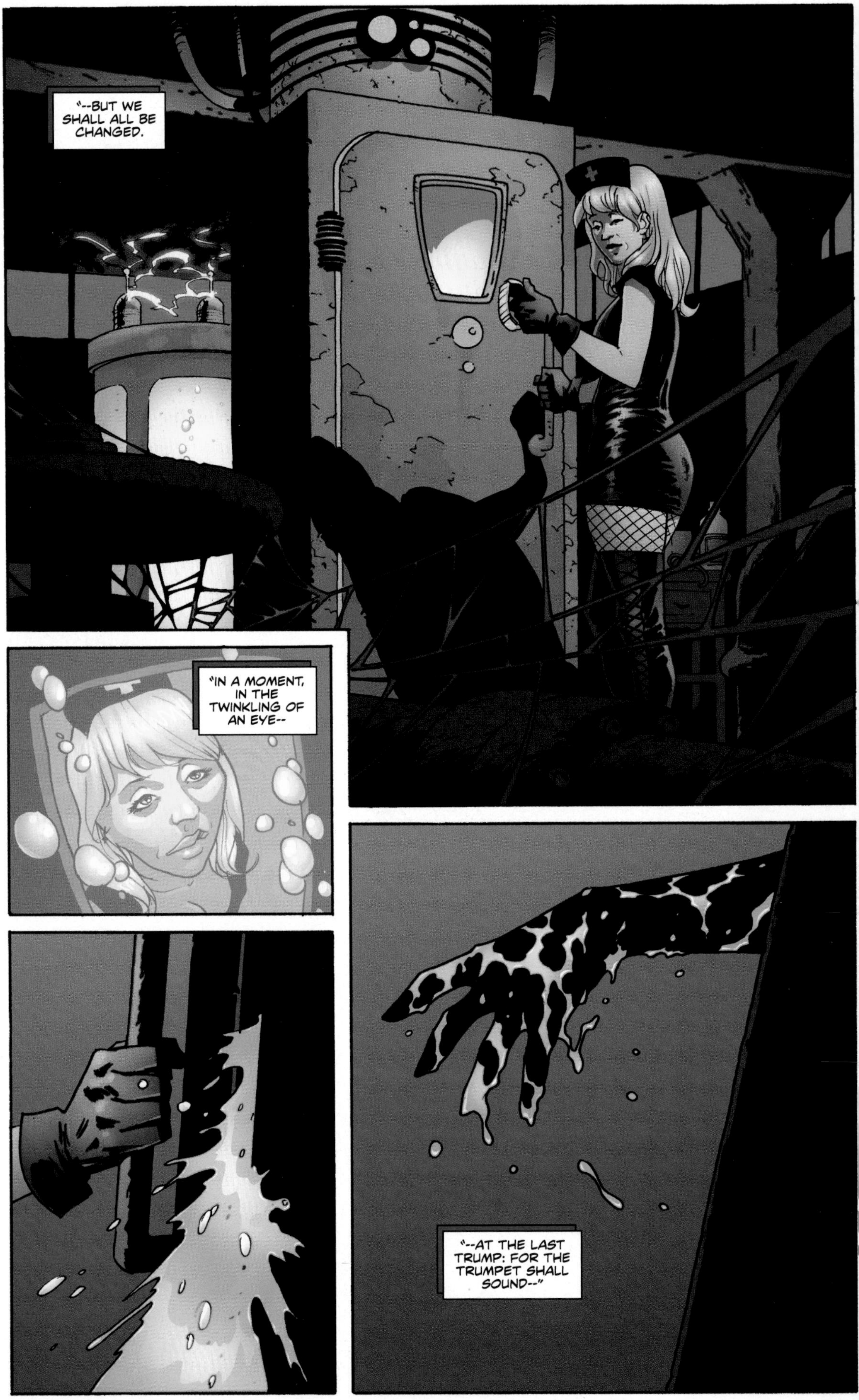
"--BUT WE SHALL ALL BE CHANGED.
"IN A MOMENT, IN THE TWINKLING OF AN EYE--
"--AT THE LAST TRUMP: FOR THE TRUMPET SHALL SOUND--"

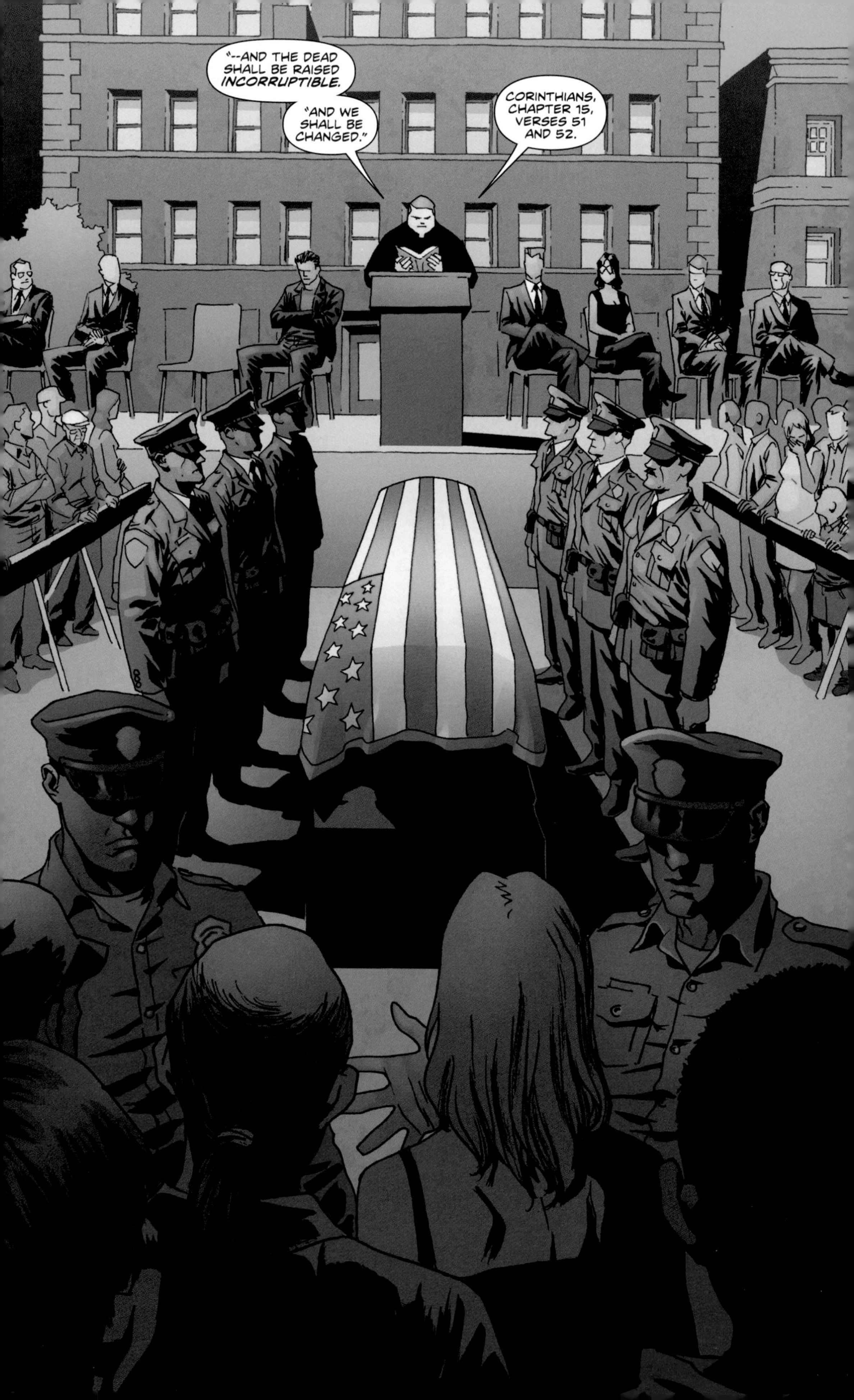
"--AND THE DEAD SHALL BE RAISED *INCORRUPTIBLE*.
"AND WE SHALL BE CHANGED."
CORINTHIANS, CHAPTER 15, VERSES 51 AND 52.

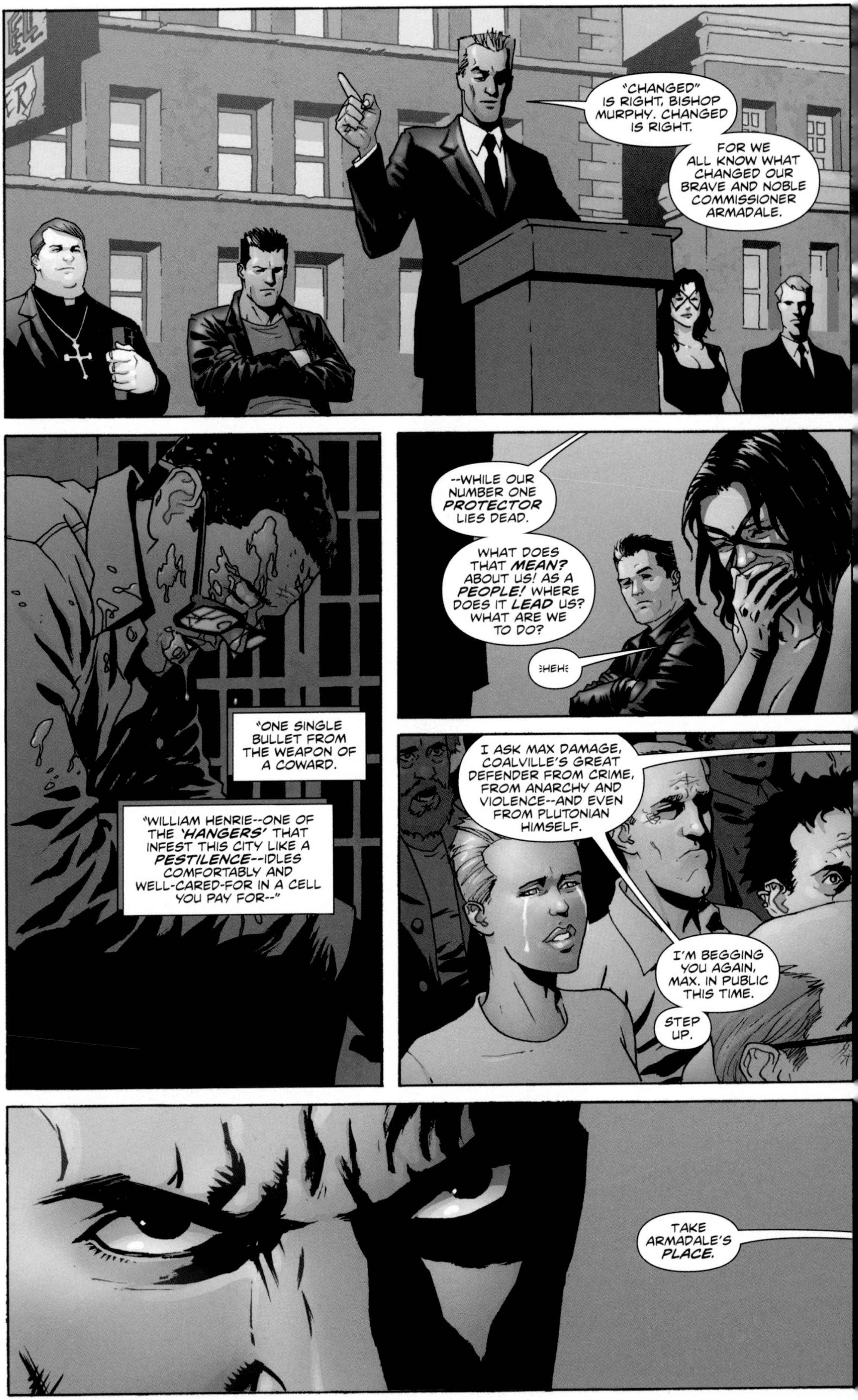
"CHANGED" IS RIGHT, BISHOP MURPHY. CHANGED IS RIGHT.
FOR WE ALL KNOW WHAT CHANGED OUR BRAVE AND NOBLE COMMISSIONER ARMADALE.
"ONE SINGLE BULLET FROM THE WEAPON OF A COWARD.
"WILLIAM HENRIE--ONE OF THE 'HANGERS' THAT INFEST THIS CITY LIKE A PESTILENCE--IDLES COMFORTABLY AND WELL-CARED-FOR IN A CELL YOU PAY FOR--"
--WHILE OUR NUMBER ONE PROTECTOR LIES DEAD.
WHAT DOES THAT MEAN? ABOUT US! AS A PEOPLE! WHERE DOES IT LEAD US? WHAT ARE WE TO DO?
HEH
I ASK MAX DAMAGE, COALVILLE'S GREAT DEFENDER FROM CRIME, FROM ANARCHY AND VIOLENCE--AND EVEN FROM PLUTONIAN HIMSELF.
I'M BEGGING YOU AGAIN, MAX. IN PUBLIC THIS TIME.
STEP UP.
TAKE ARMADALE'S PLACE.

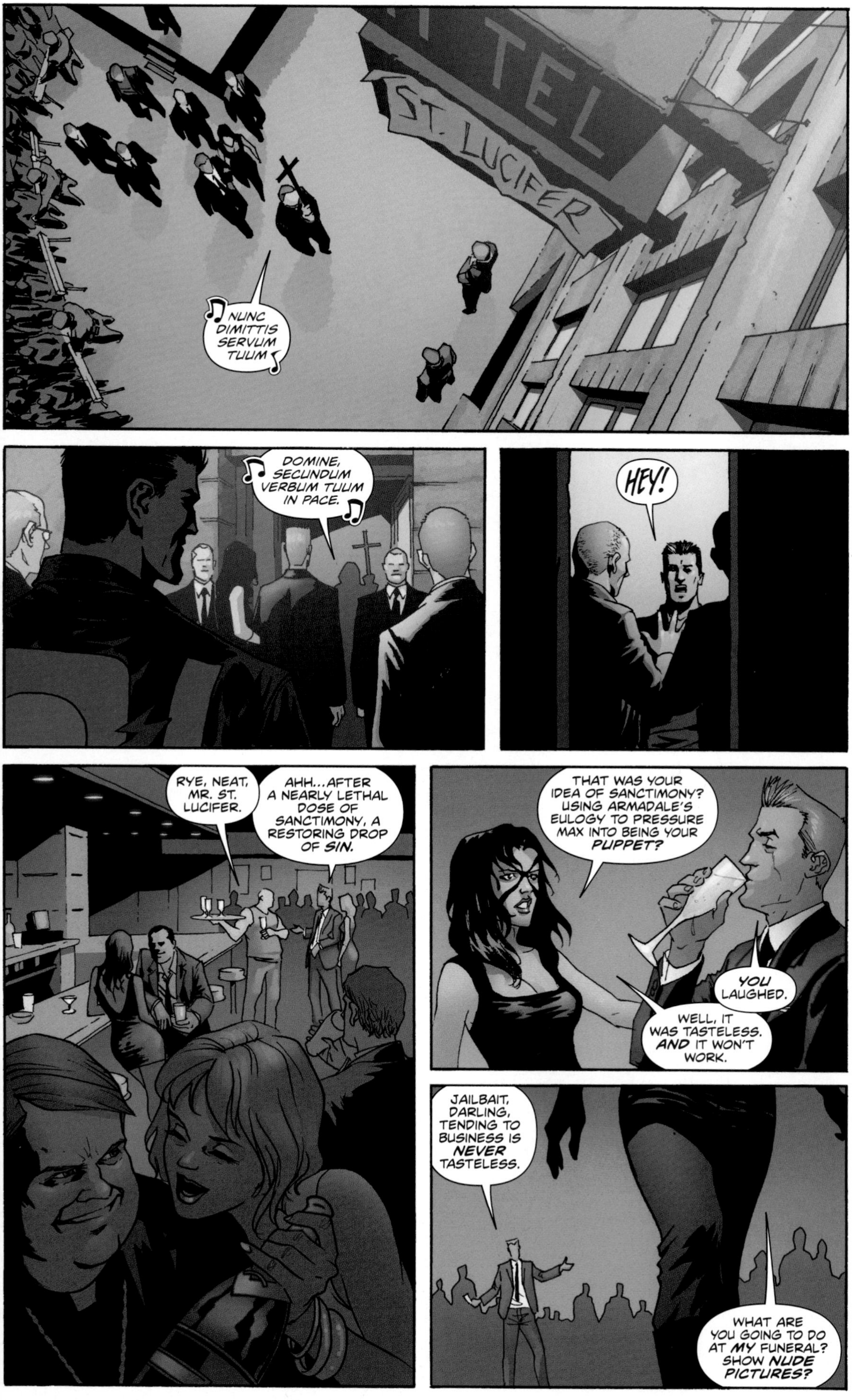
ST. LUCIFER
NUNC DIMITTIS SERVUM TUUM
DOMINE, SECUNDUM VERBUM TUUM IN PACE.
HEY!
RYE, NEAT, MR. ST. LUCIFER.
AHH...AFTER A NEARLY LETHAL DOSE OF SANCTIMONY, A RESTORING DROP OF SIN.
THAT WAS YOUR IDEA OF SANCTIMONY? USING ARMADALE'S EULOGY TO PRESSURE MAX INTO BEING YOUR PUPPET?
YOU LAUGHED.
WELL, IT WAS TASTELESS. AND IT WON'T WORK.
JAILBAIT, DARLING, TENDING TO BUSINESS IS NEVER TASTELESS.
WHAT ARE YOU GOING TO DO AT MY FUNERAL? SHOW NUDE PICTURES?

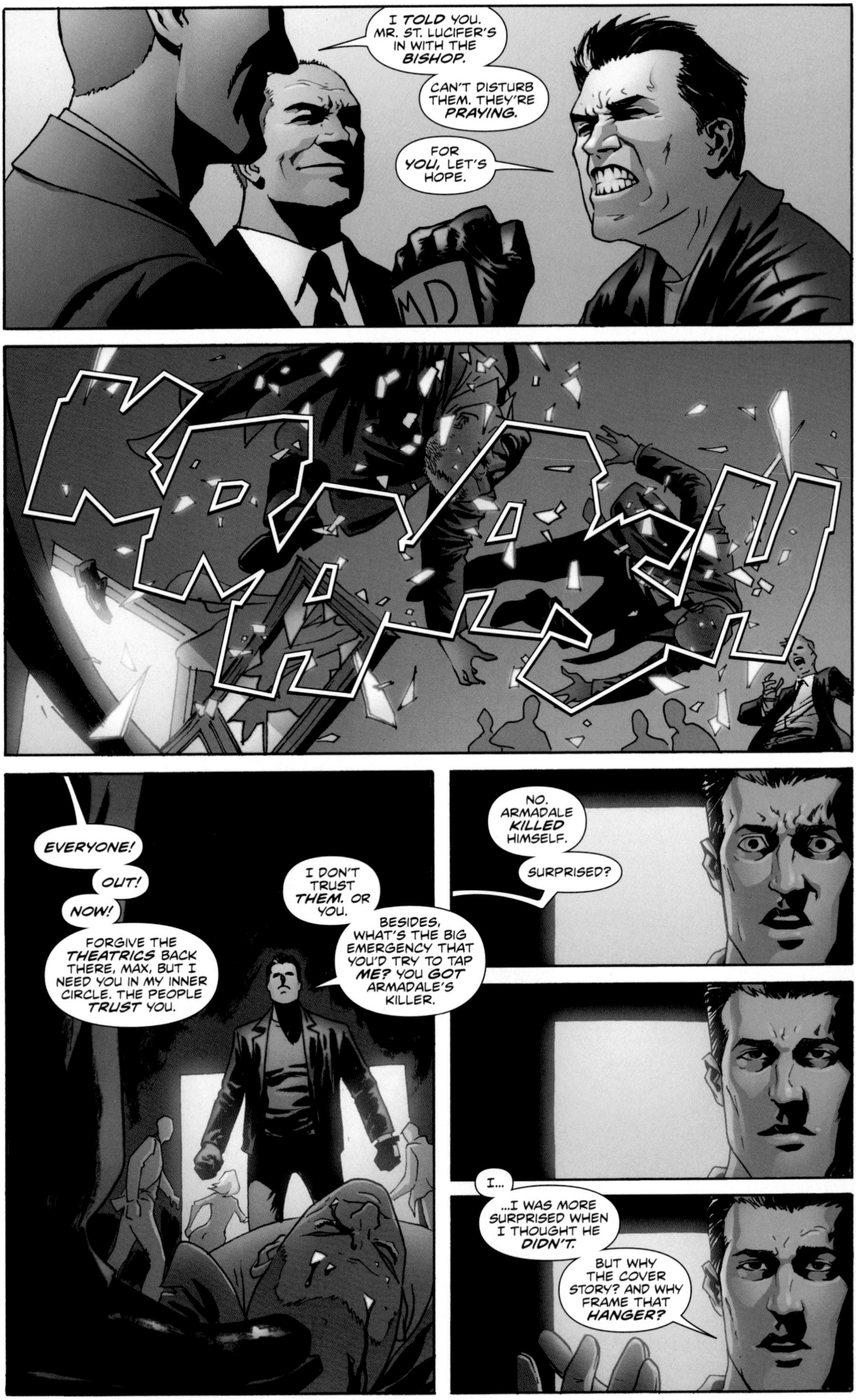
I TOLD YOU. MR. ST. LUCIFER'S IN WITH THE BISHOP.
CAN'T DISTURB THEM. THEY'RE PRAYING.
FOR YOU, LET'S HOPE.
MD
EVERYONE!
OUT!
NOW!
FORGIVE THE THEATRICS BACK THERE, MAX, BUT I NEED YOU IN MY INNER CIRCLE. THE PEOPLE TRUST YOU.
I DON'T TRUST THEM. OR YOU.
BESIDES, WHAT'S THE BIG EMERGENCY THAT YOU'D TRY TO TAP ME? YOU GOT ARMADALE'S KILLER.
NO. ARMADALE KILLED HIMSELF.
SURPRISED?
I...
...I WAS MORE SURPRISED WHEN I THOUGHT HE DIDN'T.
BUT WHY THE COVER STORY? AND WHY FRAME THAT HANGER?

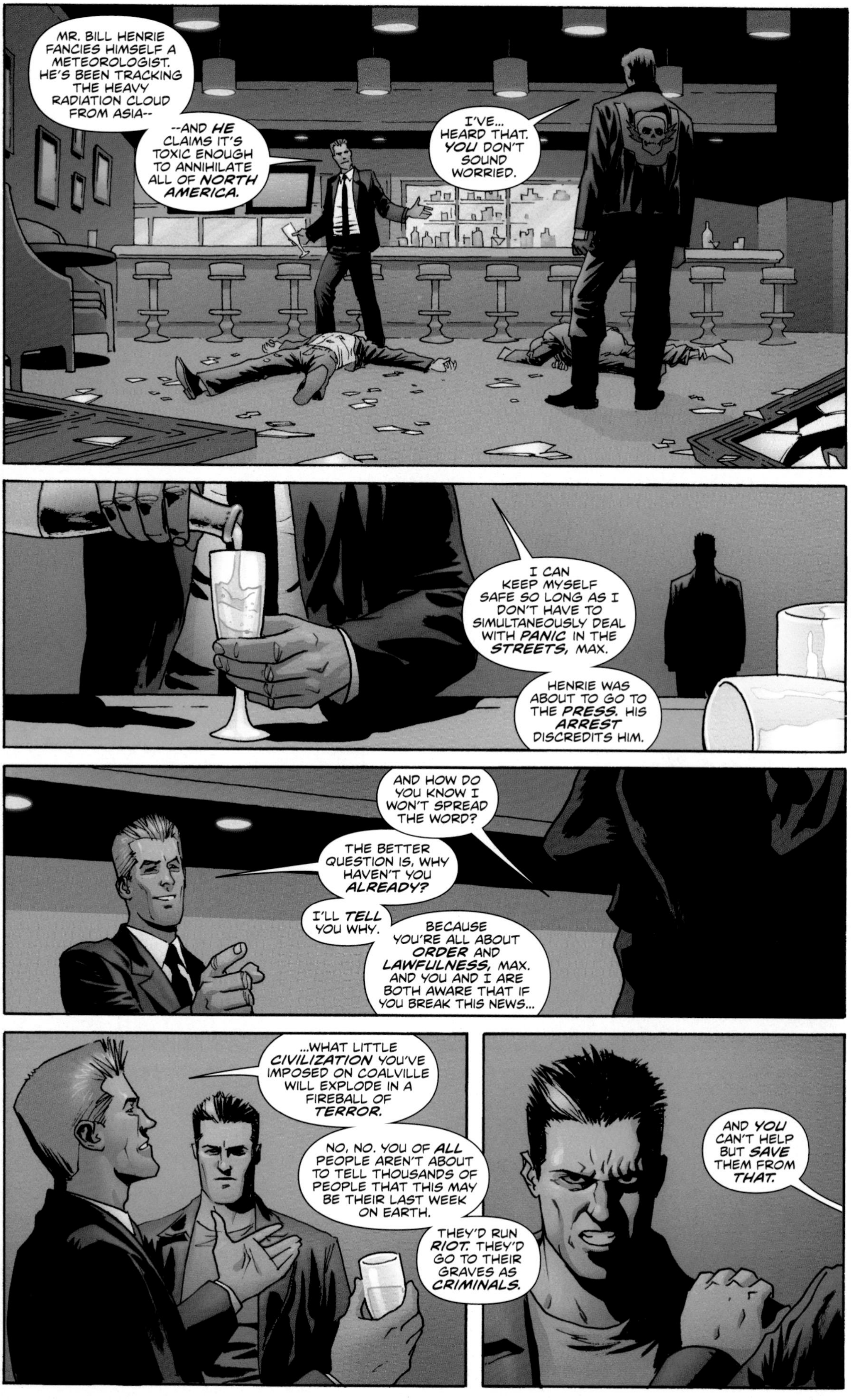
MR. BILL HENRIE FANCIES HIMSELF A METEOROLOGIST. HE'S BEEN TRACKING THE HEAVY RADIATION CLOUD FROM ASIA--
--AND HE CLAIMS IT'S TOXIC ENOUGH TO ANNIHILATE ALL OF NORTH AMERICA.
I'VE... HEARD THAT. YOU DON'T SOUND WORRIED.
I CAN KEEP MYSELF SAFE SO LONG AS I DON'T HAVE TO SIMULTANEOUSLY DEAL WITH PANIC IN THE STREETS, MAX.
HENRIE WAS ABOUT TO GO TO THE PRESS. HIS ARREST DISCREDITS HIM.
AND HOW DO YOU KNOW I WON'T SPREAD THE WORD?
THE BETTER QUESTION IS, WHY HAVEN'T YOU ALREADY?
I'LL TELL YOU WHY.
BECAUSE YOU'RE ALL ABOUT ORDER AND LAWFULNESS, MAX. AND YOU AND I ARE BOTH AWARE THAT IF YOU BREAK THIS NEWS...
...WHAT LITTLE CIVILIZATION YOU'VE IMPOSED ON COALVILLE WILL EXPLODE IN A FIREBALL OF TERROR.
NO, NO. YOU OF ALL PEOPLE AREN'T ABOUT TO TELL THOUSANDS OF PEOPLE THAT THIS MAY BE THEIR LAST WEEK ON EARTH.
THEY'D RUN RIOT. THEY'D GO TO THEIR GRAVES AS CRIMINALS.
AND YOU CAN'T HELP BUT SAVE THEM FROM THAT.

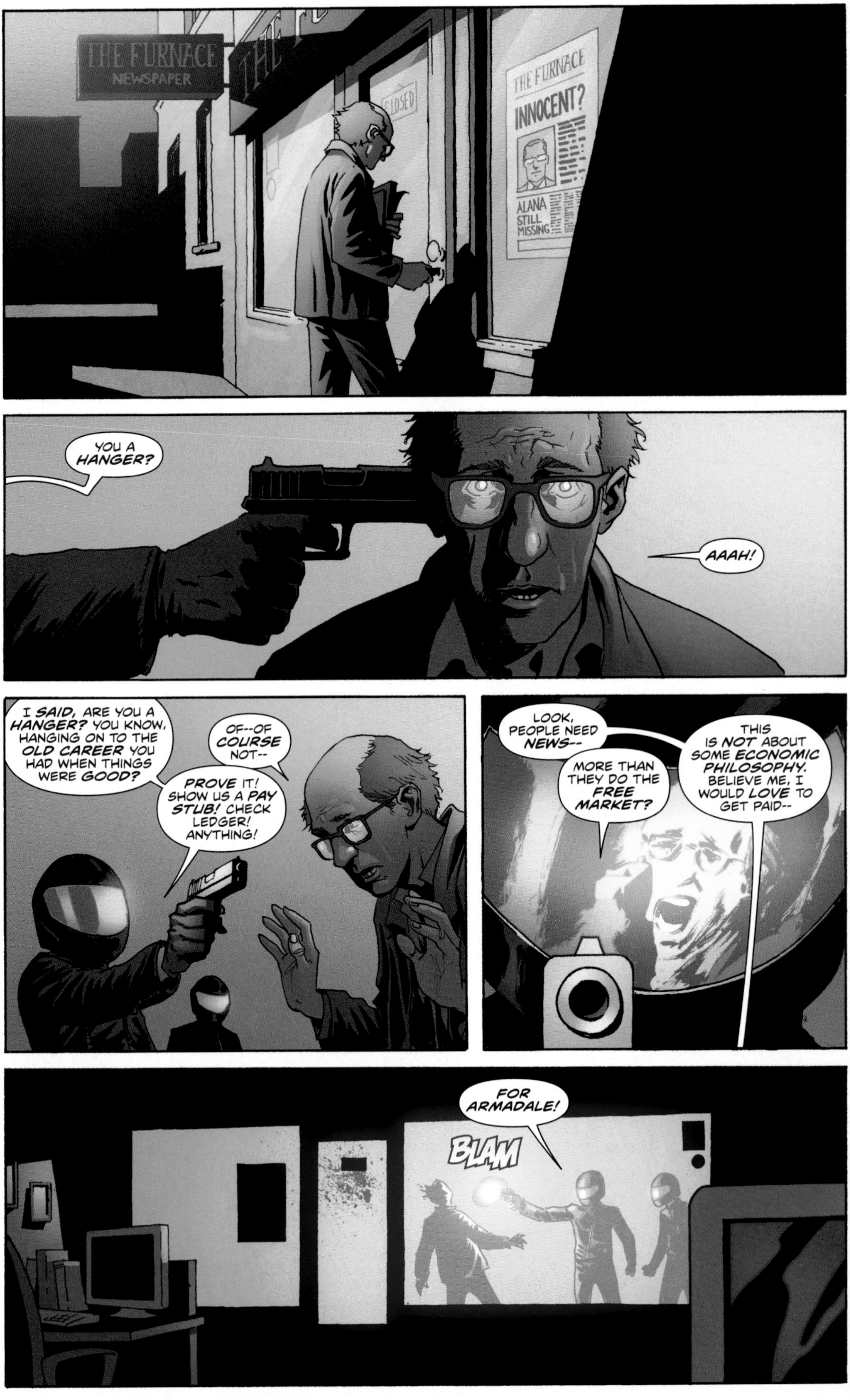
THE FURNACE
NEWSPAPER
CLOSED
THE FURNACE
INNOCENT?
ALANA STILL MISSING
YOU A HANGER?
AAAH!
I SAID, ARE YOU A HANGER? YOU KNOW, HANGING ON TO THE OLD CAREER YOU HAD WHEN THINGS WERE GOOD?
OF--OF COURSE NOT--
PROVE IT! SHOW US A PAY STUB! CHECK LEDGER! ANYTHING!
LOOK, PEOPLE NEED NEWS--
MORE THAN THEY DO THE FREE MARKET?
THIS IS NOT ABOUT SOME ECONOMIC PHILOSOPHY. BELIEVE ME, I WOULD LOVE TO GET PAID--
FOR ARMADALE!
BLAM

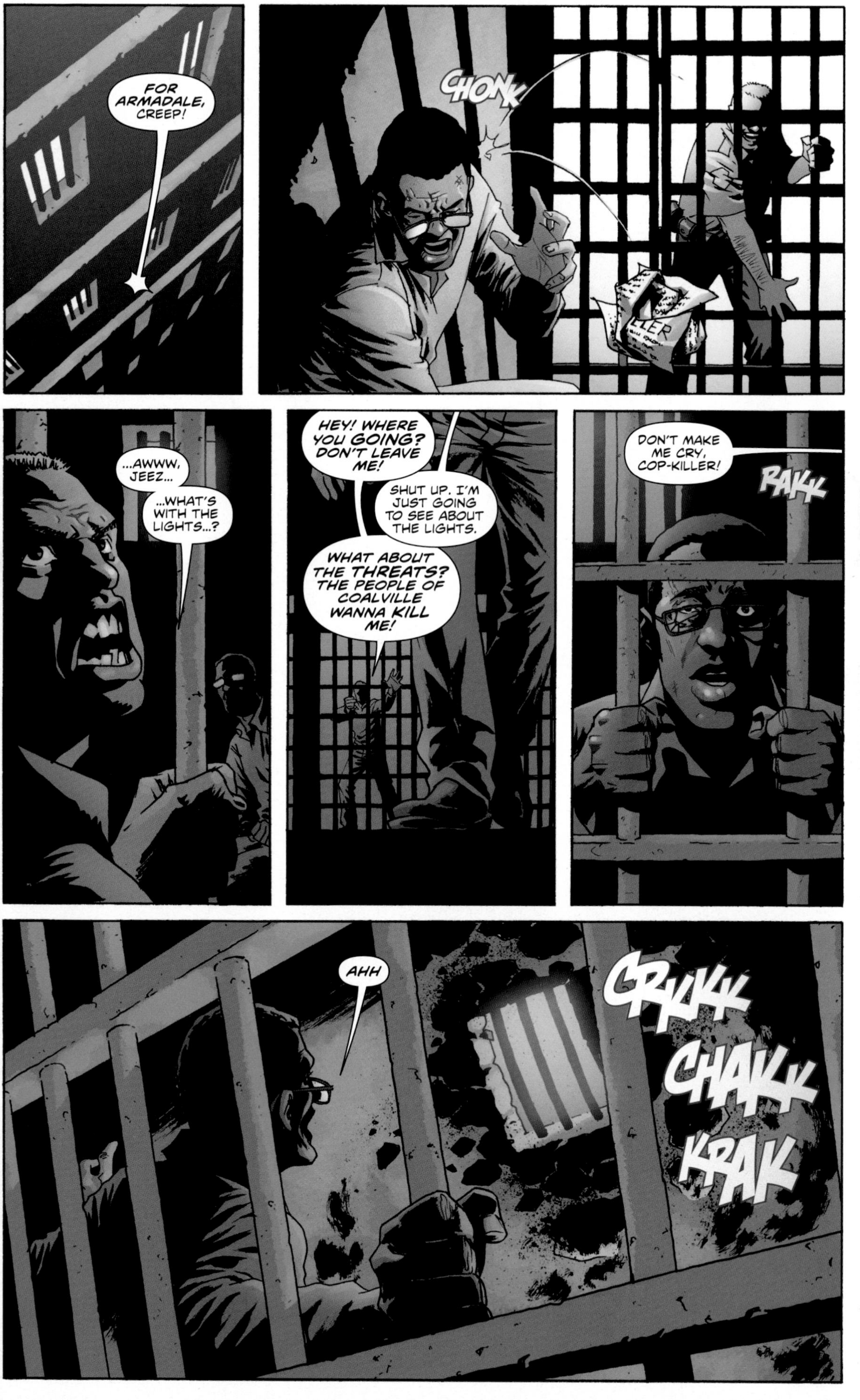
FOR ARMADALE, CREEP!
CHONK
...AWWW, JEEZ...
...WHAT'S WITH THE LIGHTS...?
HEY! WHERE YOU GOING? DON'T LEAVE ME!
SHUT UP. I'M JUST GOING TO SEE ABOUT THE LIGHTS.
WHAT ABOUT THE THREATS? THE PEOPLE OF COALVILLE WANNA KILL ME!
DON'T MAKE ME CRY, COP-KILLER!
RAKK
AHH
CRKKK
CHAKK
KRAK

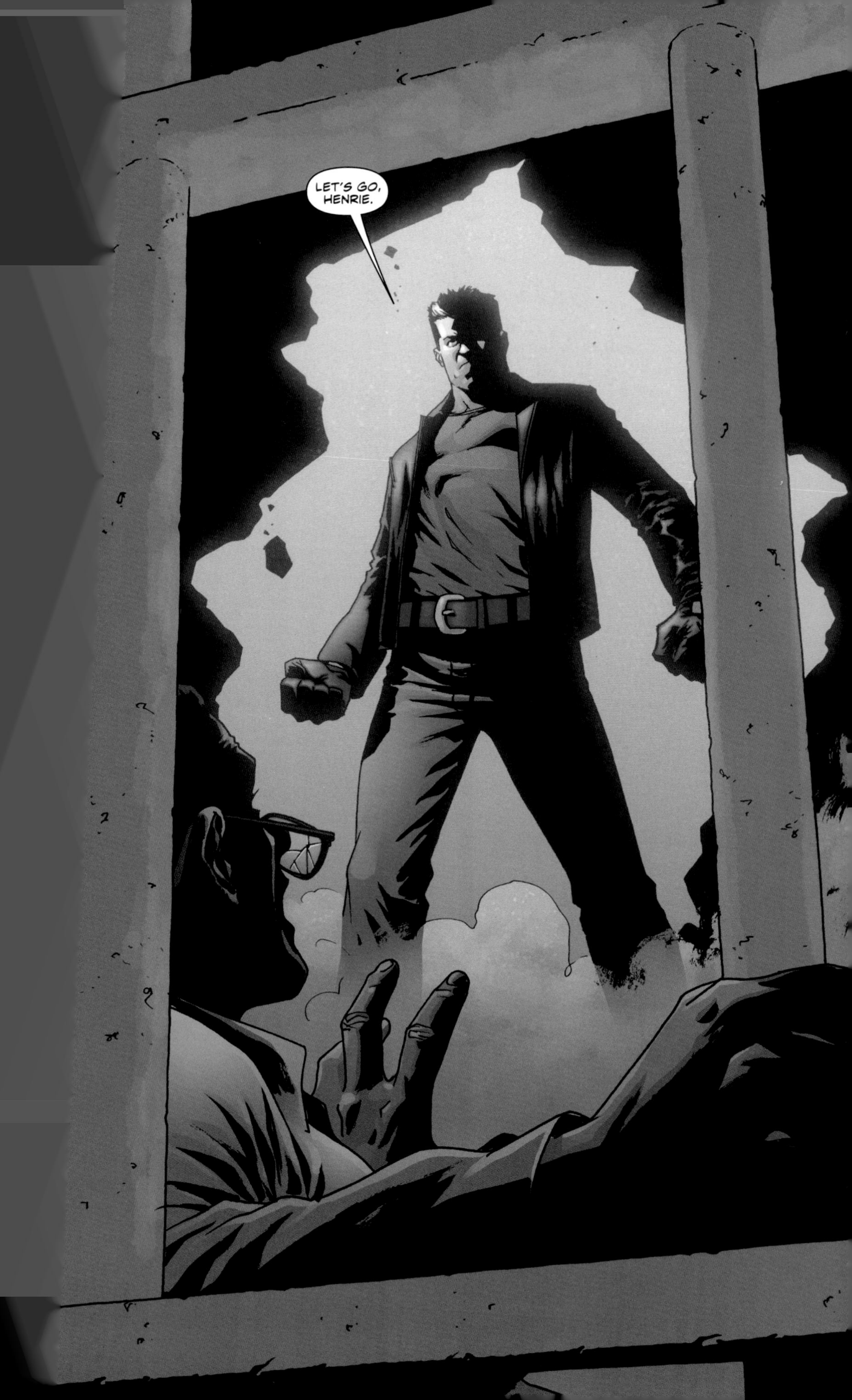
LET'S GO, HENRIE.

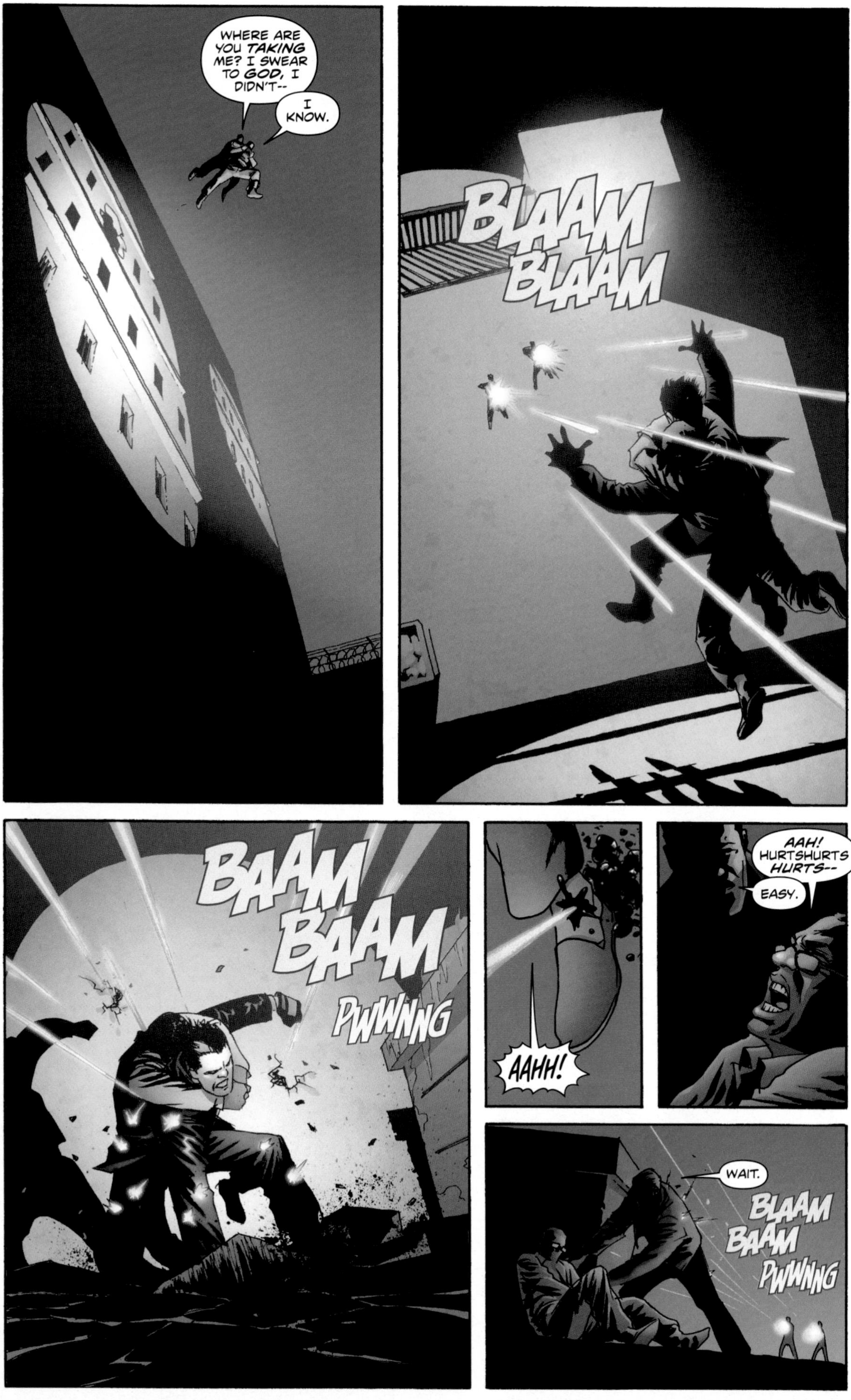
WHERE ARE YOU TAKING ME? I SWEAR TO GOD, I DIDN'T--
I KNOW.
BLAAM BLAAM
BAAM BAAM
PWWNNG
AAHH!
AAH! HURTSHURTS HURTS--
EASY.
WAIT.
BLAAM BAAM PWWNNG

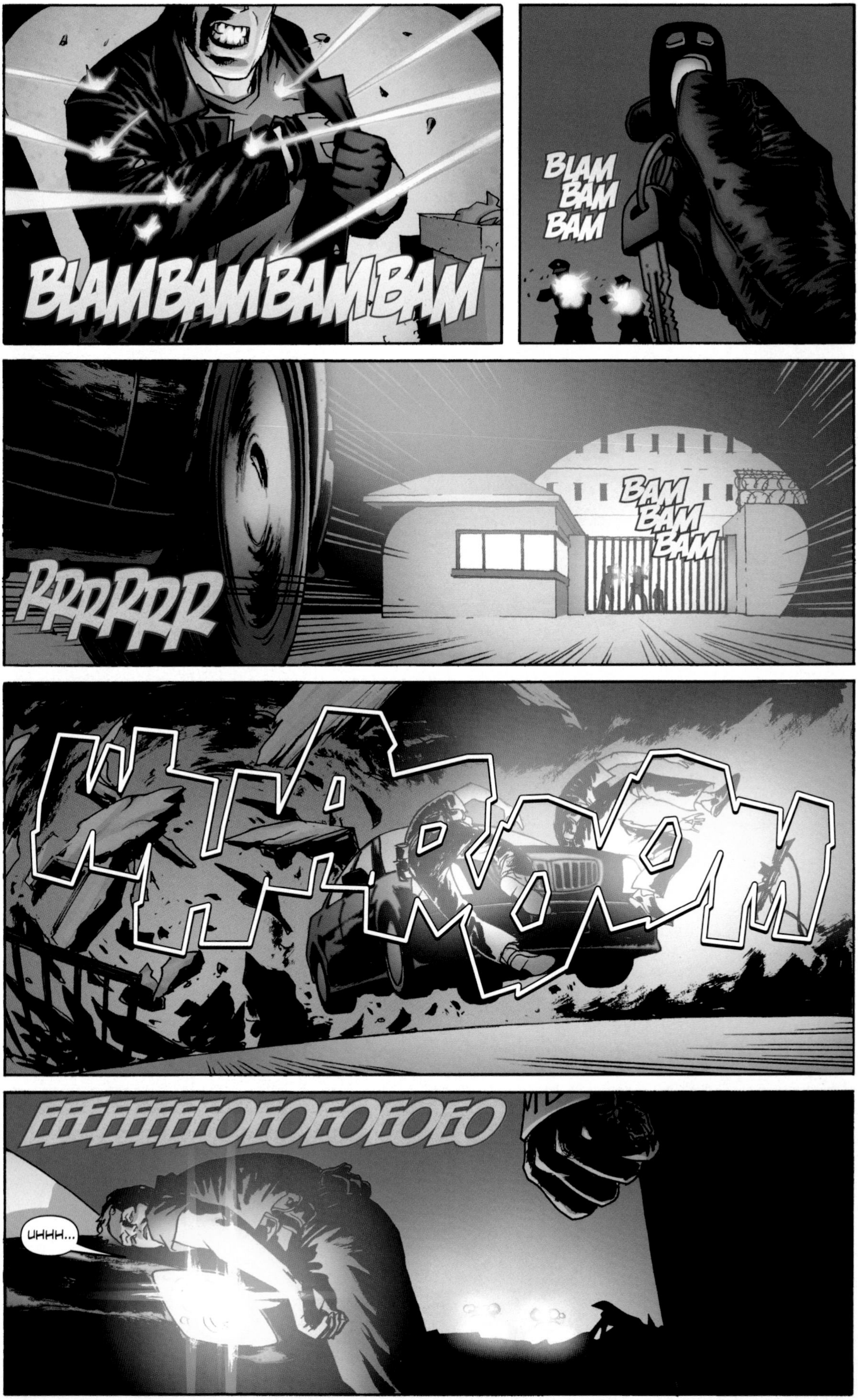
BLAM BAM BAM BAM
BLAM BAM BAM
RRRRRR
BAM BAM BAM
WHAROOOM
EEEEEEEEOEOEOEOEOEO
UHHH...

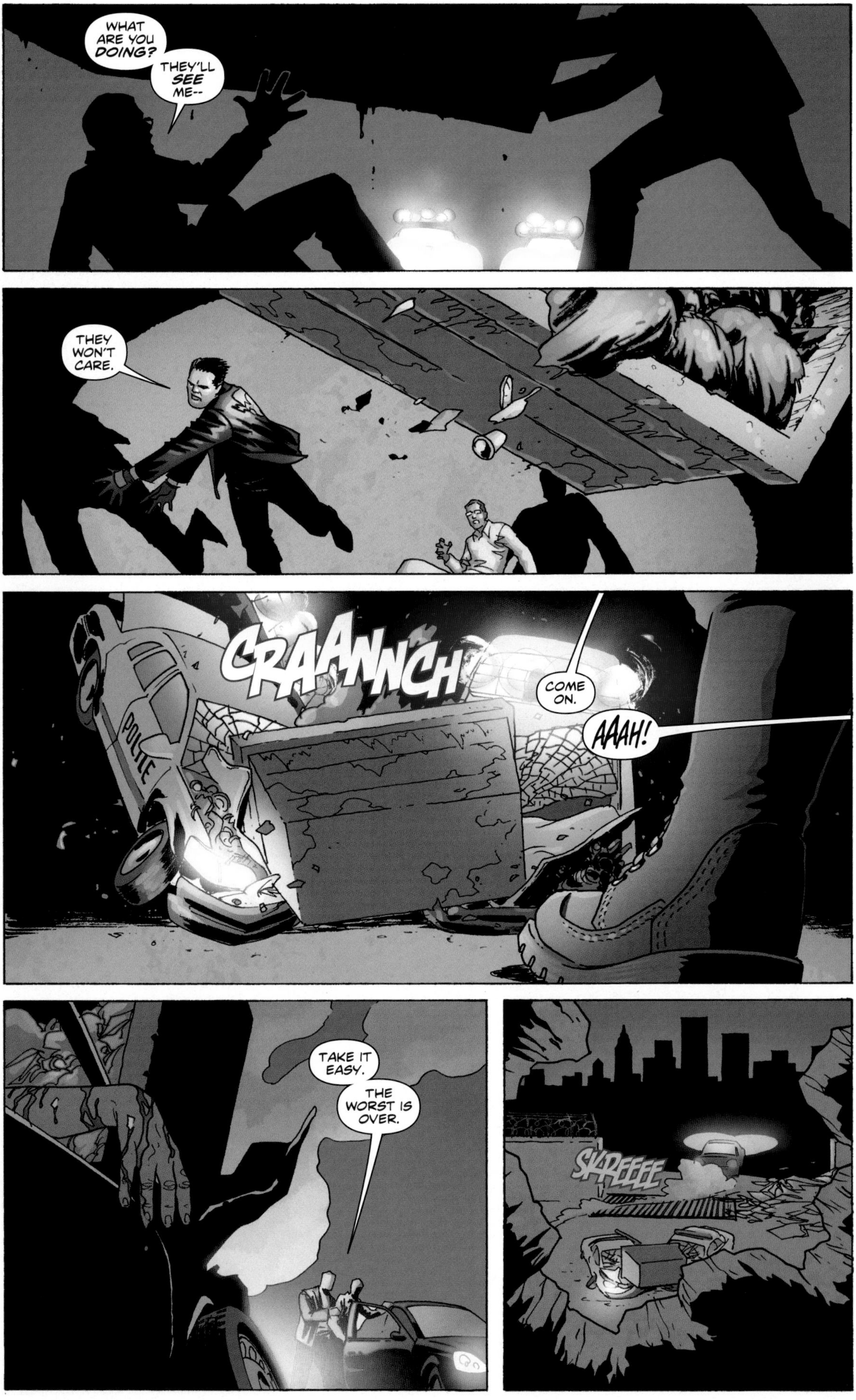
WHAT ARE YOU DOING?
THEY'LL SEE ME--
THEY WON'T CARE.
CRAANNCH
COME ON.
AAAH!
TAKE IT EASY.
THE WORST IS OVER.
SKREEEEE

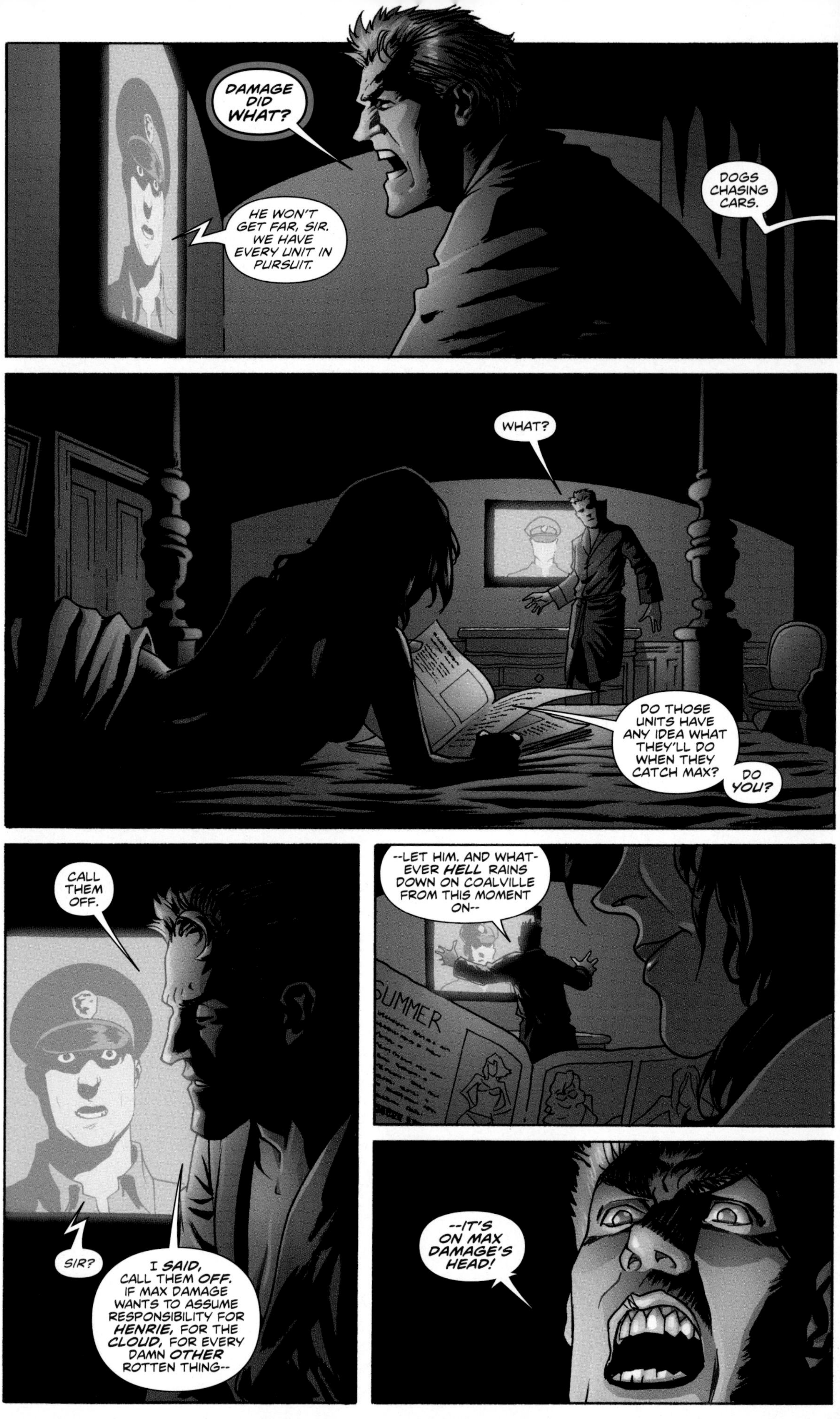
DAMAGE DID WHAT?
HE WON'T GET FAR, SIR. WE HAVE EVERY UNIT IN PURSUIT.
DOGS CHASING CARS.
WHAT?
DO THOSE UNITS HAVE ANY IDEA WHAT THEY'LL DO WHEN THEY CATCH MAX?
DO YOU?
CALL THEM OFF.
SIR?
I SAID, CALL THEM OFF. IF MAX DAMAGE WANTS TO ASSUME RESPONSIBILITY FOR HENRIE, FOR THE CLOUD, FOR EVERY DAMN OTHER ROTTEN THING--
--LET HIM. AND WHATEVER HELL RAINS DOWN ON COALVILLE FROM THIS MOMENT ON--
SUMMER
--IT'S ON MAX DAMAGE'S HEAD!

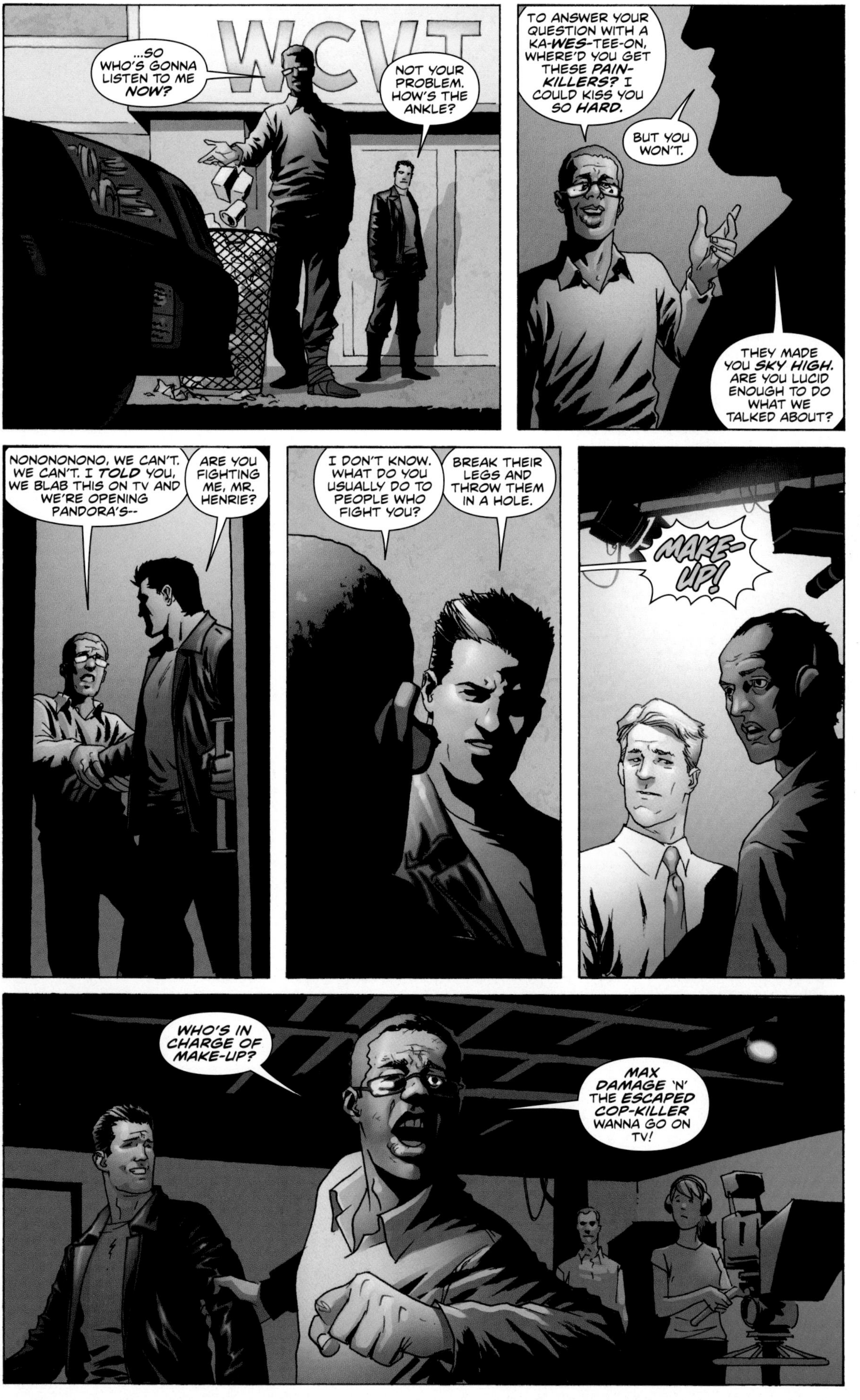

...SO WHO'S GONNA LISTEN TO ME NOW?
NOT YOUR PROBLEM. HOW'S THE ANKLE?
TO ANSWER YOUR QUESTION WITH A KA-WES-TEE-ON, WHERE'D YOU GET THESE PAIN-KILLERS? I COULD KISS YOU SO HARD.
BUT YOU WON'T.
THEY MADE YOU SKY HIGH. ARE YOU LUCID ENOUGH TO DO WHAT WE TALKED ABOUT?
NONONONONO, WE CAN'T. WE CAN'T. I TOLD YOU, WE BLAB THIS ON TV AND WE'RE OPENING PANDORA'S--
ARE YOU FIGHTING ME, MR. HENRIE?
I DON'T KNOW. WHAT DO YOU USUALLY DO TO PEOPLE WHO FIGHT YOU?
BREAK THEIR LEGS AND THROW THEM IN A HOLE.
MAKE-UP!
WHO'S IN CHARGE OF MAKE-UP?
MAX DAMAGE 'N' THE ESCAPED COP-KILLER WANNA GO ON TV!

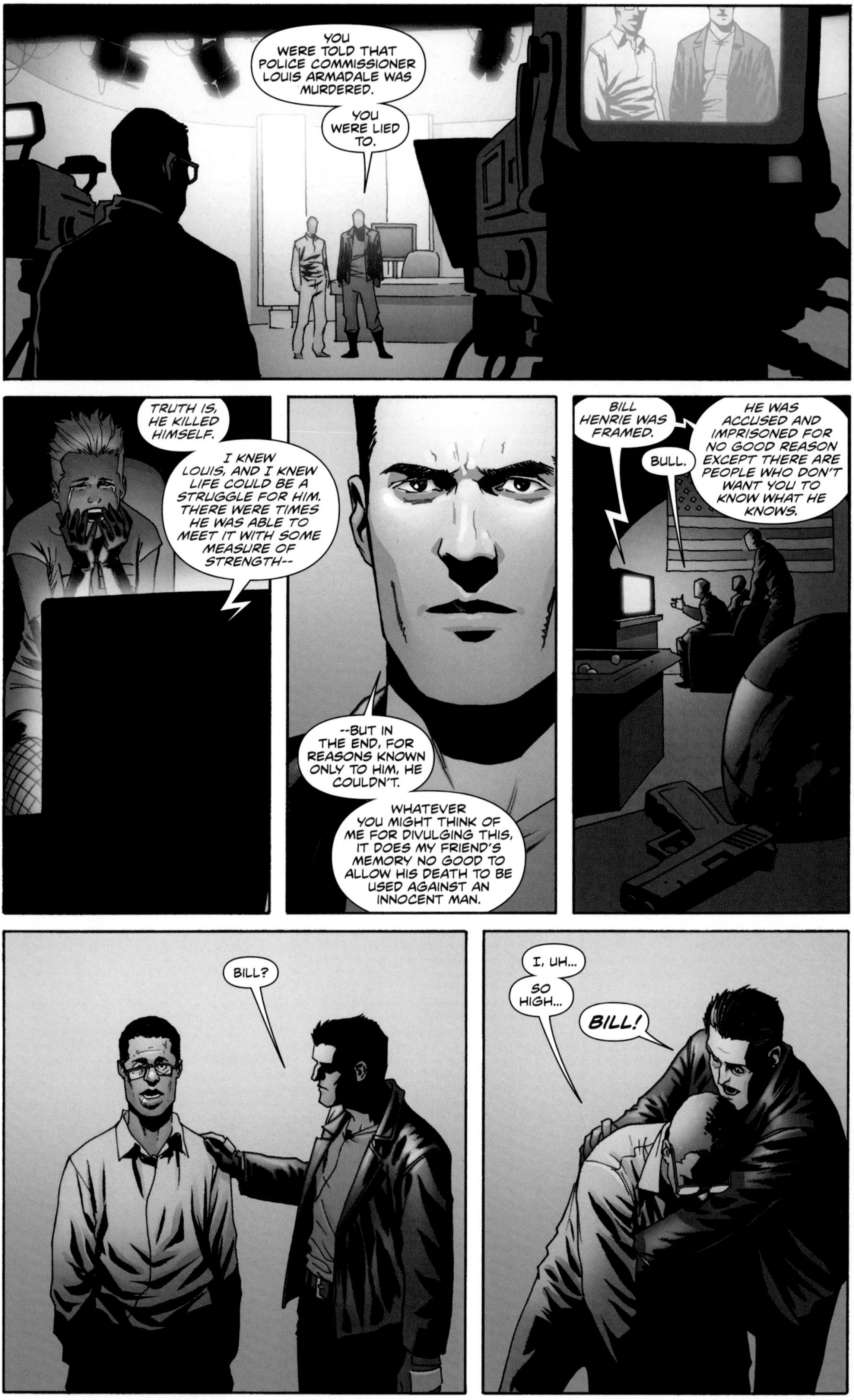
YOU WERE TOLD THAT POLICE COMMISSIONER LOUIS ARMADALE WAS MURDERED.
YOU WERE LIED TO.
TRUTH IS, HE KILLED HIMSELF.
I KNEW LOUIS, AND I KNEW LIFE COULD BE A STRUGGLE FOR HIM. THERE WERE TIMES HE WAS ABLE TO MEET IT WITH SOME MEASURE OF STRENGTH--
--BUT IN THE END, FOR REASONS KNOWN ONLY TO HIM, HE COULDN'T.
WHATEVER YOU MIGHT THINK OF ME FOR DIVULGING THIS, IT DOES MY FRIEND'S MEMORY NO GOOD TO ALLOW HIS DEATH TO BE USED AGAINST AN INNOCENT MAN.
BILL HENRIE WAS FRAMED.
HE WAS ACCUSED AND IMPRISONED FOR NO GOOD REASON EXCEPT THERE ARE PEOPLE WHO DON'T WANT YOU TO KNOW WHAT HE KNOWS.
BULL.
BILL?
I, UH...
SO HIGH...
BILL!

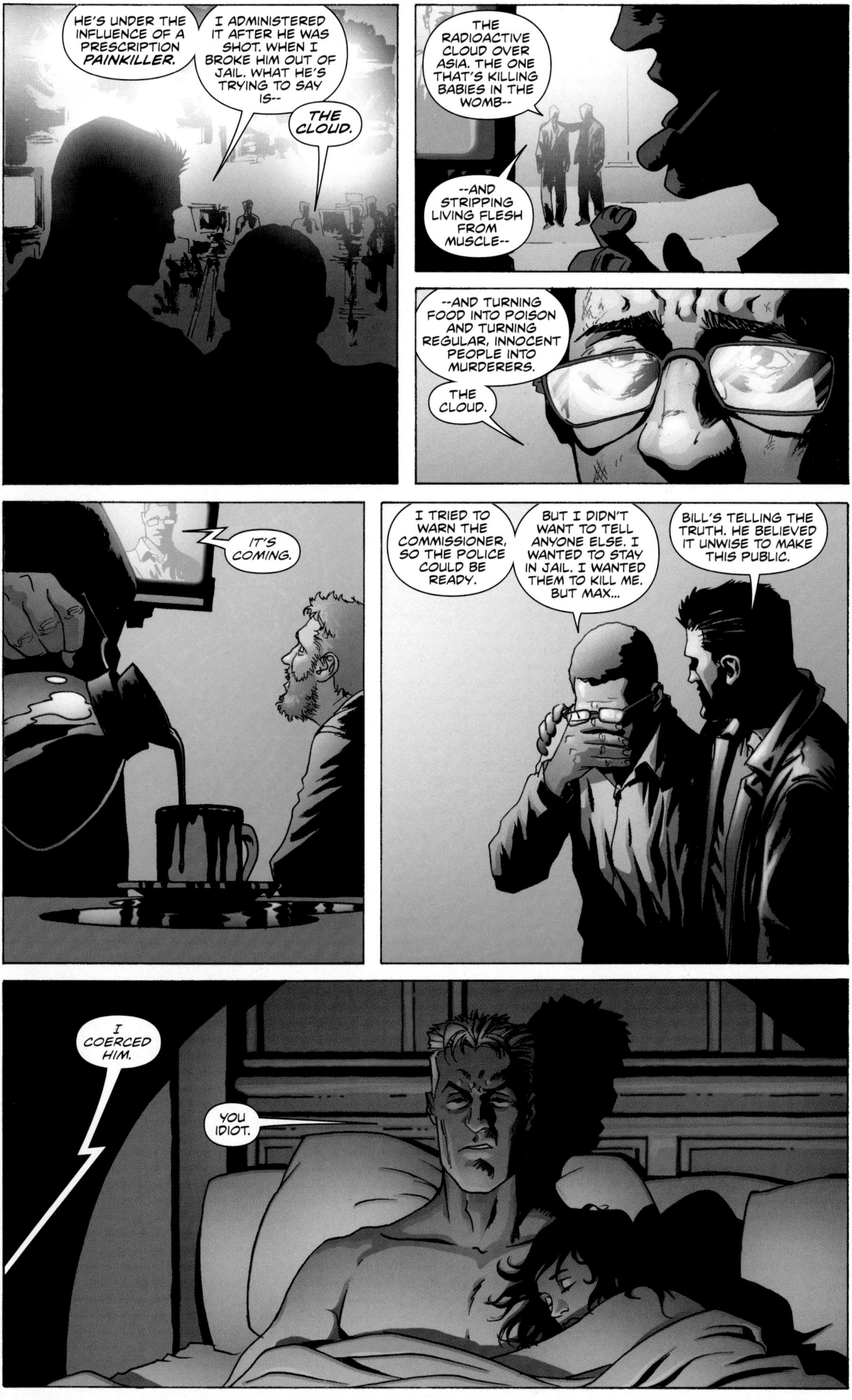
HE'S UNDER THE INFLUENCE OF A PRESCRIPTION *PAINKILLER.*
I ADMINISTERED IT AFTER HE WAS SHOT. WHEN I BROKE HIM OUT OF JAIL. WHAT HE'S TRYING TO SAY IS--
THE CLOUD.
THE RADIOACTIVE CLOUD OVER ASIA. THE ONE THAT'S KILLING BABIES IN THE WOMB--
--AND STRIPPING LIVING FLESH FROM MUSCLE--
--AND TURNING FOOD INTO POISON AND TURNING REGULAR, INNOCENT PEOPLE INTO MURDERERS.
THE CLOUD.
IT'S COMING.
I TRIED TO WARN THE COMMISSIONER, SO THE POLICE COULD BE READY.
BUT I DIDN'T WANT TO TELL ANYONE ELSE. I WANTED TO STAY IN JAIL. I WANTED THEM TO KILL ME. BUT MAX...
BILL'S TELLING THE TRUTH. HE BELIEVED IT UNWISE TO MAKE THIS PUBLIC.
I COERCED HIM.
YOU IDIOT.

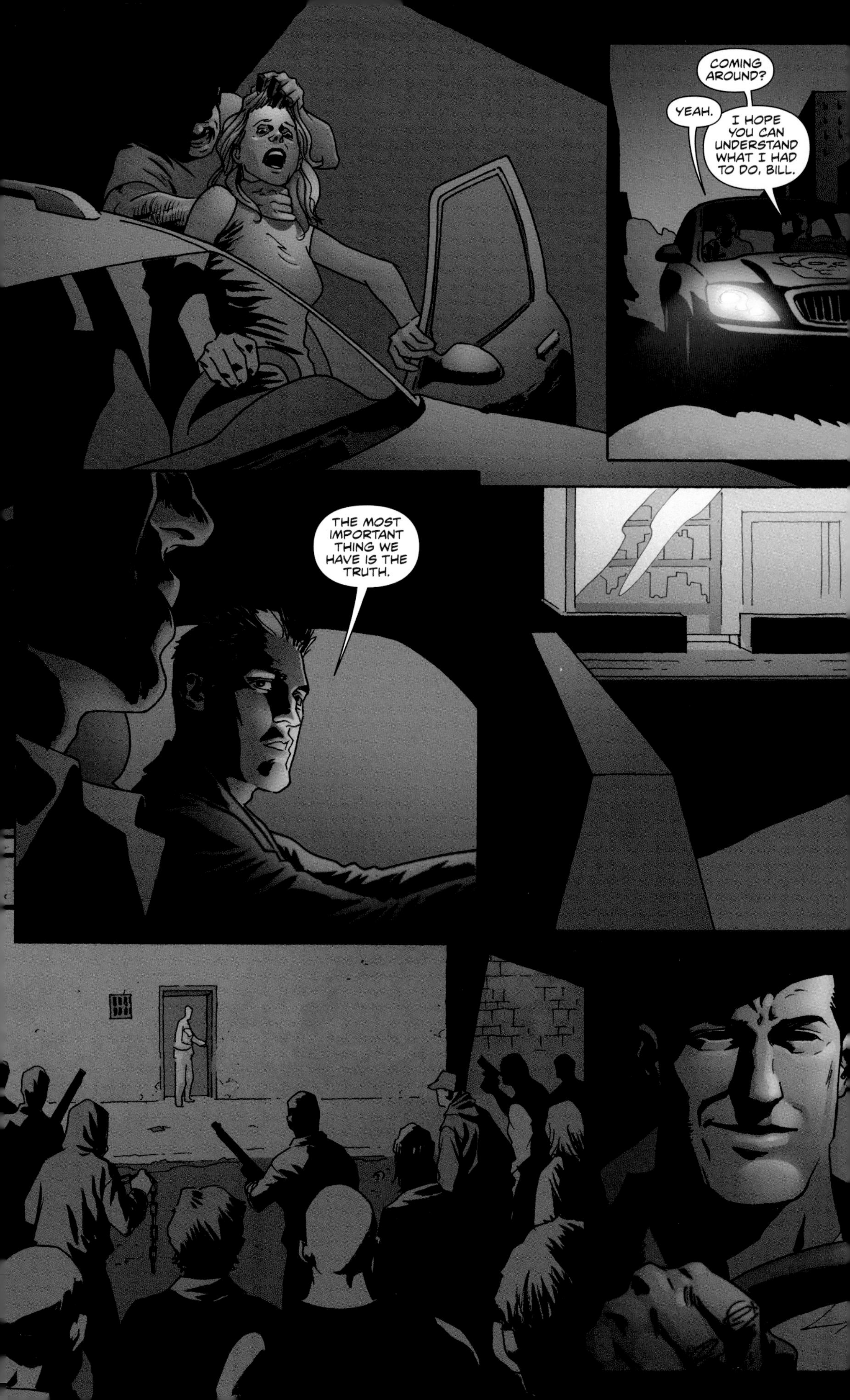
COMING AROUND?
YEAH.
I HOPE YOU CAN UNDERSTAND WHAT I HAD TO DO, BILL.
THE MOST IMPORTANT THING WE HAVE IS THE TRUTH.

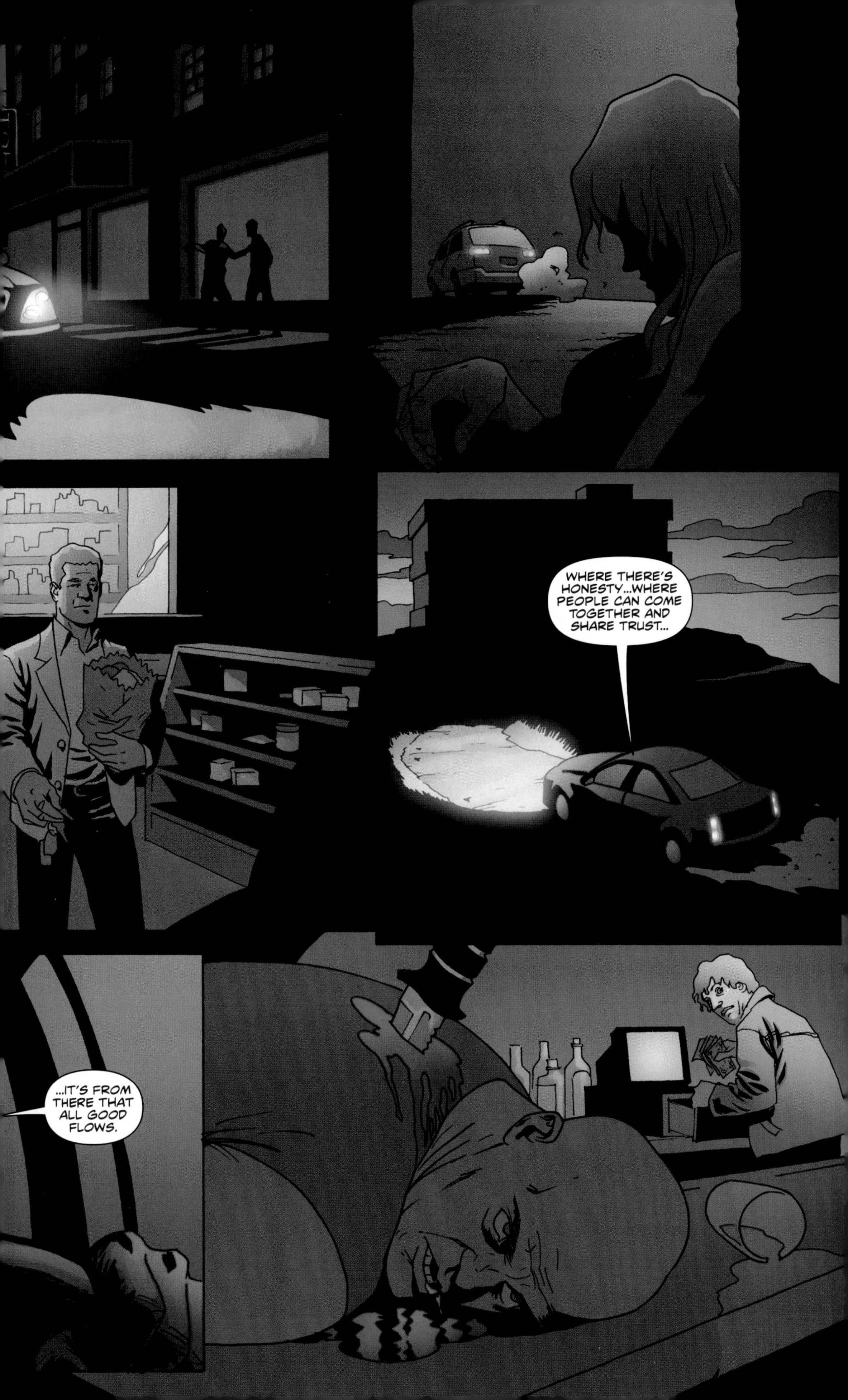
WHERE THERE'S HONESTY...WHERE PEOPLE CAN COME TOGETHER AND SHARE TRUST...
...IT'S FROM THERE THAT ALL GOOD FLOWS.

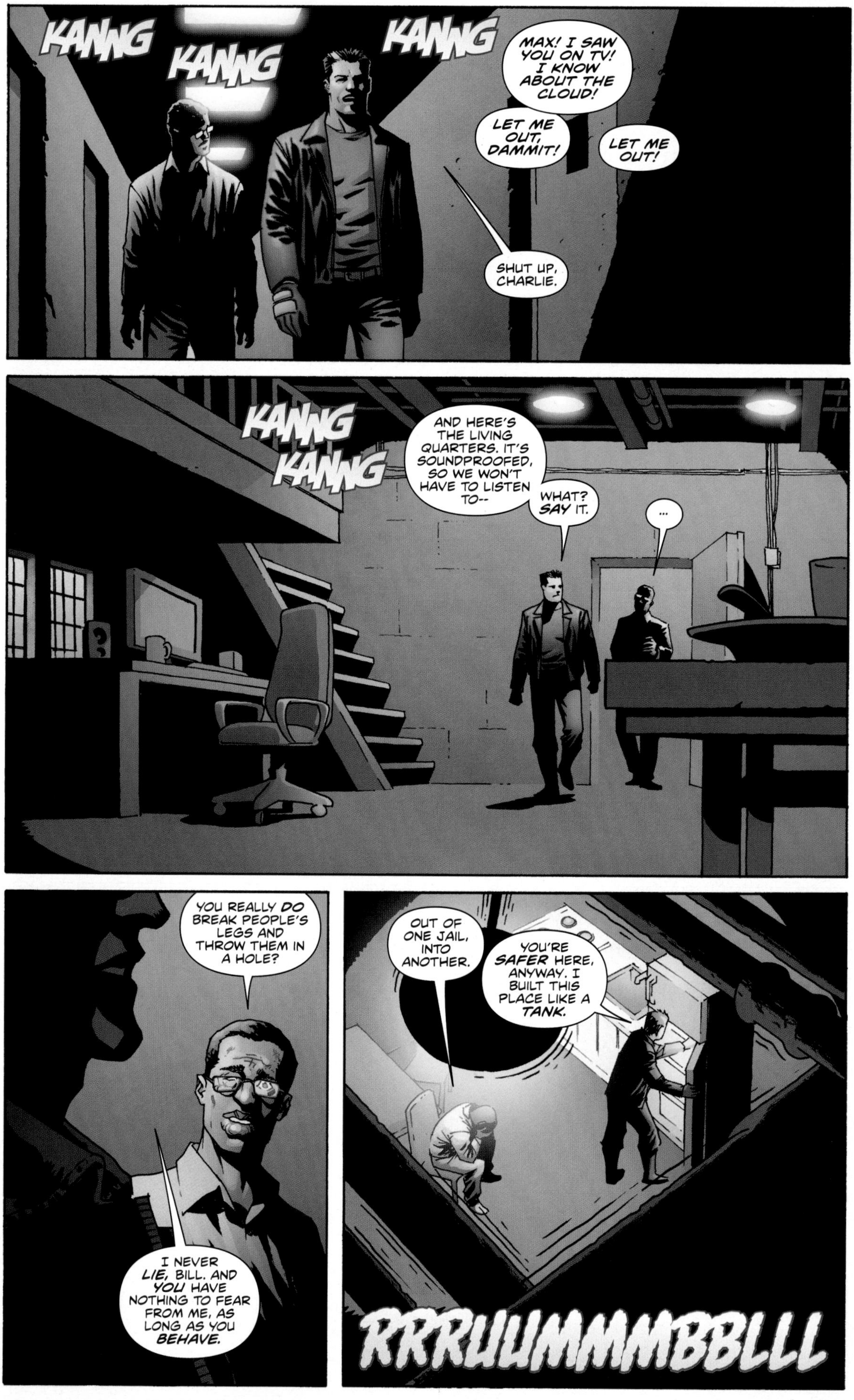
KANNG
KANNG
KANNG
MAX! I SAW YOU ON TV! I KNOW ABOUT THE CLOUD!
LET ME OUT, DAMMIT!
LET ME OUT!
SHUT UP, CHARLIE.
KANNG
KANNG
AND HERE'S THE LIVING QUARTERS. IT'S SOUNDPROOFED, SO WE WON'T HAVE TO LISTEN TO--
WHAT? SAY IT.
...
YOU REALLY DO BREAK PEOPLE'S LEGS AND THROW THEM IN A HOLE?
I NEVER LIE, BILL. AND YOU HAVE NOTHING TO FEAR FROM ME, AS LONG AS YOU BEHAVE.
OUT OF ONE JAIL, INTO ANOTHER.
YOU'RE SAFER HERE, ANYWAY. I BUILT THIS PLACE LIKE A TANK.
RRRUUMMMMBBLLL

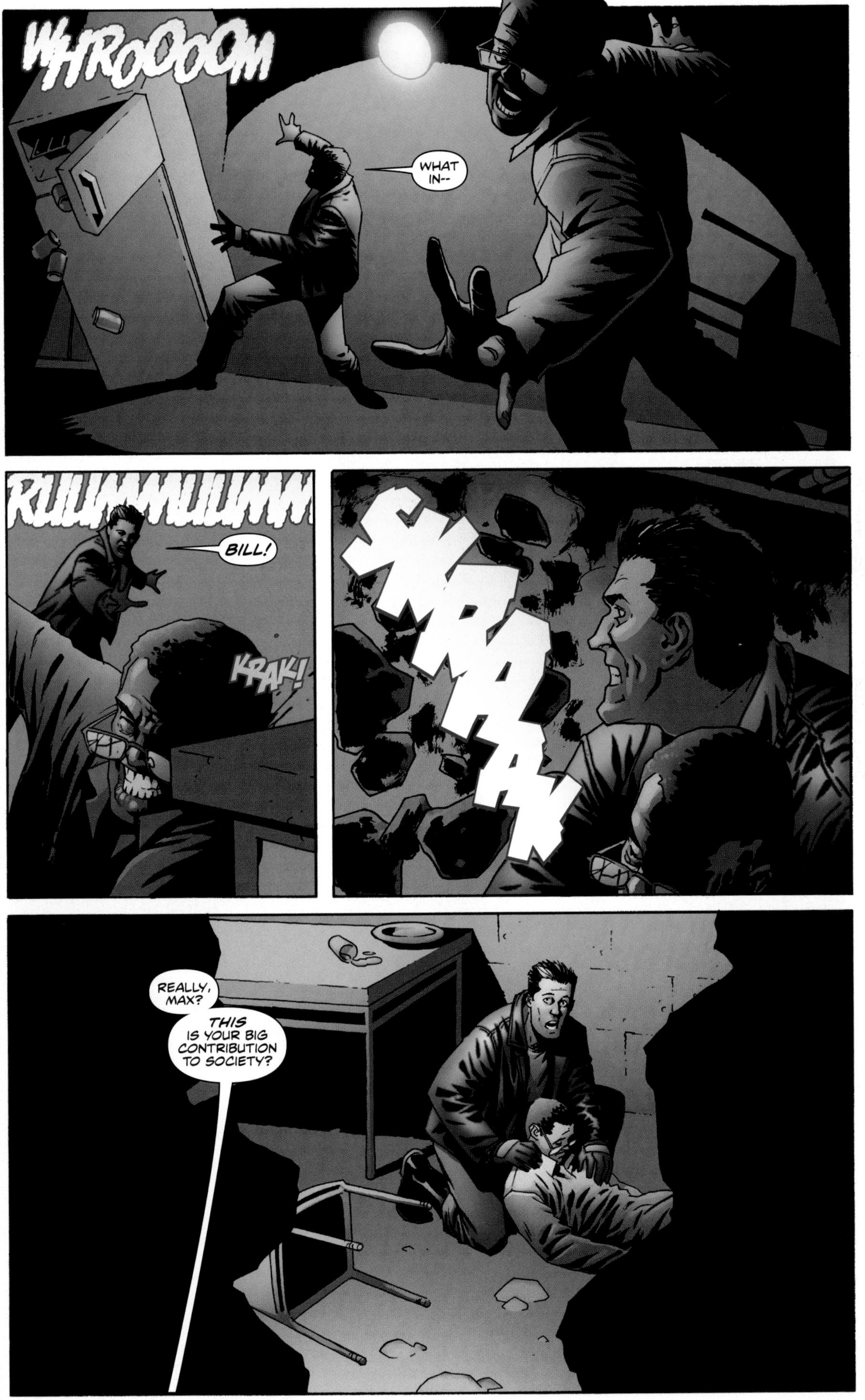
WHROOOOM
WHAT IN--
RUUMMMUUMM
BILL!
KRAK!
SKRAKAK
REALLY, MAX?
THIS IS YOUR BIG CONTRIBUTION TO SOCIETY?

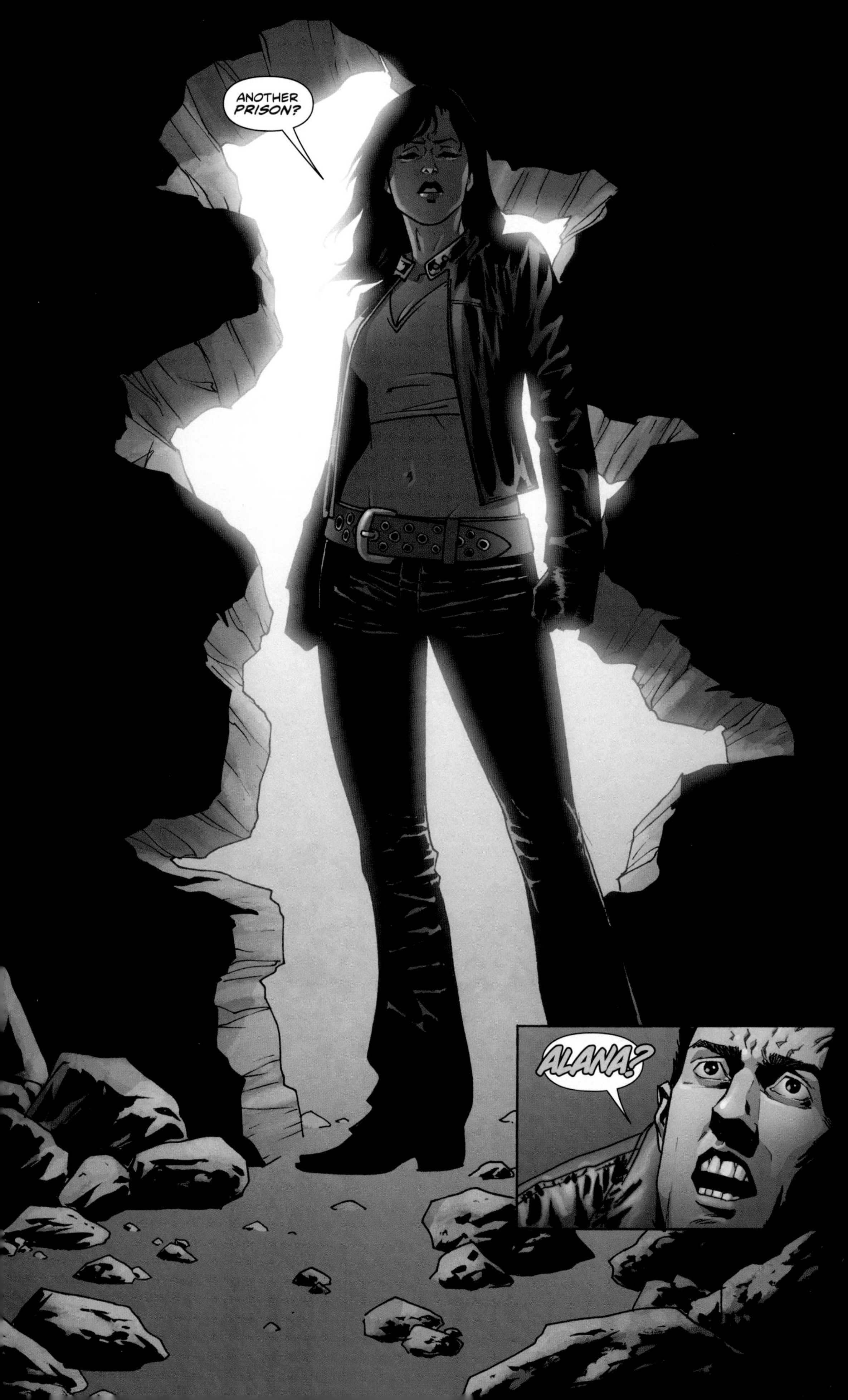
ANOTHER PRISON?
ALANA?

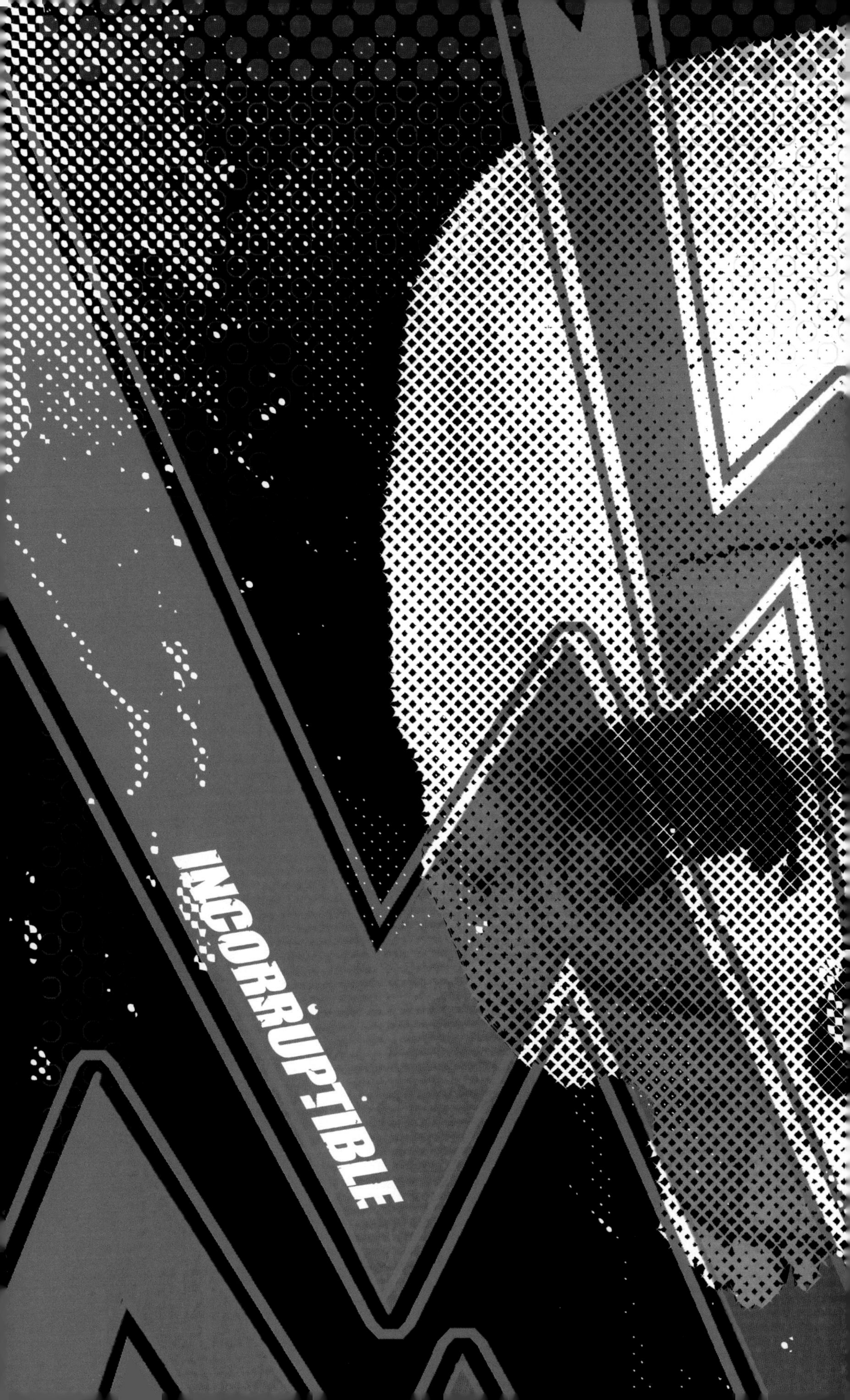
INCORRUPTIBLE

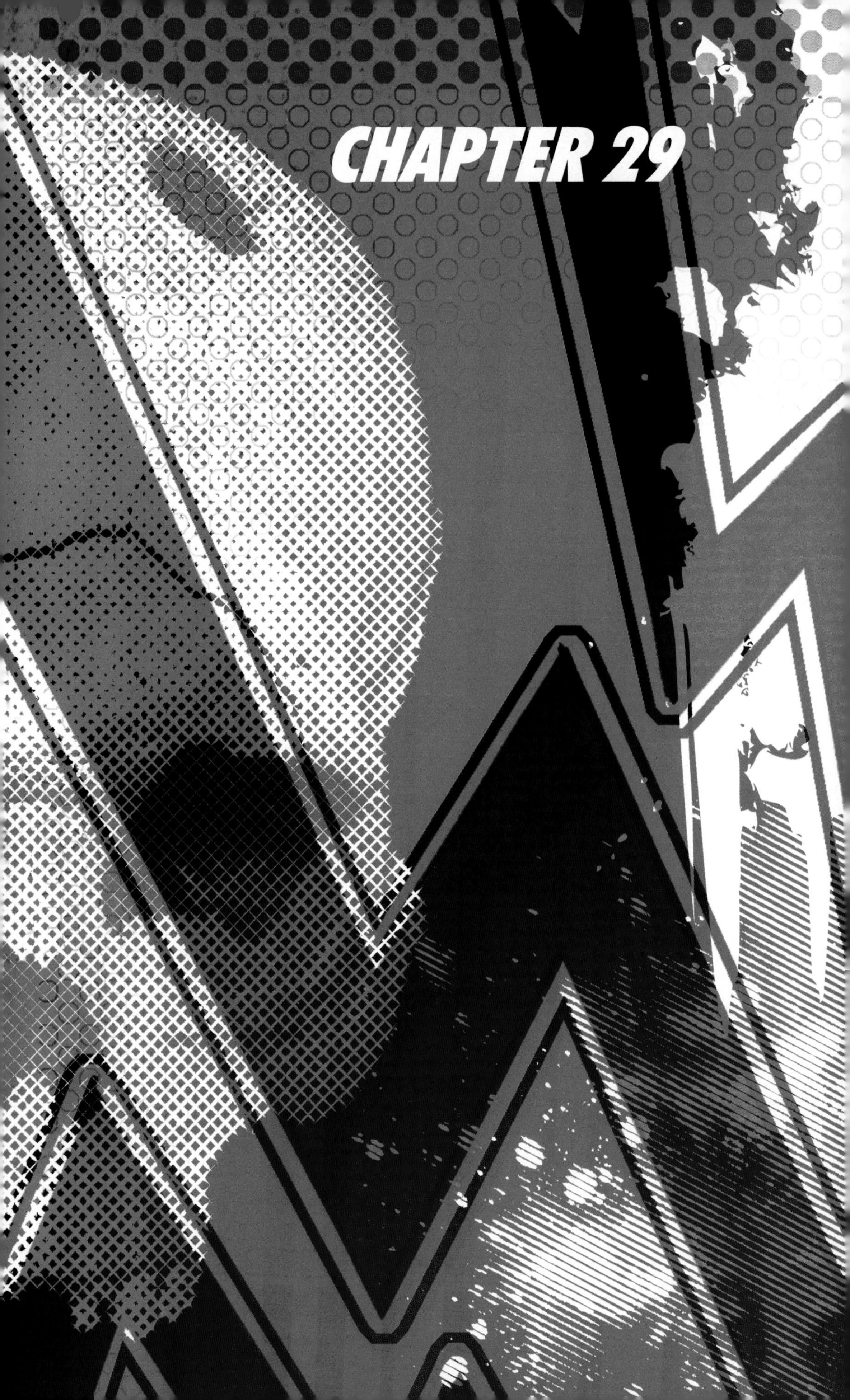
CHAPTER 29

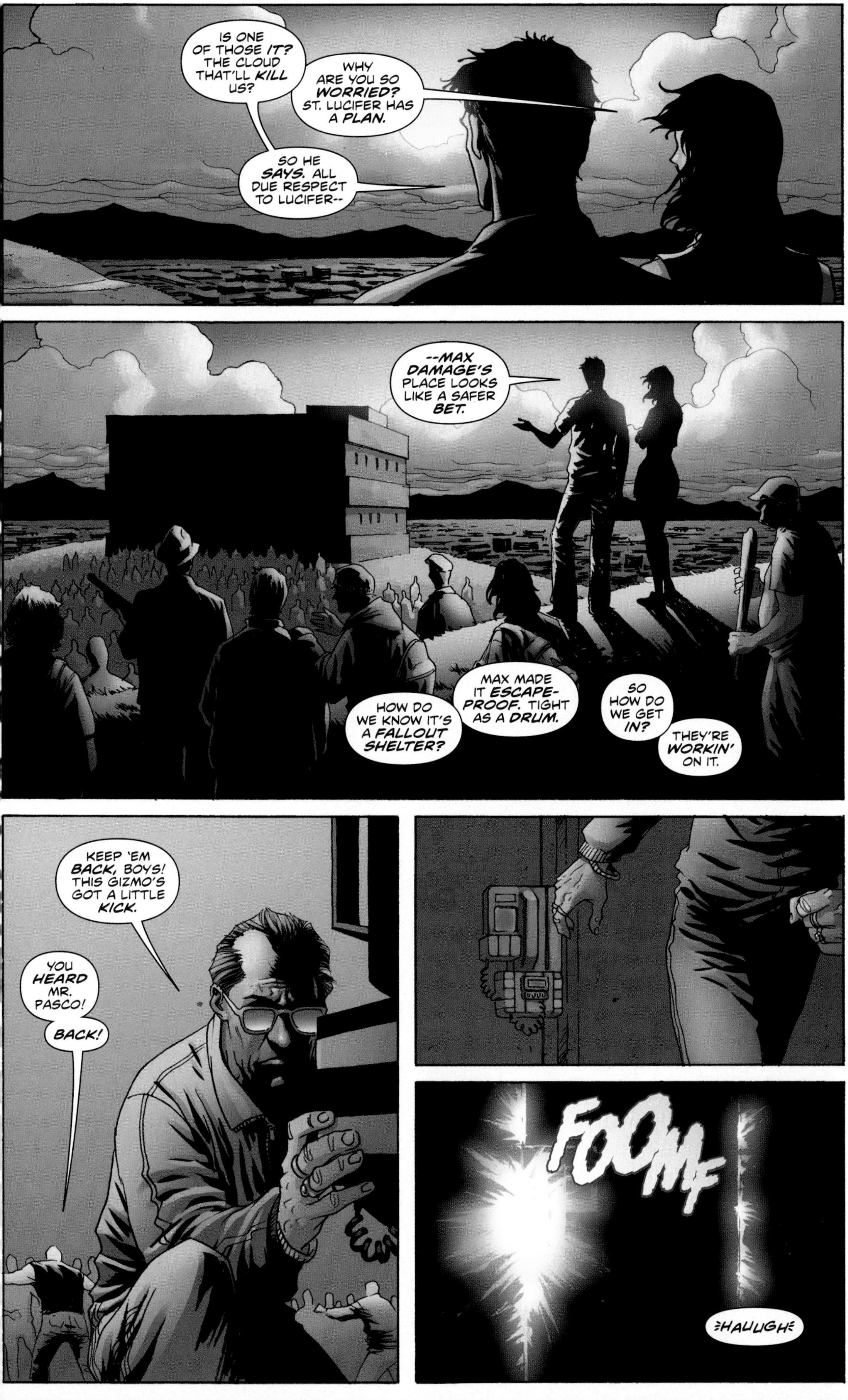
IS ONE OF THOSE IT? THE CLOUD THAT'LL KILL US?
WHY ARE YOU SO WORRIED? ST. LUCIFER HAS A PLAN.
SO HE SAYS. ALL DUE RESPECT TO LUCIFER--
--MAX DAMAGE'S PLACE LOOKS LIKE A SAFER BET.
HOW DO WE KNOW IT'S A FALLOUT SHELTER?
MAX MADE IT ESCAPE-PROOF. TIGHT AS A DRUM.
SO HOW DO WE GET IN?
THEY'RE WORKIN' ON IT.
KEEP 'EM BACK, BOYS! THIS GIZMO'S GOT A LITTLE KICK.
YOU HEARD MR. PASCO!
BACK!
FOOMF
HAUUGH

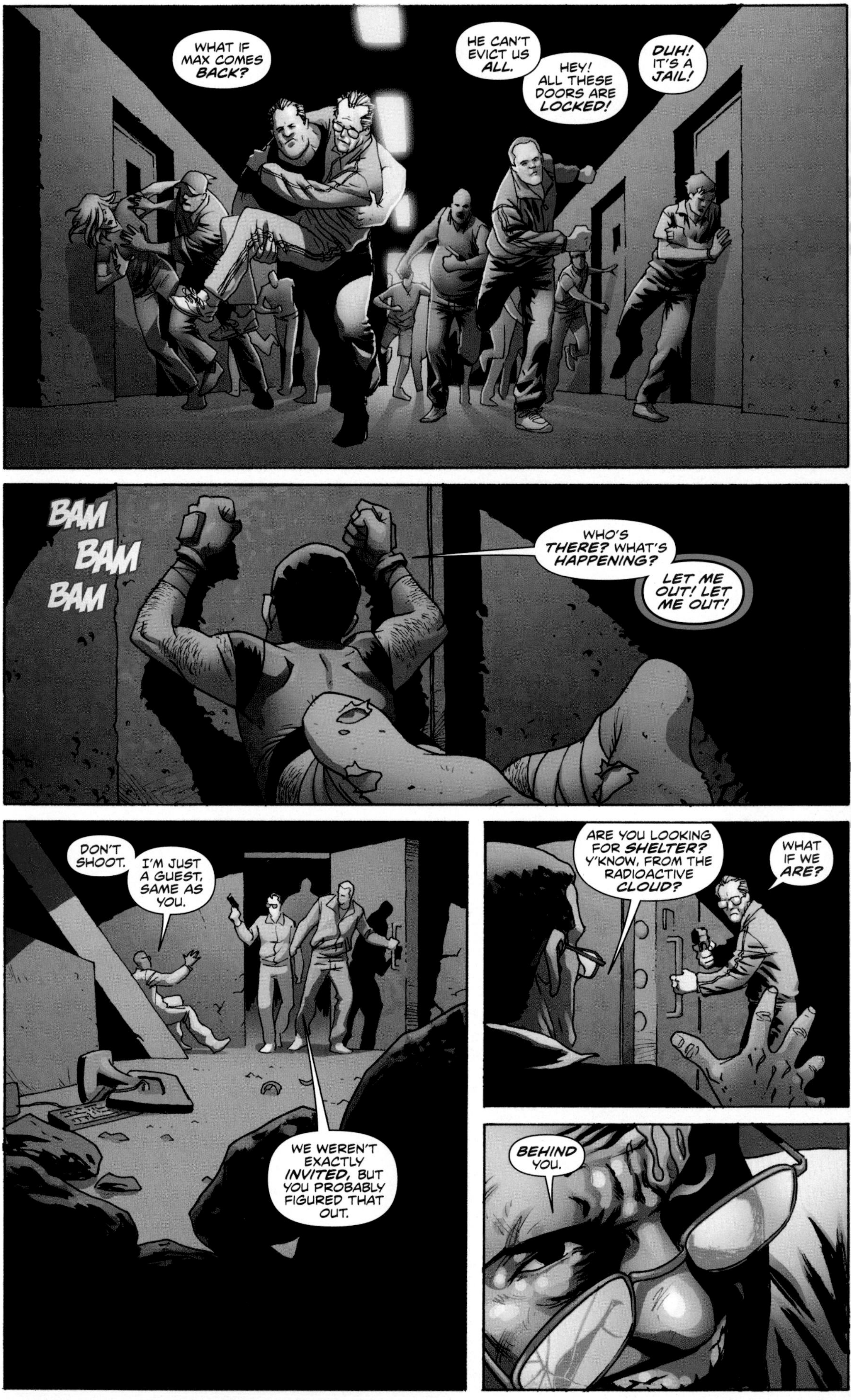
WHAT IF MAX COMES BACK?
HE CAN'T EVICT US ALL.
HEY! ALL THESE DOORS ARE LOCKED!
DUH! IT'S A JAIL!
BAM BAM BAM
WHO'S THERE? WHAT'S HAPPENING?
LET ME OUT! LET ME OUT!
DON'T SHOOT.
I'M JUST A GUEST, SAME AS YOU.
WE WEREN'T EXACTLY INVITED, BUT YOU PROBABLY FIGURED THAT OUT.
ARE YOU LOOKING FOR SHELTER? Y'KNOW, FROM THE RADIOACTIVE CLOUD?
WHAT IF WE ARE?
BEHIND YOU.

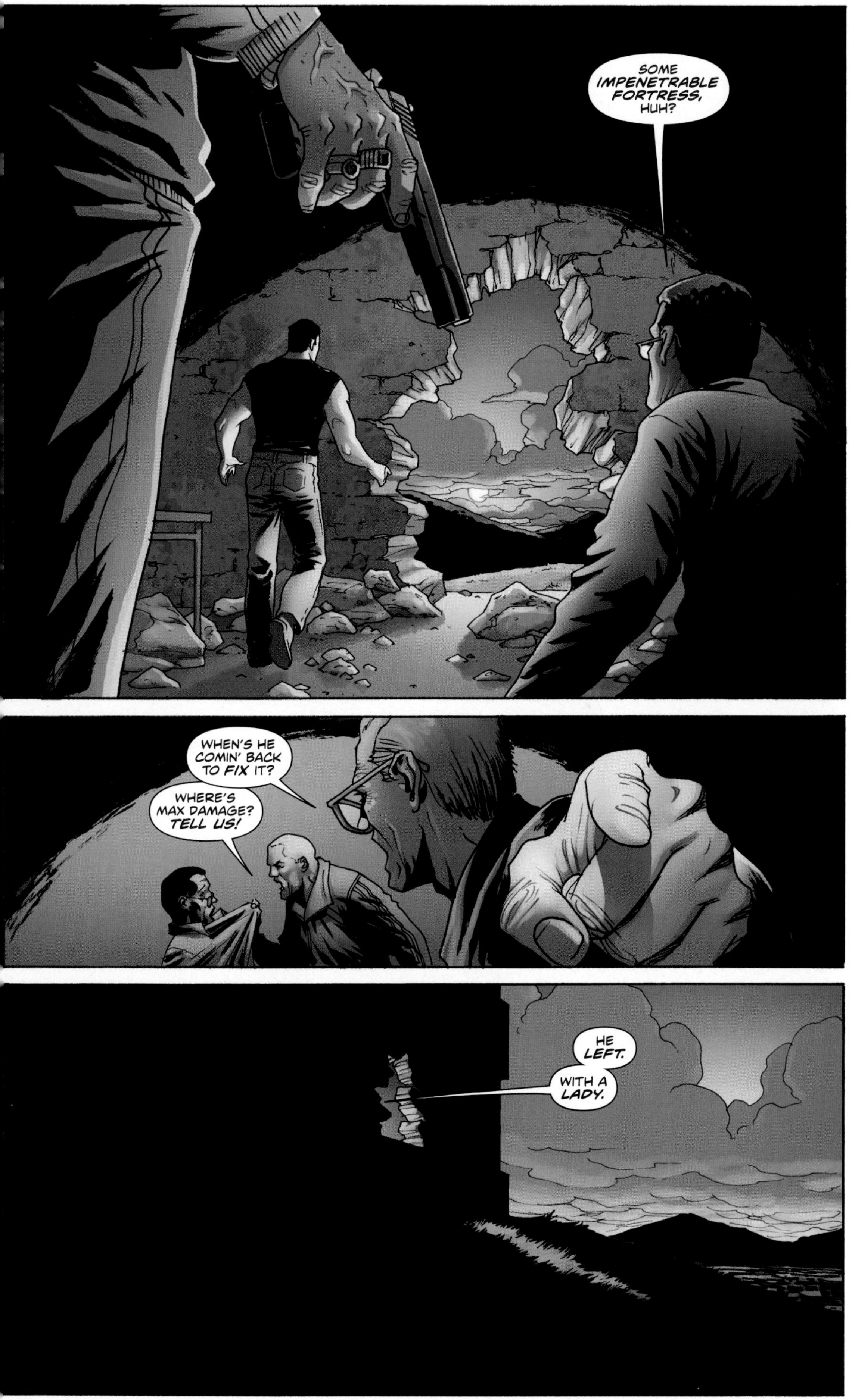

SOME IMPENETRABLE FORTRESS, HUH?
WHEN'S HE COMIN' BACK TO FIX IT?
WHERE'S MAX DAMAGE? TELL US!
HE LEFT.
WITH A LADY.

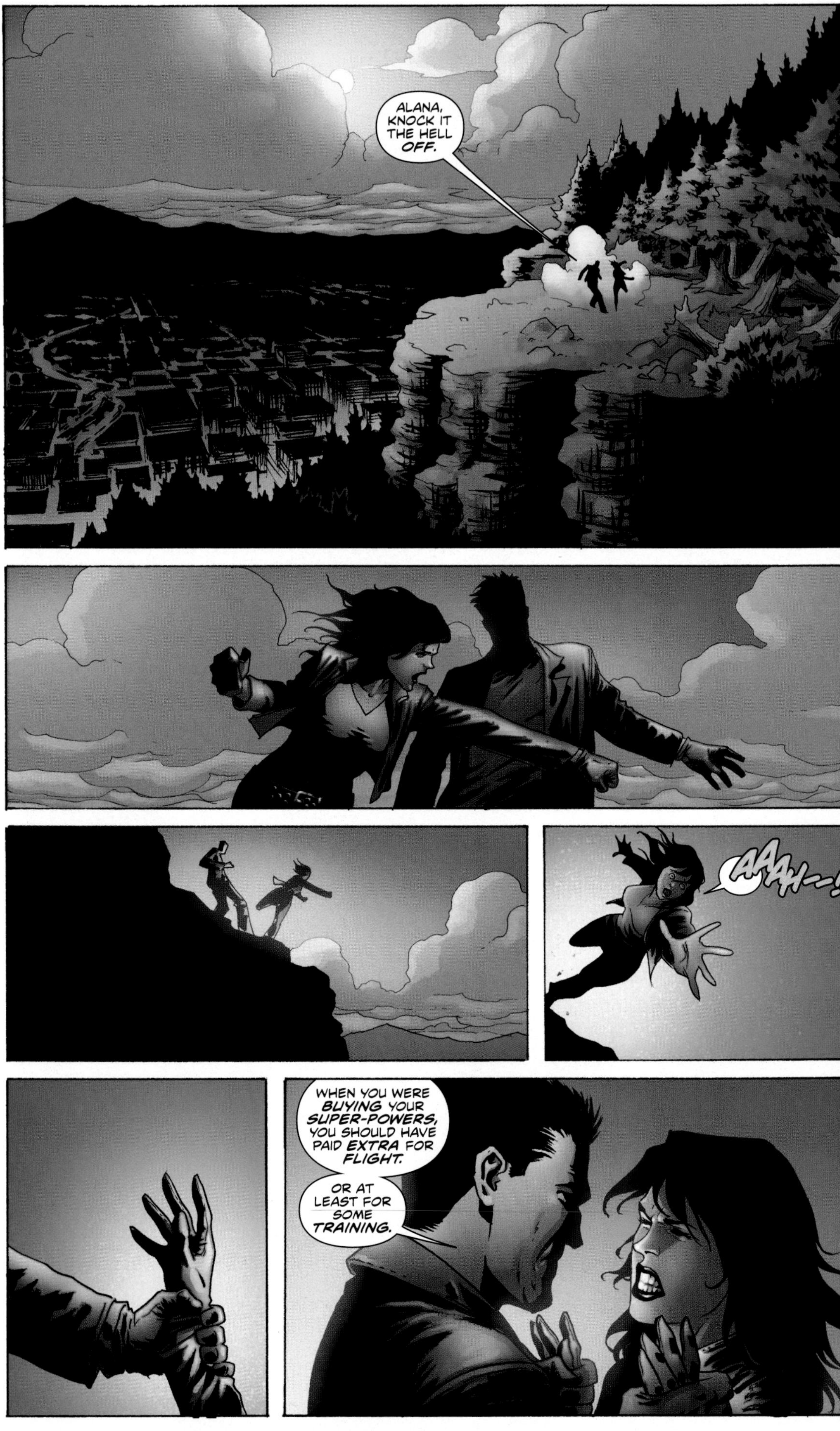

ALANA, KNOCK IT THE HELL OFF.
AAAH--!
WHEN YOU WERE BUYING YOUR SUPER-POWERS, YOU SHOULD HAVE PAID EXTRA FOR FLIGHT.
OR AT LEAST FOR SOME TRAINING.

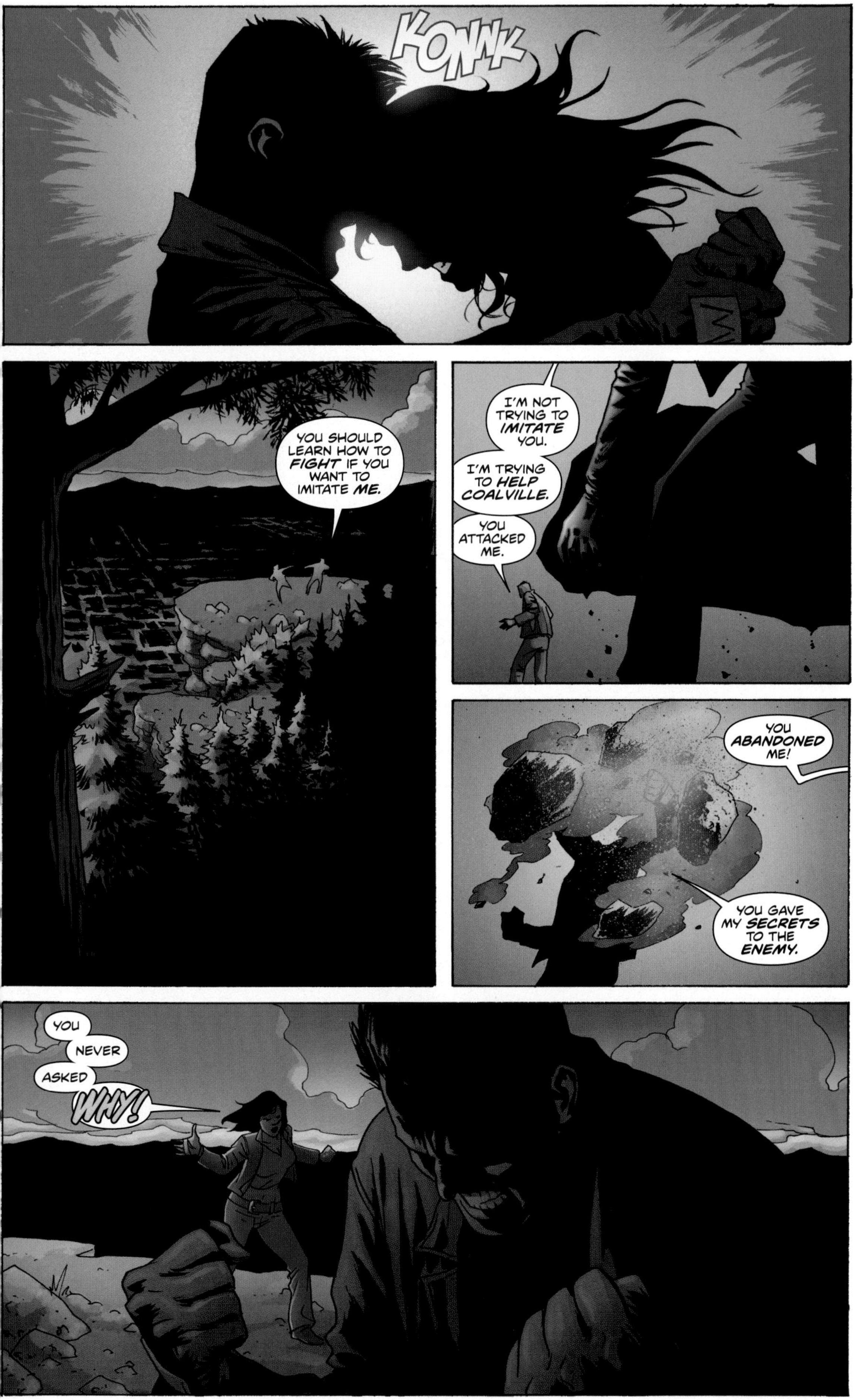
KONNK
YOU SHOULD LEARN HOW TO FIGHT IF YOU WANT TO IMITATE ME.
I'M NOT TRYING TO IMITATE YOU.
I'M TRYING TO HELP COALVILLE.
YOU ATTACKED ME.
YOU ABANDONED ME!
YOU GAVE MY SECRETS TO THE ENEMY.
YOU
NEVER
ASKED
WHY!

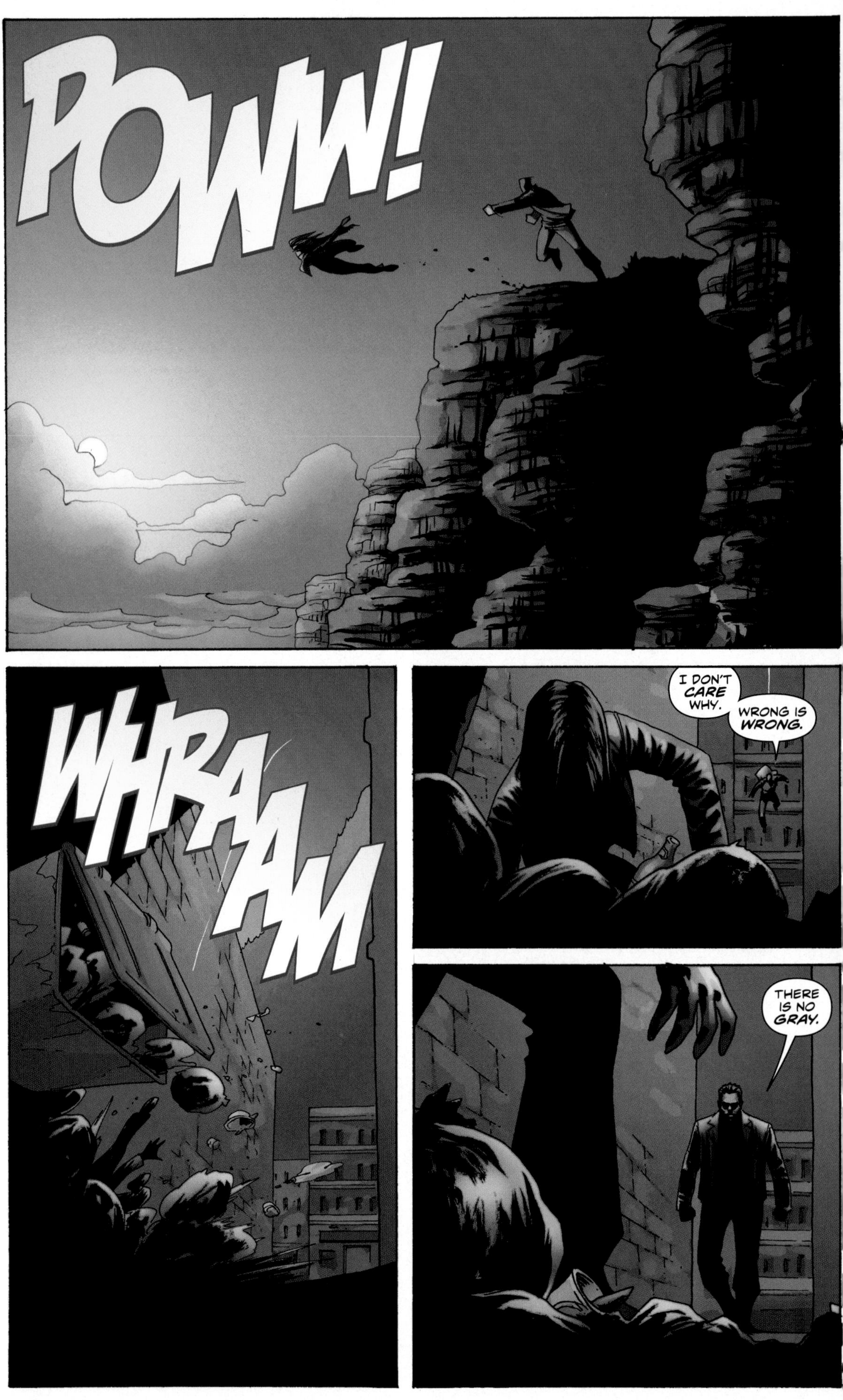
POWW!
WHRAAM
I DON'T *CARE* WHY.
WRONG IS *WRONG.*
THERE IS NO *GRAY.*

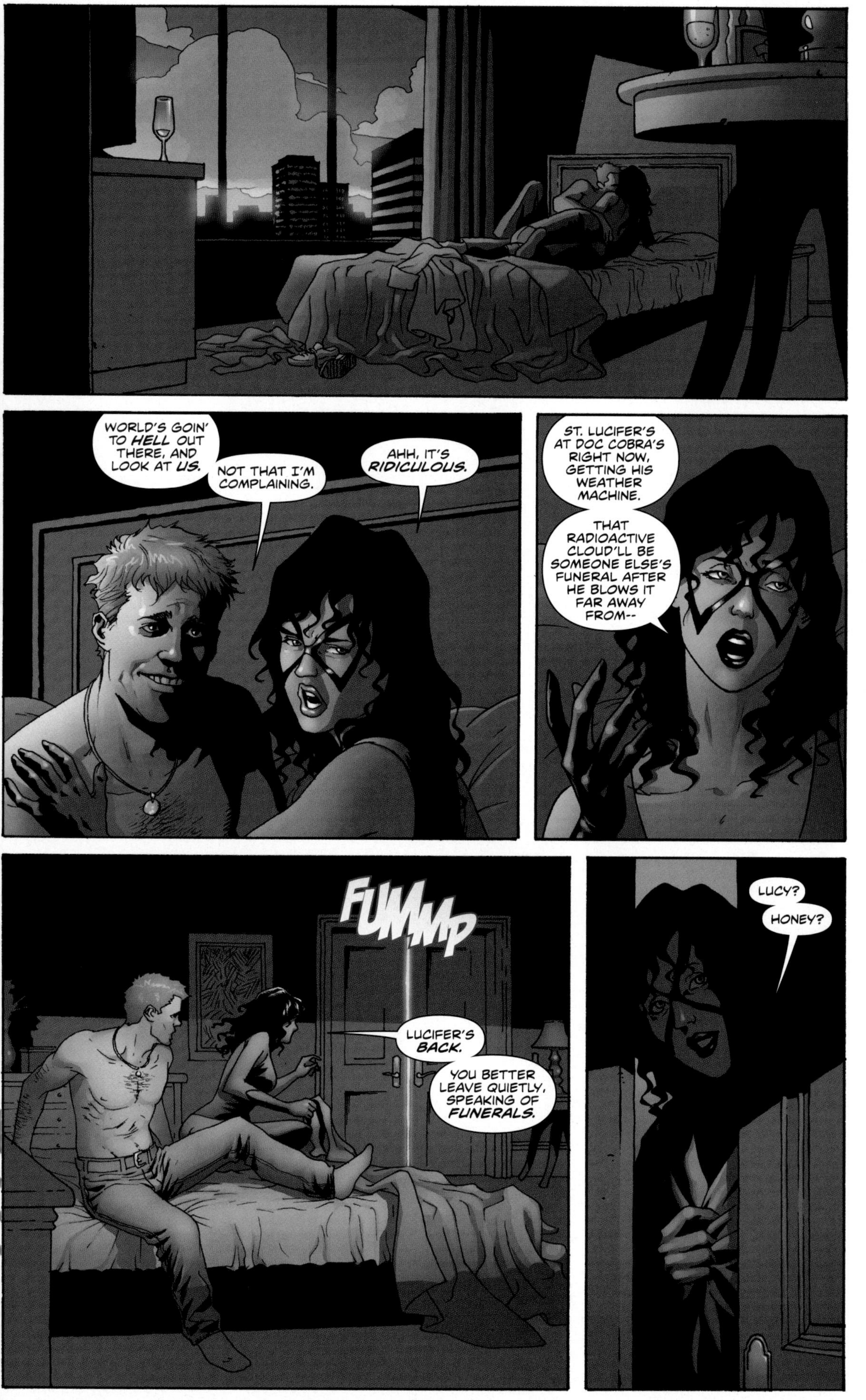
WORLD'S GOIN' TO HELL OUT THERE, AND LOOK AT US.
NOT THAT I'M COMPLAINING.
AHH, IT'S RIDICULOUS.
ST. LUCIFER'S AT DOC COBRA'S RIGHT NOW, GETTING HIS WEATHER MACHINE.
THAT RADIOACTIVE CLOUD'LL BE SOMEONE ELSE'S FUNERAL AFTER HE BLOWS IT FAR AWAY FROM--
FUMMP
LUCIFER'S BACK.
YOU BETTER LEAVE QUIETLY, SPEAKING OF FUNERALS.
LUCY?
HONEY?

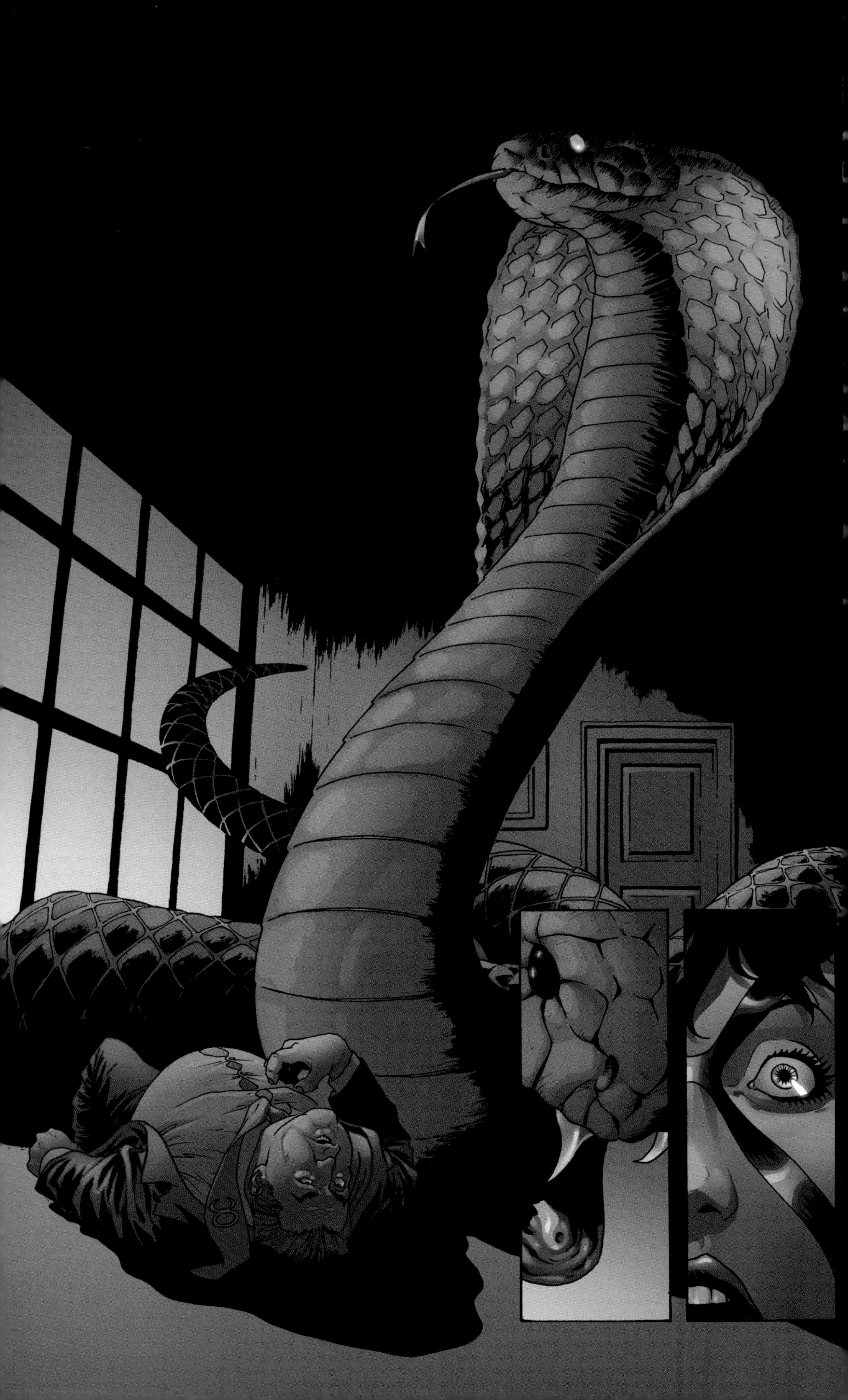

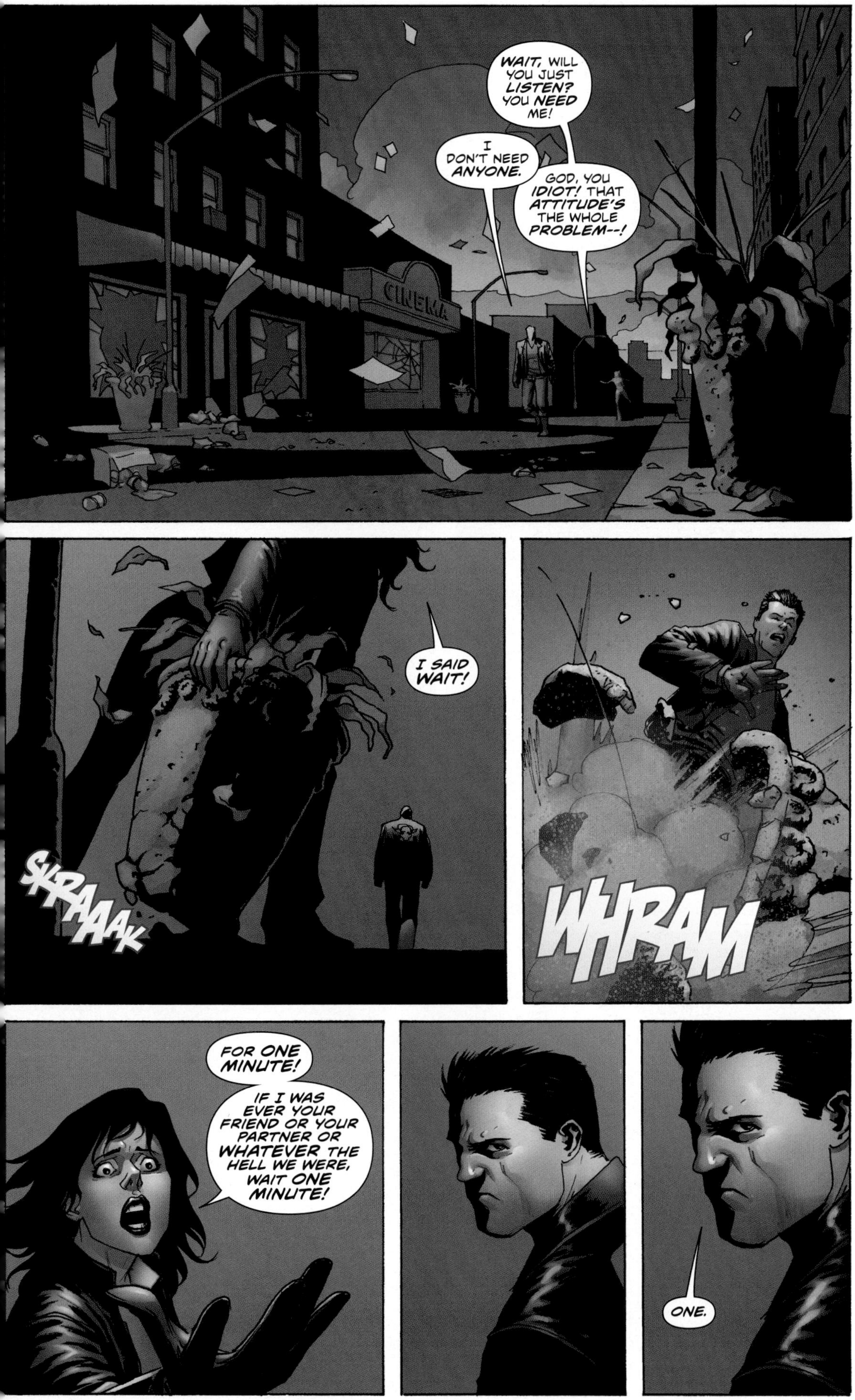
WAIT, WILL YOU JUST LISTEN? YOU NEED ME!
I DON'T NEED ANYONE.
GOD, YOU IDIOT! THAT ATTITUDE'S THE WHOLE PROBLEM--!
CINEMA
I SAID WAIT!
SKRAAAK
WHRAM
FOR ONE MINUTE!
IF I WAS EVER YOUR FRIEND OR YOUR PARTNER OR WHATEVER THE HELL WE WERE, WAIT ONE MINUTE!
ONE.

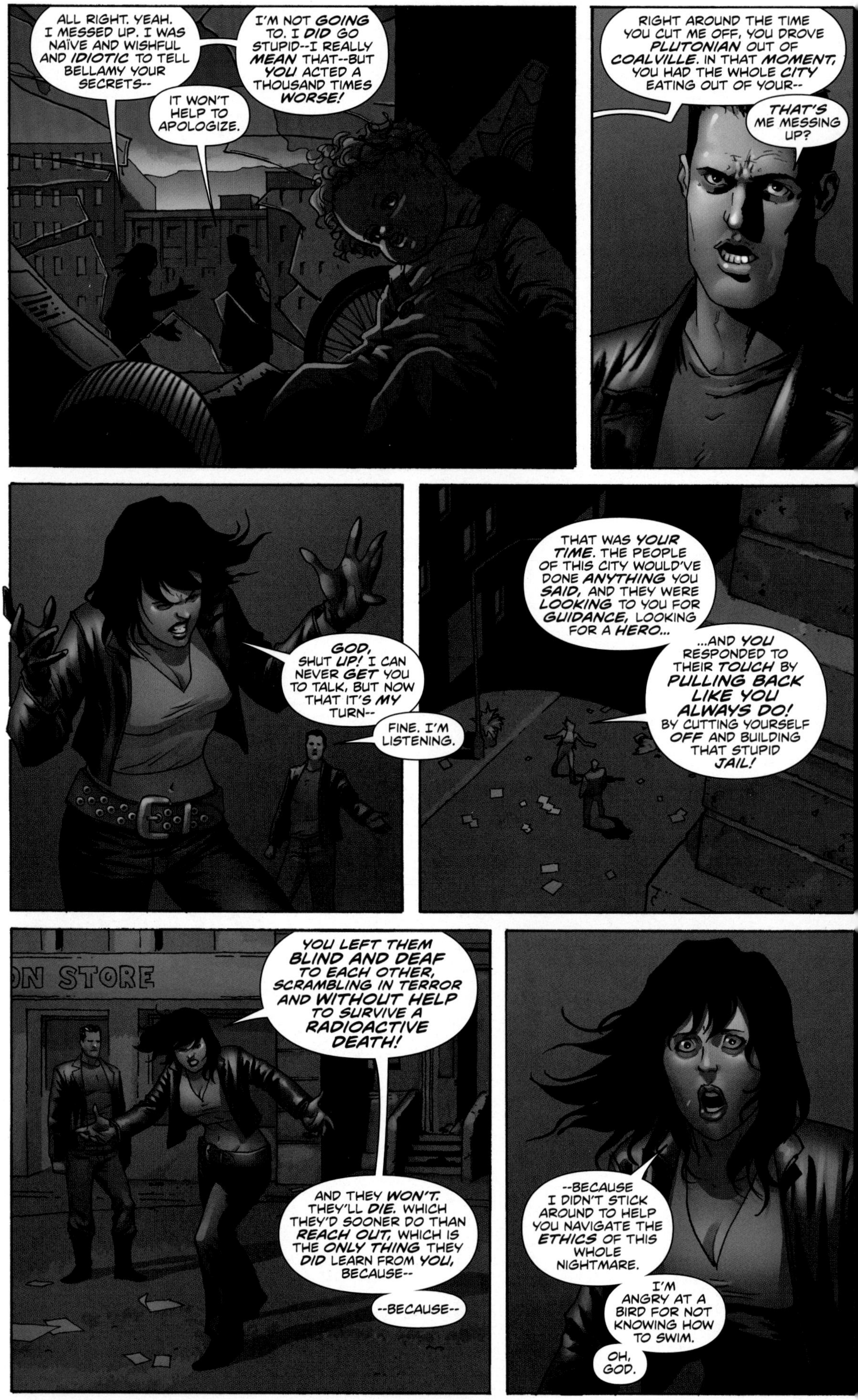

ALL RIGHT. YEAH. I MESSED UP. I WAS NAÏVE AND WISHFUL AND IDIOTIC TO TELL BELLAMY YOUR SECRETS--
IT WON'T HELP TO APOLOGIZE.
I'M NOT GOING TO. I DID GO STUPID--I REALLY MEAN THAT--BUT YOU ACTED A THOUSAND TIMES WORSE!
RIGHT AROUND THE TIME YOU CUT ME OFF, YOU DROVE PLUTONIAN OUT OF COALVILLE. IN THAT MOMENT, YOU HAD THE WHOLE CITY EATING OUT OF YOUR--
THAT'S ME MESSING UP?
GOD, SHUT UP! I CAN NEVER GET YOU TO TALK, BUT NOW THAT IT'S MY TURN--
FINE. I'M LISTENING.
THAT WAS YOUR TIME. THE PEOPLE OF THIS CITY WOULD'VE DONE ANYTHING YOU SAID, AND THEY WERE LOOKING TO YOU FOR GUIDANCE, LOOKING FOR A HERO...
...AND YOU RESPONDED TO THEIR TOUCH BY PULLING BACK LIKE YOU ALWAYS DO! BY CUTTING YOURSELF OFF AND BUILDING THAT STUPID JAIL!
ON STORE
YOU LEFT THEM BLIND AND DEAF TO EACH OTHER, SCRAMBLING IN TERROR AND WITHOUT HELP TO SURVIVE A RADIOACTIVE DEATH!
AND THEY WON'T. THEY'LL DIE. WHICH THEY'D SOONER DO THAN REACH OUT, WHICH IS THE ONLY THING THEY DID LEARN FROM YOU, BECAUSE--
--BECAUSE--
--BECAUSE I DIDN'T STICK AROUND TO HELP YOU NAVIGATE THE ETHICS OF THIS WHOLE NIGHTMARE.
I'M ANGRY AT A BIRD FOR NOT KNOWING HOW TO SWIM.
OH, GOD.

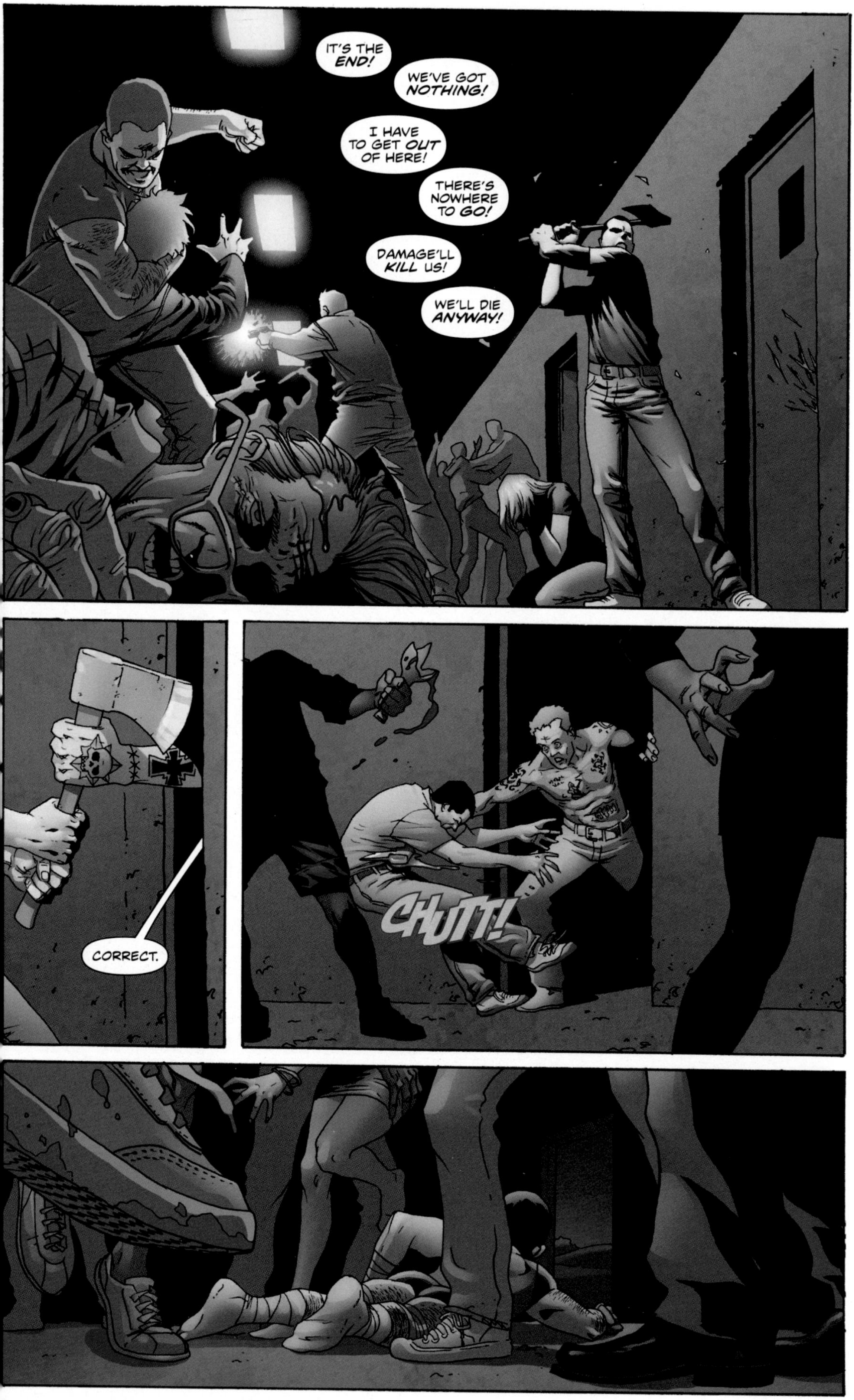
IT'S THE END!
WE'VE GOT NOTHING!
I HAVE TO GET OUT OF HERE!
THERE'S NOWHERE TO GO!
DAMAGE'LL KILL US!
WE'LL DIE ANYWAY!
CORRECT.
CHUTT!

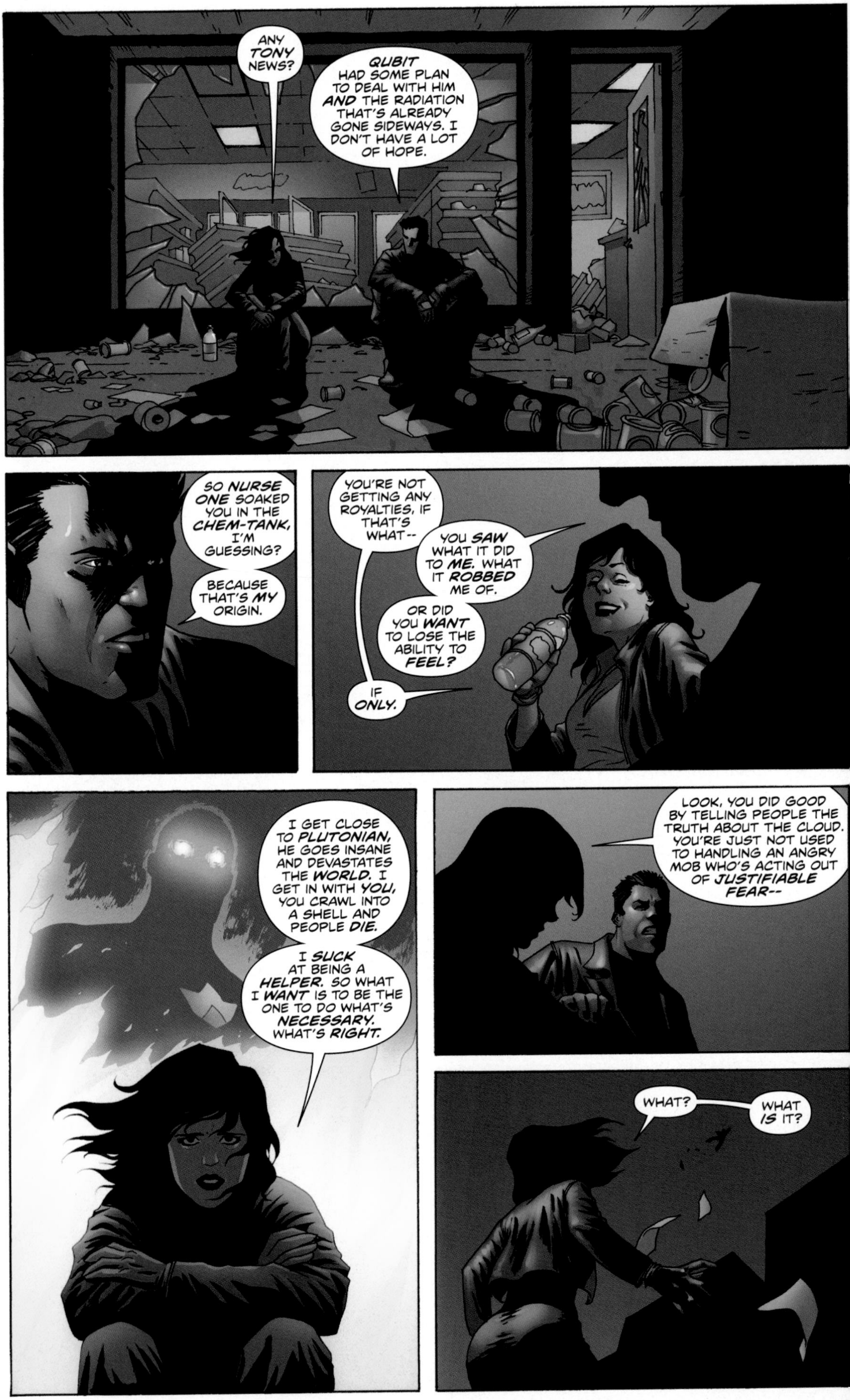
ANY TONY NEWS?
QUBIT HAD SOME PLAN TO DEAL WITH HIM AND THE RADIATION THAT'S ALREADY GONE SIDEWAYS. I DON'T HAVE A LOT OF HOPE.
SO NURSE ONE SOAKED YOU IN THE CHEM-TANK, I'M GUESSING?
BECAUSE THAT'S MY ORIGIN.
YOU'RE NOT GETTING ANY ROYALTIES, IF THAT'S WHAT--
YOU SAW WHAT IT DID TO ME. WHAT IT ROBBED ME OF.
OR DID YOU WANT TO LOSE THE ABILITY TO FEEL?
IF ONLY.
I GET CLOSE TO PLUTONIAN, HE GOES INSANE AND DEVASTATES THE WORLD. I GET IN WITH YOU, YOU CRAWL INTO A SHELL AND PEOPLE DIE.
I SUCK AT BEING A HELPER. SO WHAT I WANT IS TO BE THE ONE TO DO WHAT'S NECESSARY. WHAT'S RIGHT.
LOOK, YOU DID GOOD BY TELLING PEOPLE THE TRUTH ABOUT THE CLOUD. YOU'RE JUST NOT USED TO HANDLING AN ANGRY MOB WHO'S ACTING OUT OF JUSTIFIABLE FEAR--
WHAT?
WHAT IS IT?

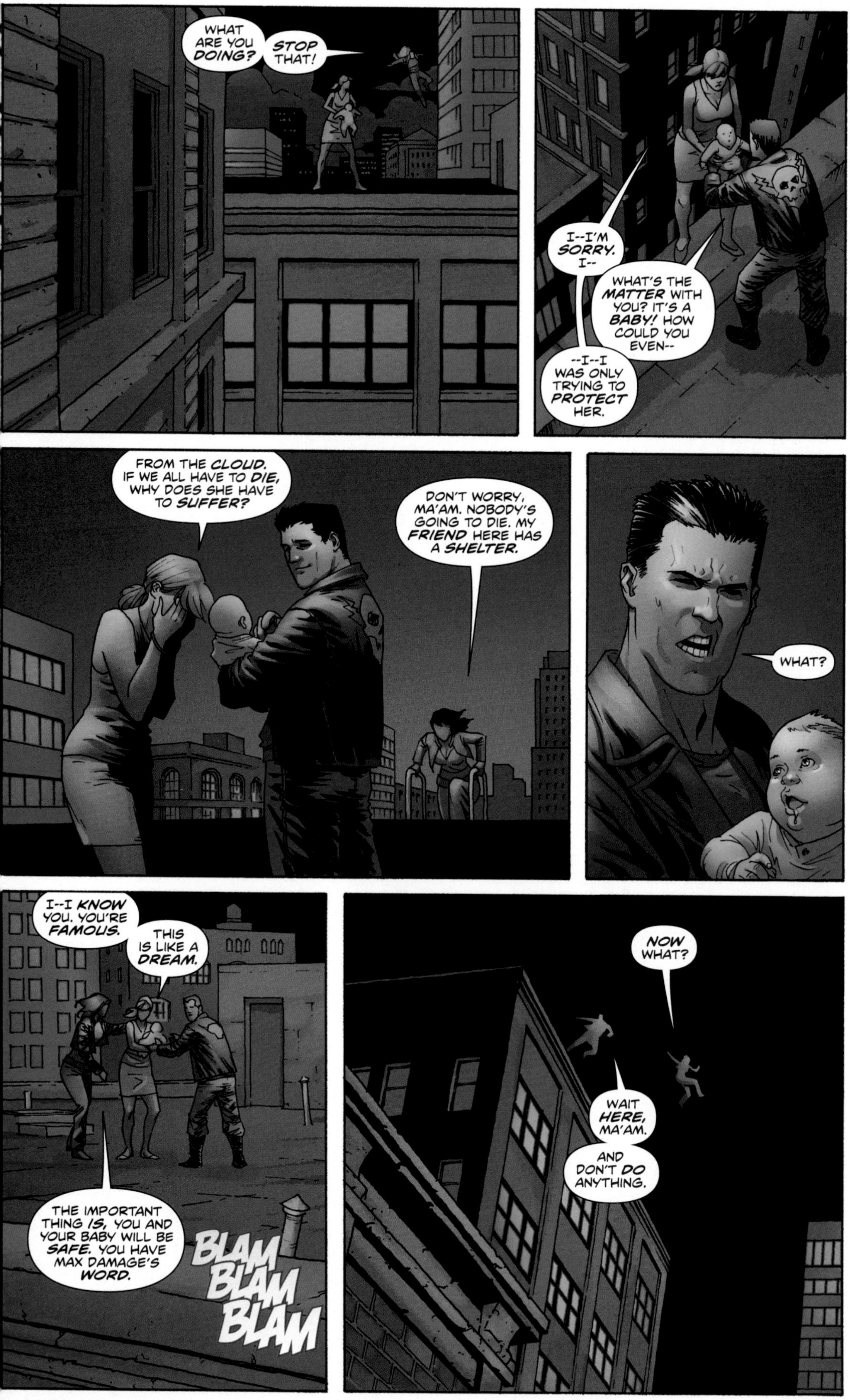
WHAT ARE YOU DOING?
STOP THAT!
I--I'M SORRY. I--
WHAT'S THE MATTER WITH YOU? IT'S A BABY! HOW COULD YOU EVEN--
--I--I WAS ONLY TRYING TO PROTECT HER.
FROM THE CLOUD. IF WE ALL HAVE TO DIE, WHY DOES SHE HAVE TO SUFFER?
DON'T WORRY, MA'AM. NOBODY'S GOING TO DIE. MY FRIEND HERE HAS A SHELTER.
WHAT?
I--I KNOW YOU. YOU'RE FAMOUS.
THIS IS LIKE A DREAM.
THE IMPORTANT THING IS, YOU AND YOUR BABY WILL BE SAFE. YOU HAVE MAX DAMAGE'S WORD.
BLAM BLAM BLAM
NOW WHAT?
WAIT HERE, MA'AM.
AND DON'T DO ANYTHING.

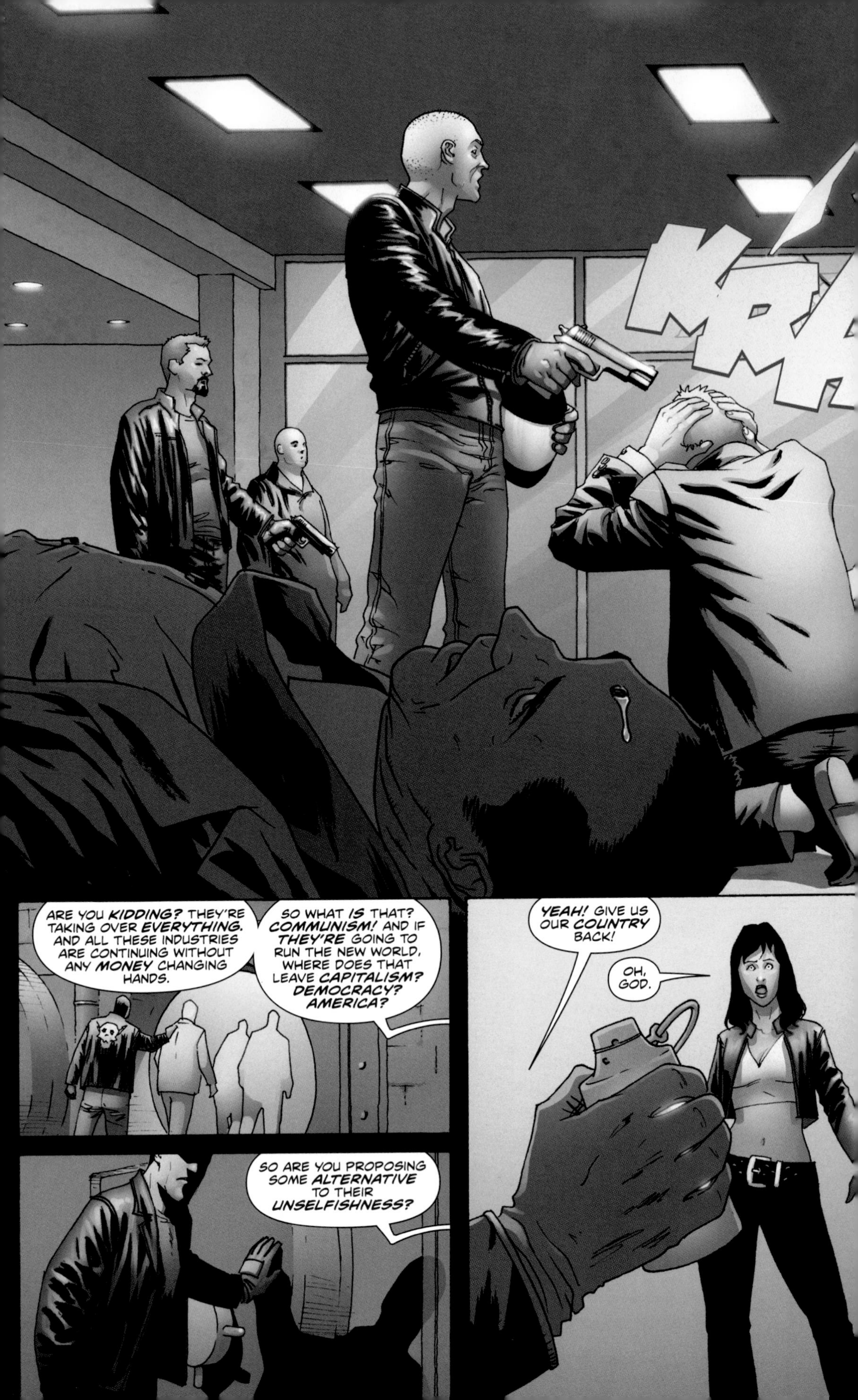
KRA
ARE YOU KIDDING? THEY'RE TAKING OVER EVERYTHING. AND ALL THESE INDUSTRIES ARE CONTINUING WITHOUT ANY MONEY CHANGING HANDS.
SO WHAT IS THAT? COMMUNISM! AND IF THEY'RE GOING TO RUN THE NEW WORLD, WHERE DOES THAT LEAVE CAPITALISM? DEMOCRACY? AMERICA?
SO ARE YOU PROPOSING SOME ALTERNATIVE TO THEIR UNSELFISHNESS?
YEAH! GIVE US OUR COUNTRY BACK!
OH, GOD.

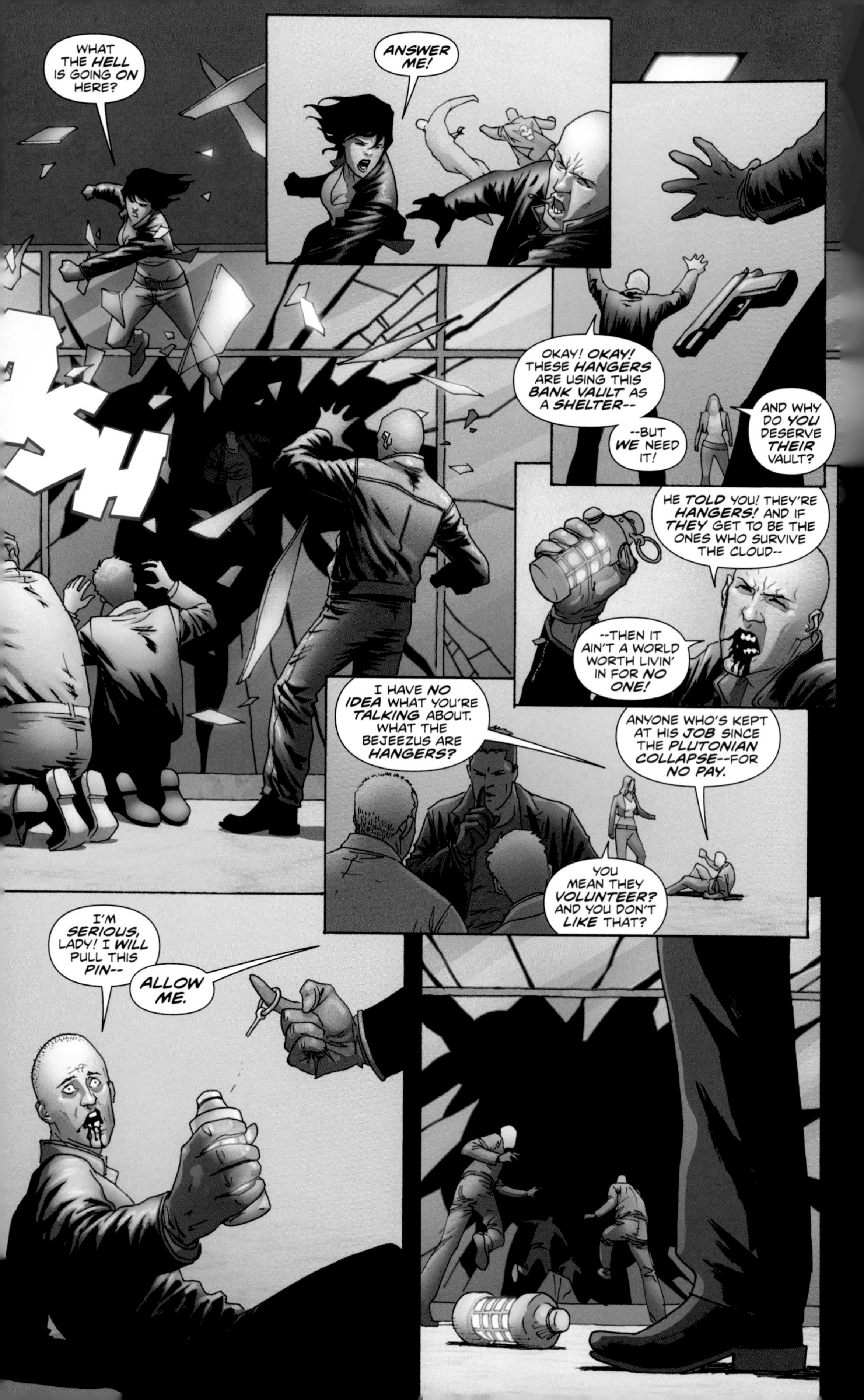
WHAT THE HELL IS GOING ON HERE?
ANSWER ME!
OKAY! OKAY! THESE HANGERS ARE USING THIS BANK VAULT AS A SHELTER--
--BUT WE NEED IT!
AND WHY DO YOU DESERVE THEIR VAULT?
HE TOLD YOU! THEY'RE HANGERS! AND IF THEY GET TO BE THE ONES WHO SURVIVE THE CLOUD--
--THEN IT AIN'T A WORLD WORTH LIVIN' IN FOR NO ONE!
I HAVE NO IDEA WHAT YOU'RE TALKING ABOUT. WHAT THE BEJEEZUS ARE HANGERS?
ANYONE WHO'S KEPT AT HIS JOB SINCE THE PLUTONIAN COLLAPSE--FOR NO PAY.
YOU MEAN THEY VOLUNTEER? AND YOU DON'T LIKE THAT?
I'M SERIOUS, LADY! I WILL PULL THIS PIN--
ALLOW ME.

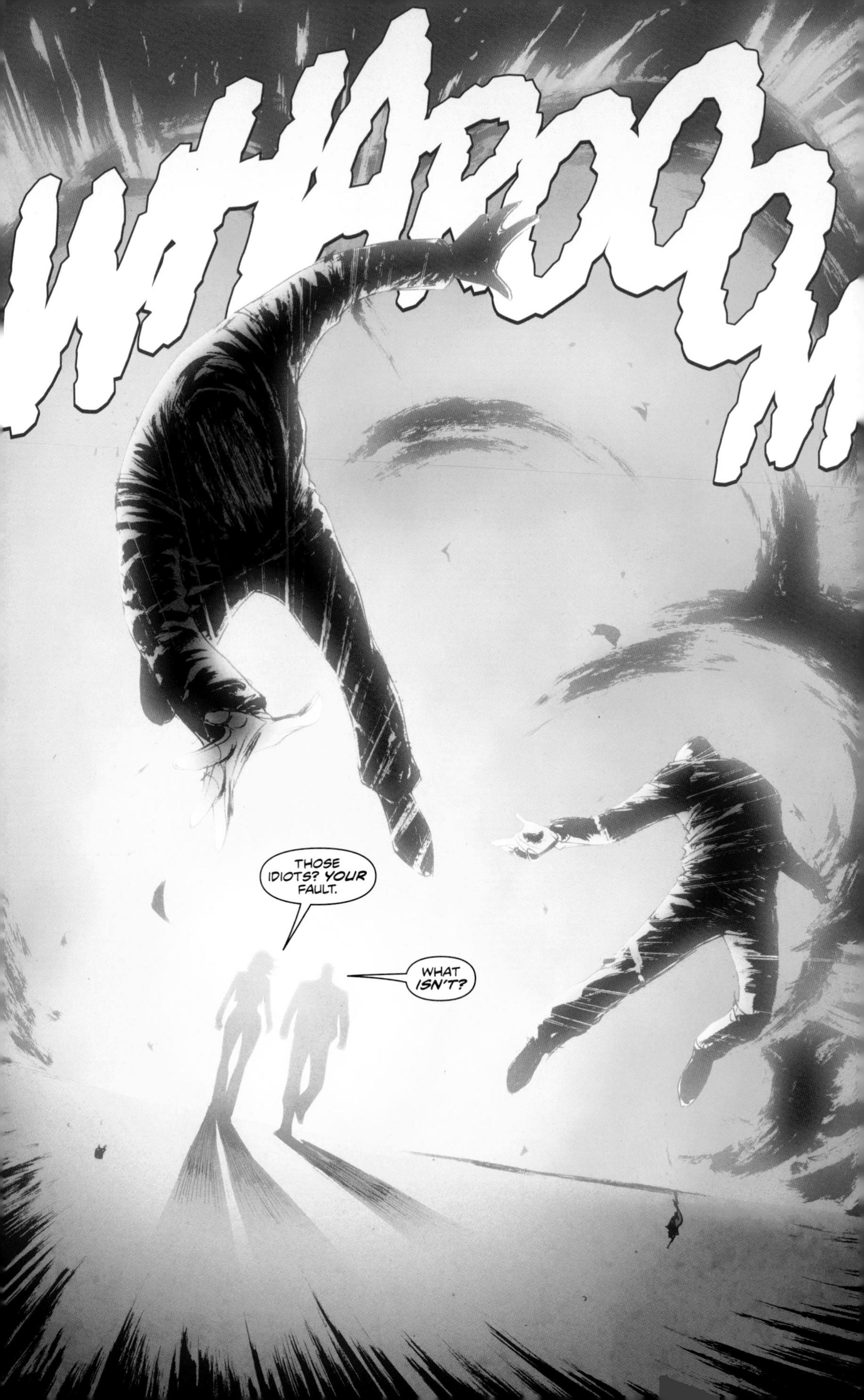
THOSE IDIOTS? YOUR FAULT.
WHAT ISN'T?

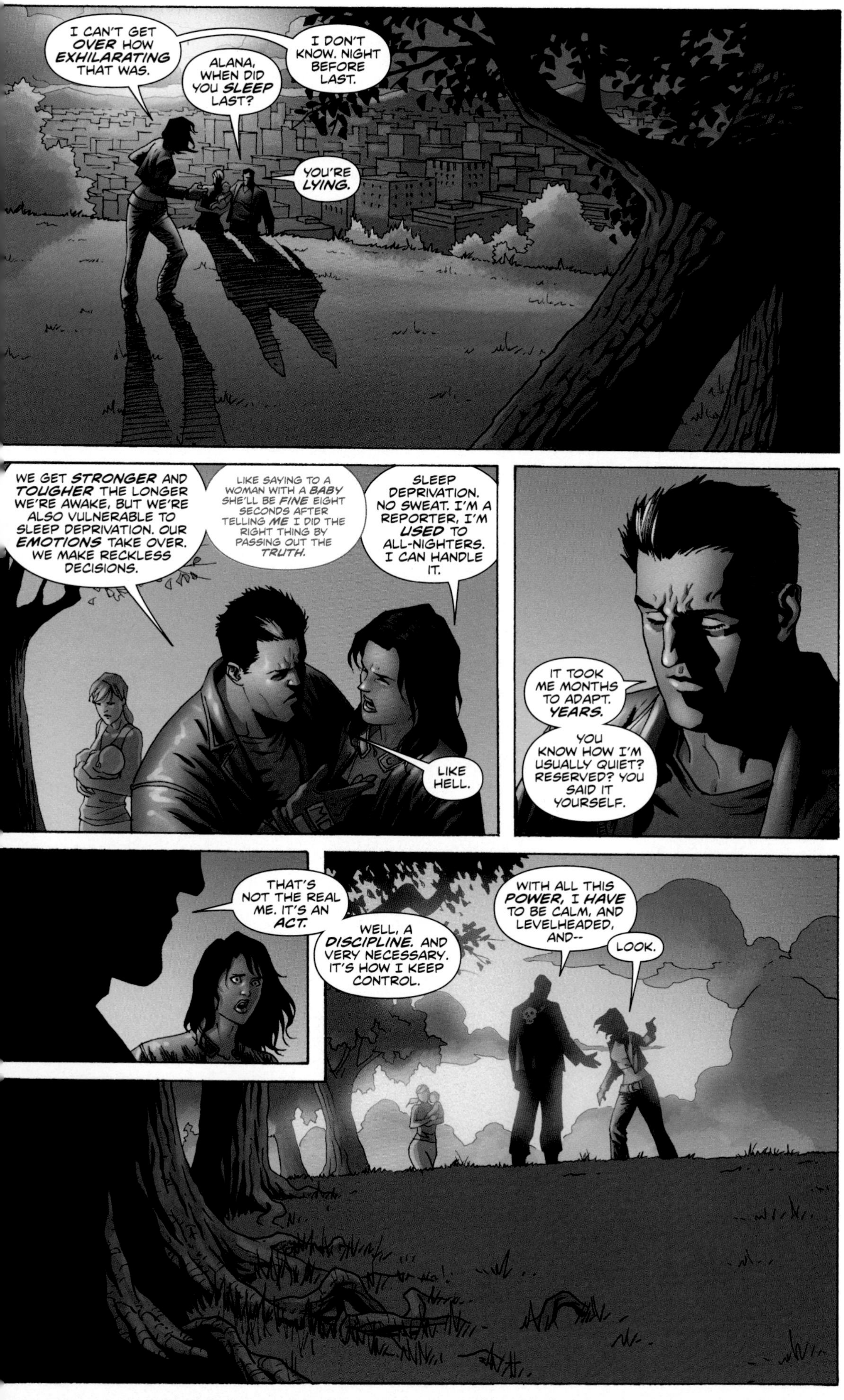
I CAN'T GET OVER HOW EXHILARATING THAT WAS.
ALANA, WHEN DID YOU SLEEP LAST?
I DON'T KNOW. NIGHT BEFORE LAST.
YOU'RE LYING.
WE GET STRONGER AND TOUGHER THE LONGER WE'RE AWAKE, BUT WE'RE ALSO VULNERABLE TO SLEEP DEPRIVATION. OUR EMOTIONS TAKE OVER. WE MAKE RECKLESS DECISIONS.
LIKE SAYING TO A WOMAN WITH A BABY SHE'LL BE FINE EIGHT SECONDS AFTER TELLING ME I DID THE RIGHT THING BY PASSING OUT THE TRUTH.
SLEEP DEPRIVATION. NO SWEAT. I'M A REPORTER, I'M USED TO ALL-NIGHTERS. I CAN HANDLE IT.
LIKE HELL.
IT TOOK ME MONTHS TO ADAPT. YEARS.
YOU KNOW HOW I'M USUALLY QUIET? RESERVED? YOU SAID IT YOURSELF.
THAT'S NOT THE REAL ME. IT'S AN ACT.
WELL, A DISCIPLINE. AND VERY NECESSARY. IT'S HOW I KEEP CONTROL.
WITH ALL THIS POWER, I HAVE TO BE CALM, AND LEVELHEADED, AND--
LOOK.

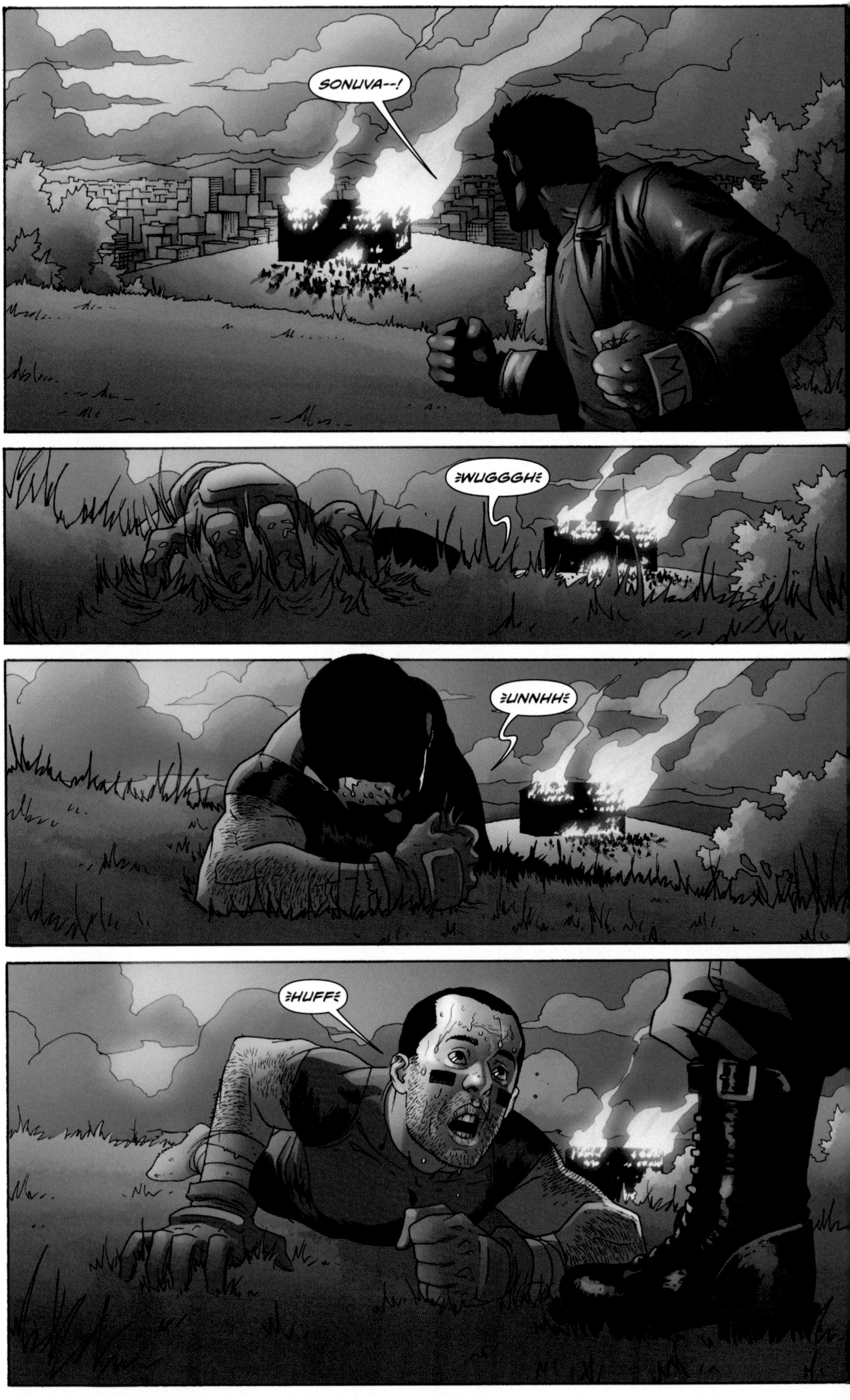
SONUVA--!
WUGGGH
UNNHH
HUFF

NICE JOB OF *GUARDING* THE PLACE, CHARLIE.

MAX...

...PLEASE... I KNOW WE'VE HAD OUR *DIFFERENCES*, BUT...

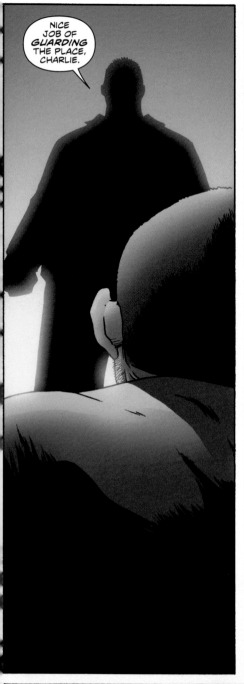

FOOMP

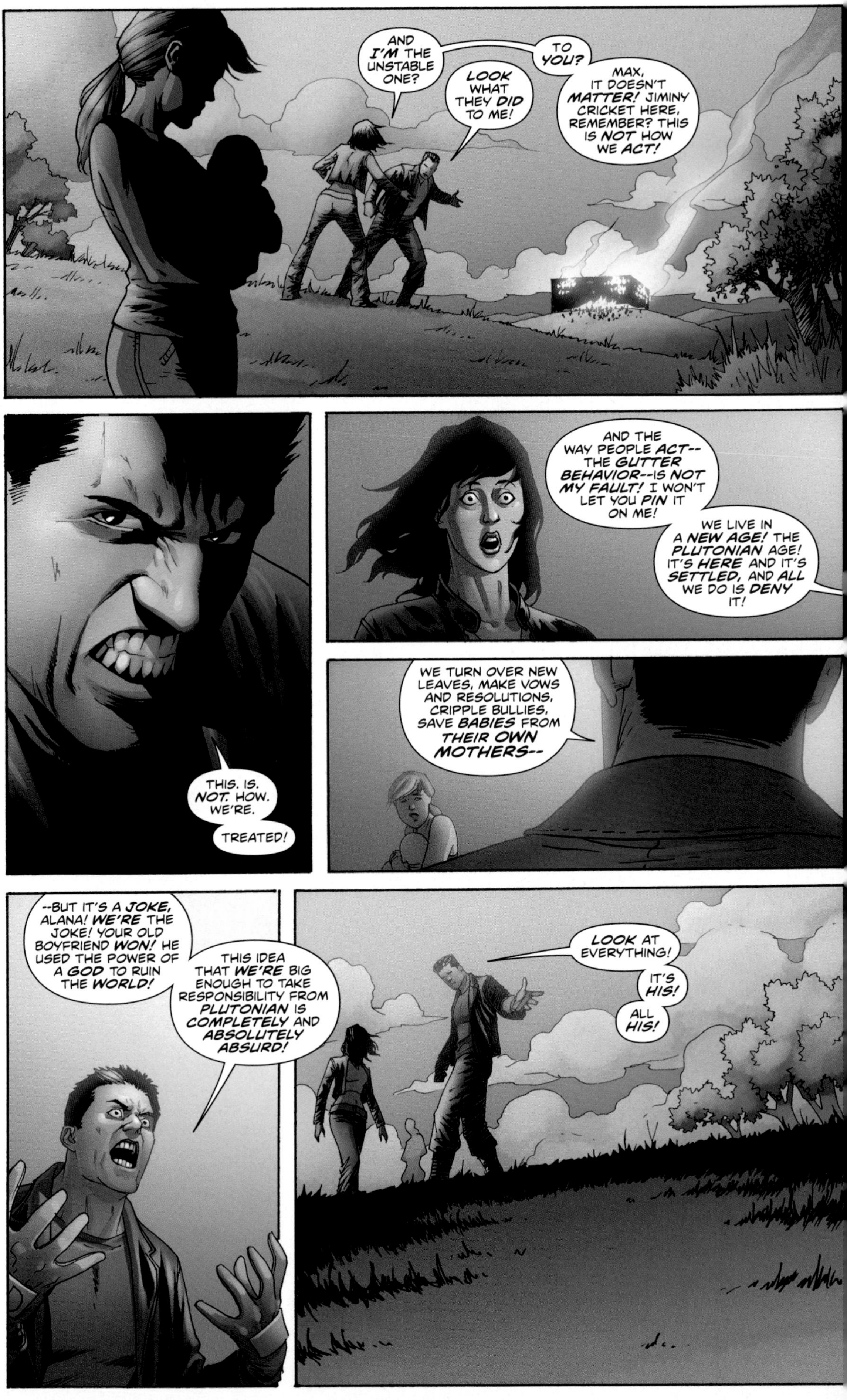
AND I'M THE UNSTABLE ONE?
TO YOU?
LOOK WHAT THEY DID TO ME!
MAX, IT DOESN'T MATTER! JIMINY CRICKET HERE, REMEMBER? THIS IS NOT HOW WE ACT!
THIS. IS. NOT. HOW. WE'RE.
TREATED!
AND THE WAY PEOPLE ACT-- THE GUTTER BEHAVIOR--IS NOT MY FAULT! I WON'T LET YOU PIN IT ON ME!
WE LIVE IN A NEW AGE! THE PLUTONIAN AGE! IT'S HERE AND IT'S SETTLED, AND ALL WE DO IS DENY IT!
WE TURN OVER NEW LEAVES, MAKE VOWS AND RESOLUTIONS, CRIPPLE BULLIES, SAVE BABIES FROM THEIR OWN MOTHERS--
--BUT IT'S A JOKE, ALANA! WE'RE THE JOKE! YOUR OLD BOYFRIEND WON! HE USED THE POWER OF A GOD TO RUIN THE WORLD!
THIS IDEA THAT WE'RE BIG ENOUGH TO TAKE RESPONSIBILITY FROM PLUTONIAN IS COMPLETELY AND ABSOLUTELY ABSURD!
LOOK AT EVERYTHING!
IT'S HIS!
ALL HIS!

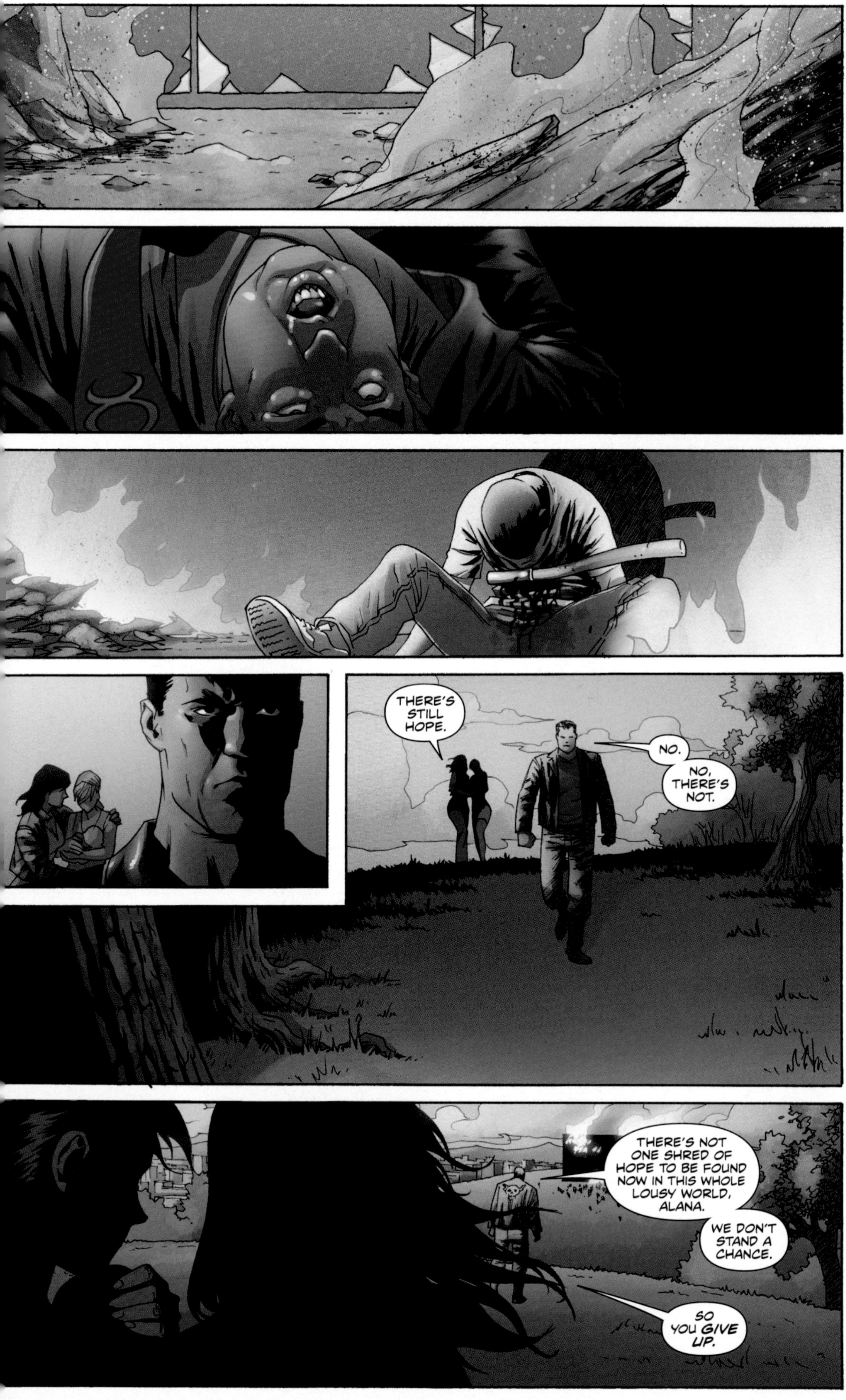
THERE'S STILL HOPE.
NO.
NO, THERE'S NOT.
THERE'S NOT ONE SHRED OF HOPE TO BE FOUND NOW IN THIS WHOLE LOUSY WORLD, ALANA.
WE DON'T STAND A CHANCE.
SO YOU GIVE UP.

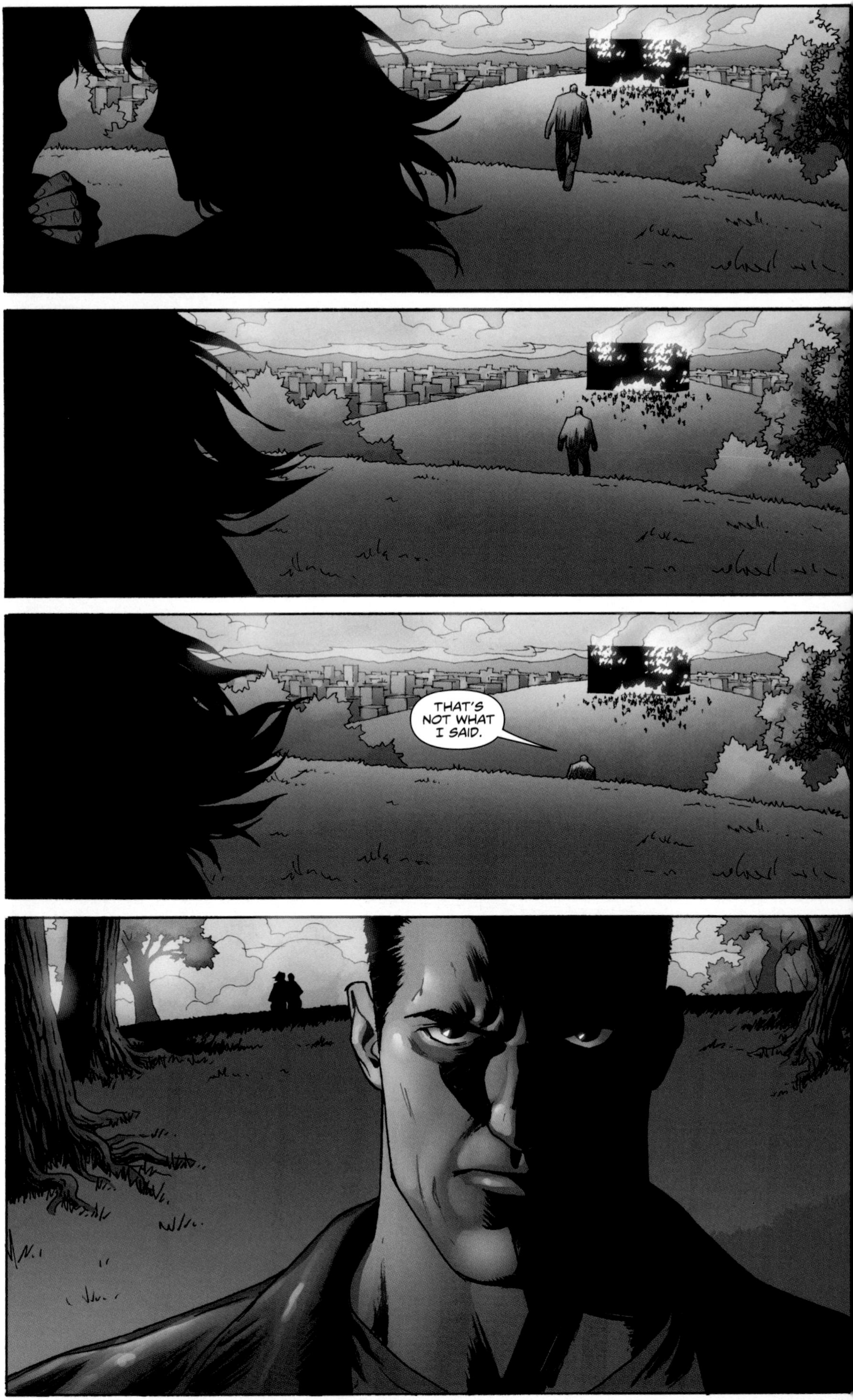
THAT'S NOT WHAT I SAID.

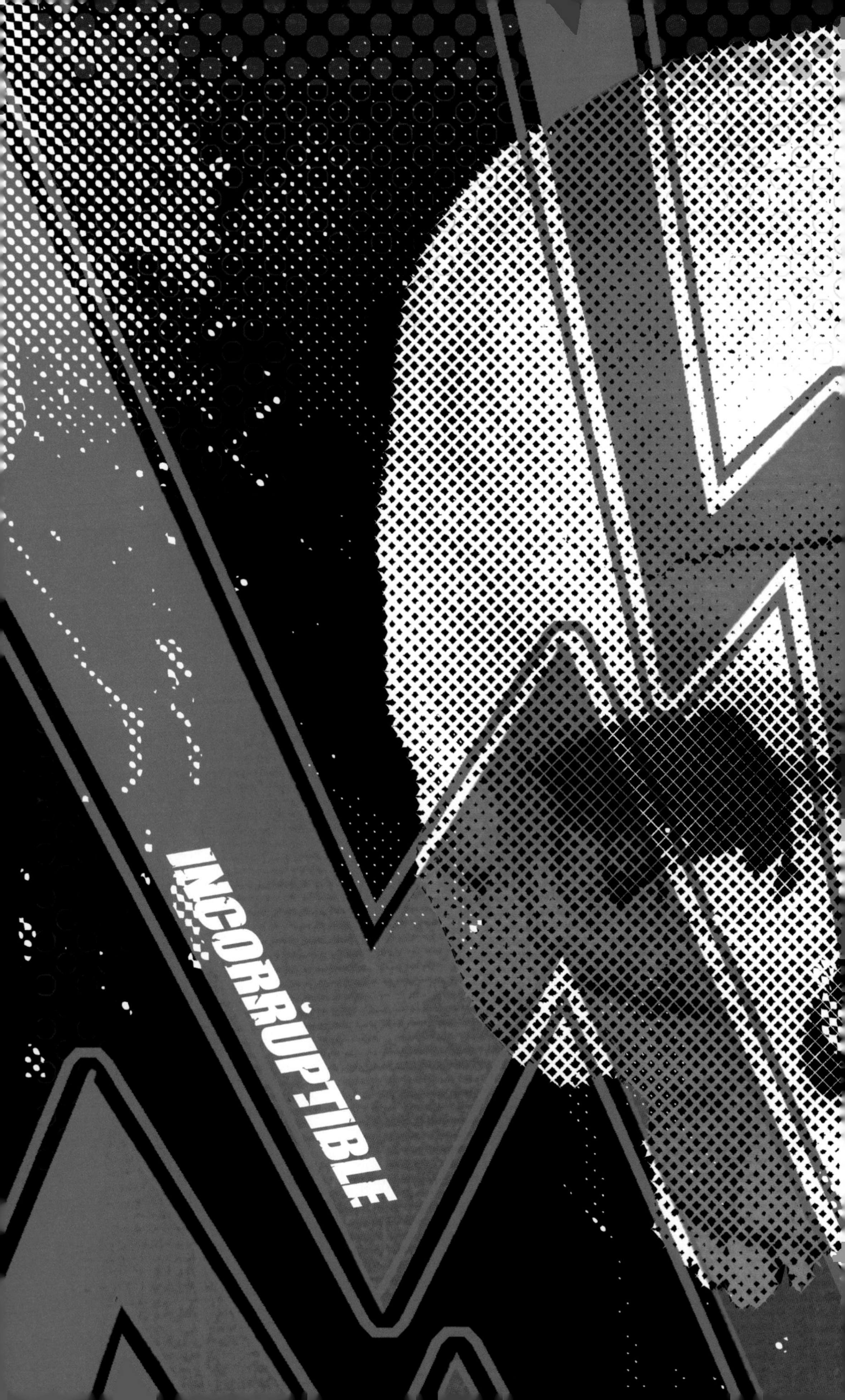
INCORRUPTIBLE

CHAPTER 30

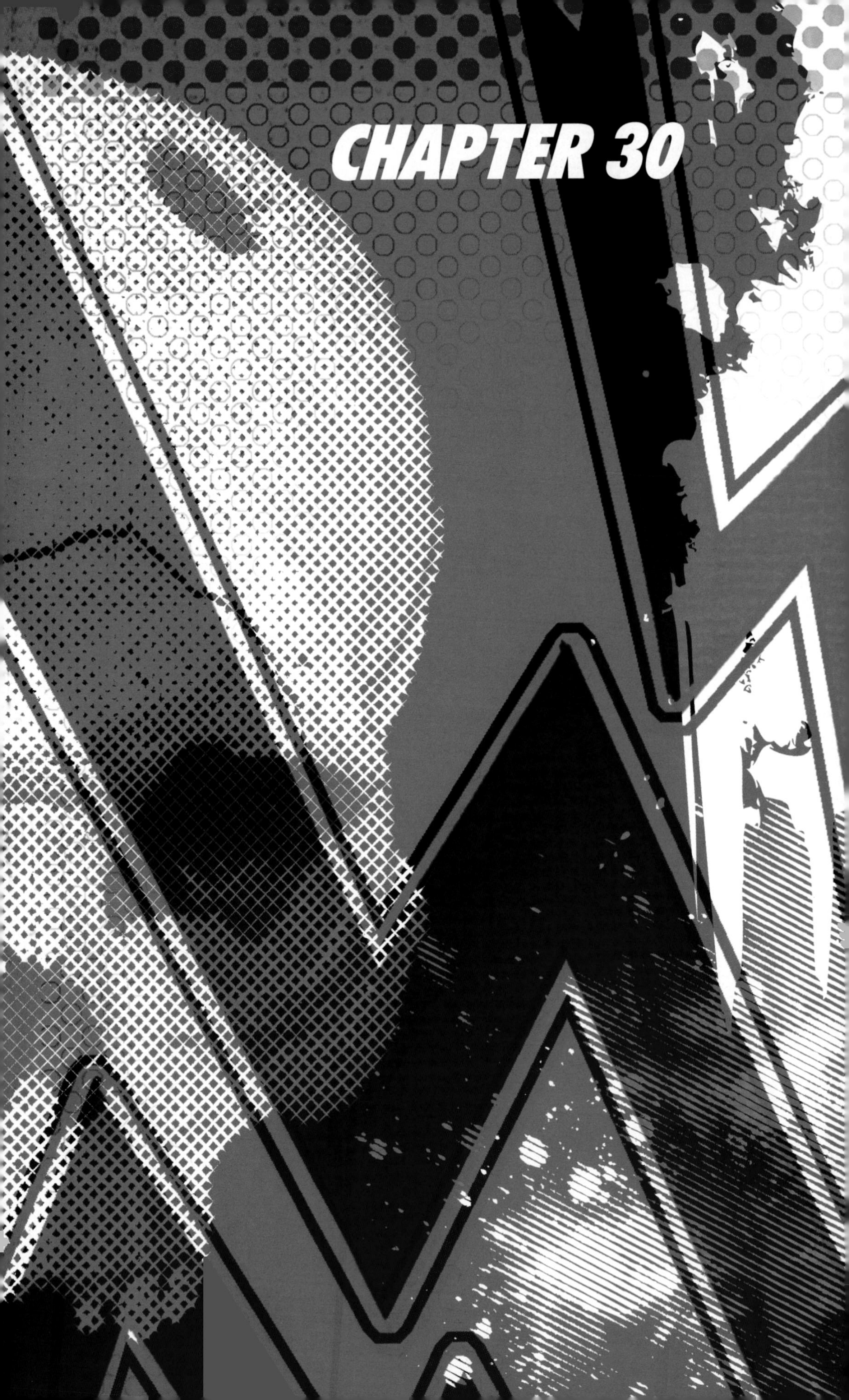

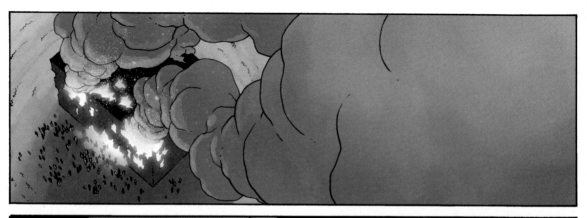

WHAT ARE YOU, THE **WARDEN** HERE?

NO--

YOU **WORK** FOR MAX DAMAGE?

--NO--

YOU **KNOW** HE HAD NO RIGHT TO **KEEP** ME HERE! **SAY** IT!

--I DON'T!

TOO **SLOW!** YOU **LOSE**--

SKAAAK

AAAHHRR

KRIK

KRAK

I DON'T HAVE THE **TIME** OR THE **PATIENCE** FOR YOU, BOONE.

MAX--!

UP, BILL.

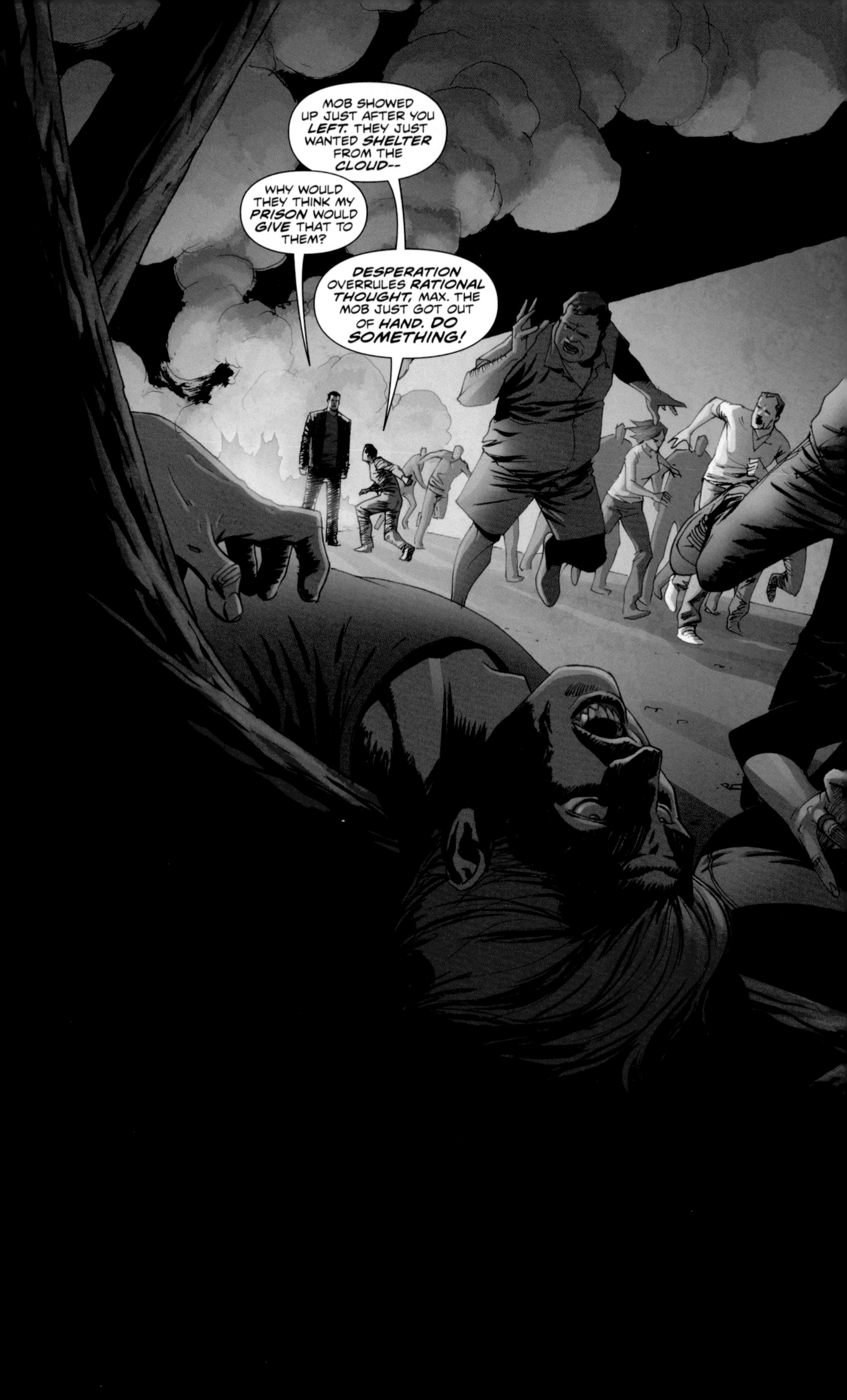
MOB SHOWED UP JUST AFTER YOU LEFT. THEY JUST WANTED SHELTER FROM THE CLOUD--
WHY WOULD THEY THINK MY PRISON WOULD GIVE THAT TO THEM?
DESPERATION OVERRULES RATIONAL THOUGHT, MAX. THE MOB JUST GOT OUT OF HAND. DO SOMETHING!

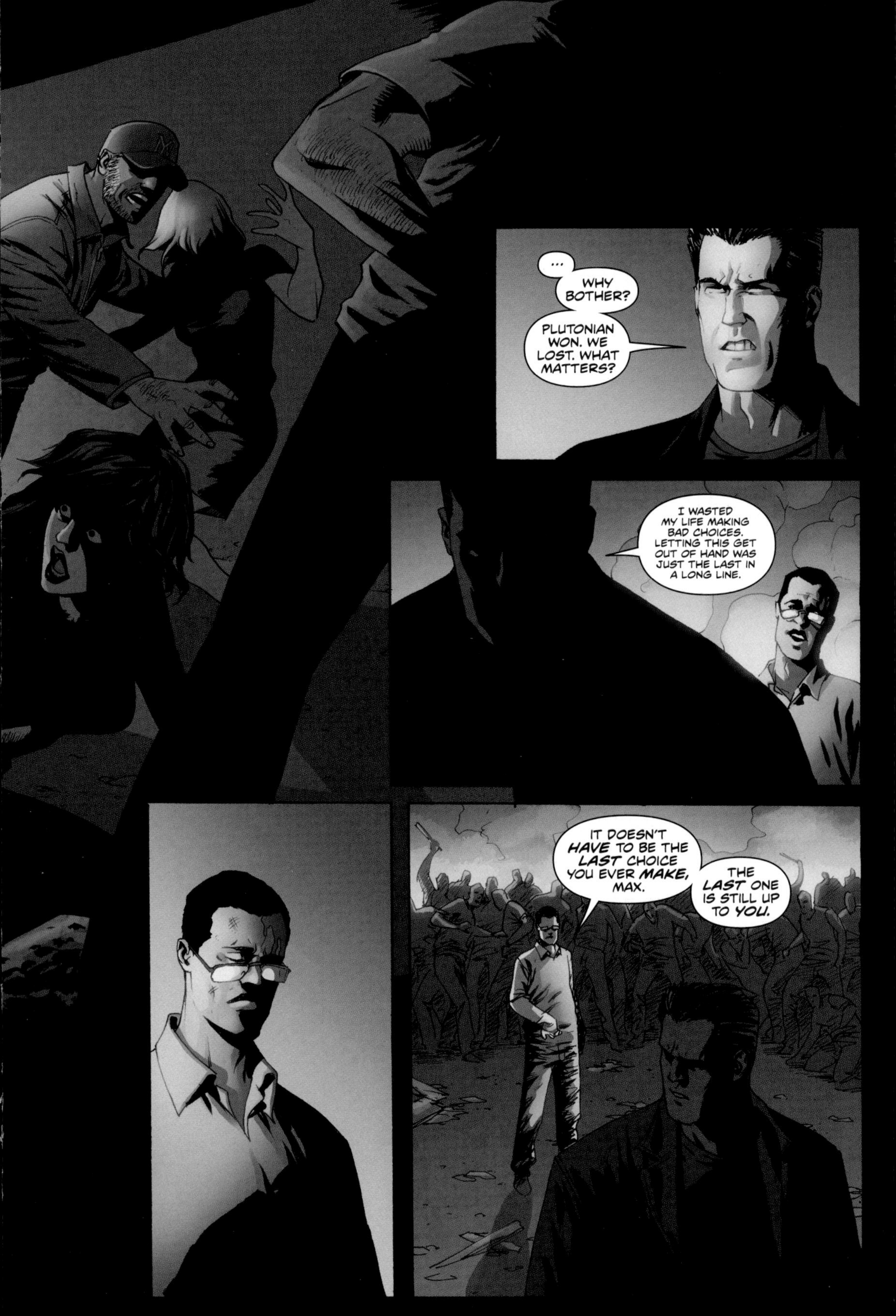
...
WHY BOTHER?
PLUTONIAN WON. WE LOST. WHAT MATTERS?
I WASTED MY LIFE MAKING BAD CHOICES. LETTING THIS GET OUT OF HAND WAS JUST THE LAST IN A LONG LINE.
IT DOESN'T *HAVE* TO BE THE *LAST* CHOICE YOU EVER *MAKE,* MAX.
THE *LAST* ONE IS STILL UP TO *YOU.*

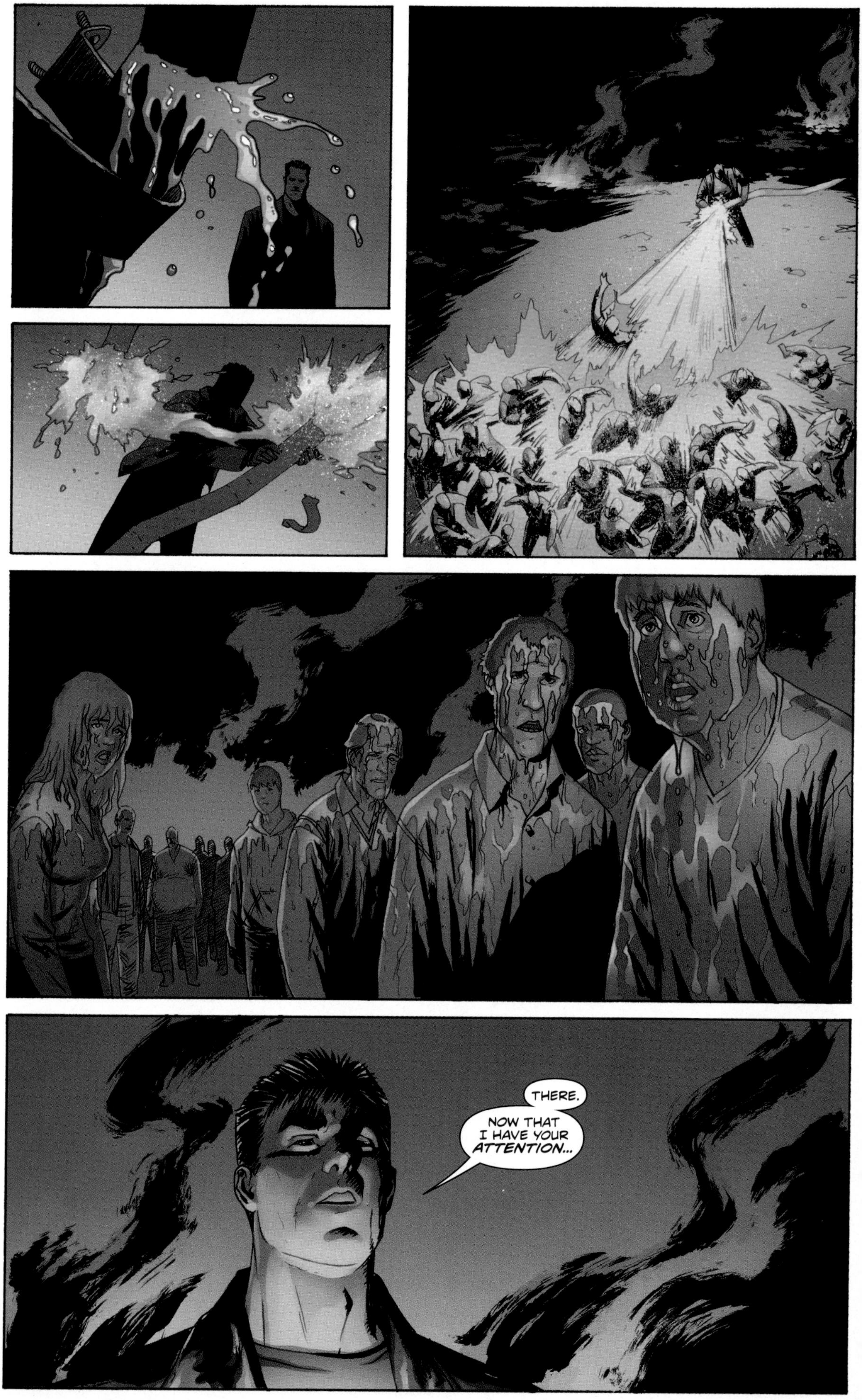
THERE.
NOW THAT I HAVE YOUR *ATTENTION*...

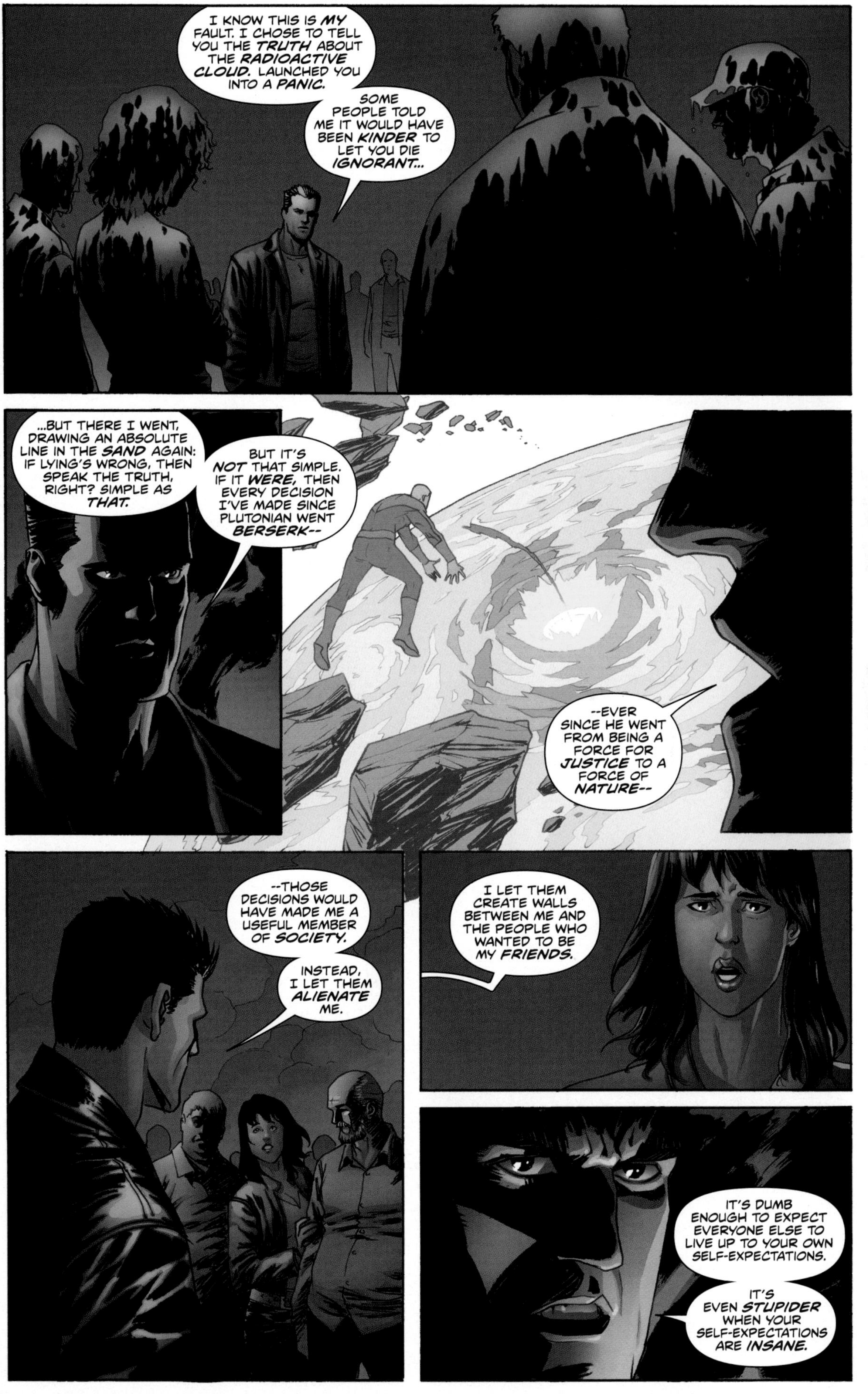
I KNOW THIS IS MY FAULT. I CHOSE TO TELL YOU THE TRUTH ABOUT THE RADIOACTIVE CLOUD. LAUNCHED YOU INTO A PANIC.
SOME PEOPLE TOLD ME IT WOULD HAVE BEEN KINDER TO LET YOU DIE IGNORANT...
...BUT THERE I WENT, DRAWING AN ABSOLUTE LINE IN THE SAND AGAIN: IF LYING'S WRONG, THEN SPEAK THE TRUTH, RIGHT? SIMPLE AS THAT.
BUT IT'S NOT THAT SIMPLE. IF IT WERE, THEN EVERY DECISION I'VE MADE SINCE PLUTONIAN WENT BERSERK--
--EVER SINCE HE WENT FROM BEING A FORCE FOR JUSTICE TO A FORCE OF NATURE--
--THOSE DECISIONS WOULD HAVE MADE ME A USEFUL MEMBER OF SOCIETY.
INSTEAD, I LET THEM ALIENATE ME.
I LET THEM CREATE WALLS BETWEEN ME AND THE PEOPLE WHO WANTED TO BE MY FRIENDS.
IT'S DUMB ENOUGH TO EXPECT EVERYONE ELSE TO LIVE UP TO YOUR OWN SELF-EXPECTATIONS.
IT'S EVEN STUPIDER WHEN YOUR SELF-EXPECTATIONS ARE INSANE.

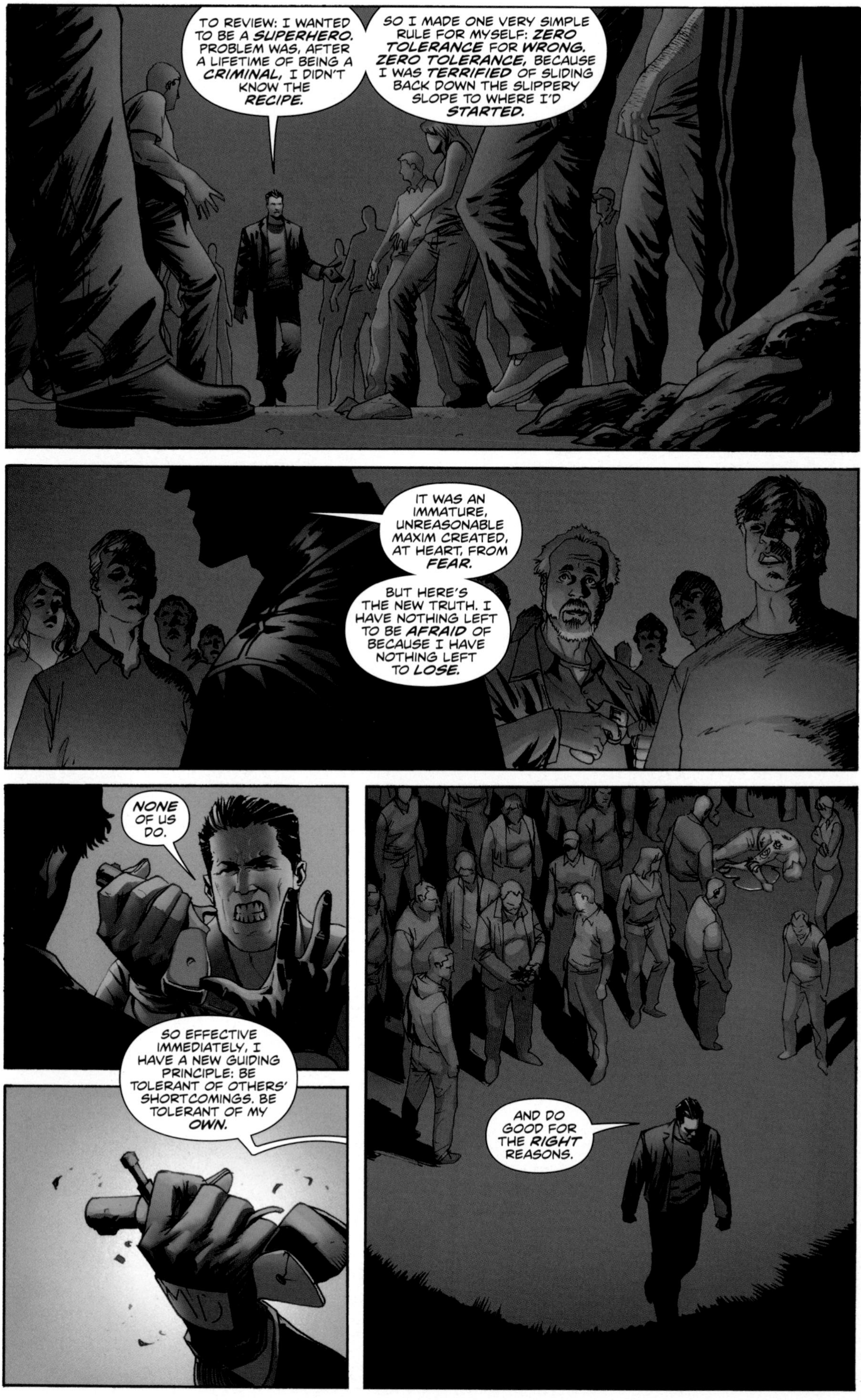
TO REVIEW: I WANTED TO BE A SUPERHERO. PROBLEM WAS, AFTER A LIFETIME OF BEING A CRIMINAL, I DIDN'T KNOW THE RECIPE.
SO I MADE ONE VERY SIMPLE RULE FOR MYSELF: ZERO TOLERANCE FOR WRONG. ZERO TOLERANCE, BECAUSE I WAS TERRIFIED OF SLIDING BACK DOWN THE SLIPPERY SLOPE TO WHERE I'D STARTED.
IT WAS AN IMMATURE, UNREASONABLE MAXIM CREATED, AT HEART, FROM FEAR.
BUT HERE'S THE NEW TRUTH. I HAVE NOTHING LEFT TO BE AFRAID OF BECAUSE I HAVE NOTHING LEFT TO LOSE.
NONE OF US DO.
SO EFFECTIVE IMMEDIATELY, I HAVE A NEW GUIDING PRINCIPLE: BE TOLERANT OF OTHERS' SHORTCOMINGS. BE TOLERANT OF MY OWN.
AND DO GOOD FOR THE RIGHT REASONS.

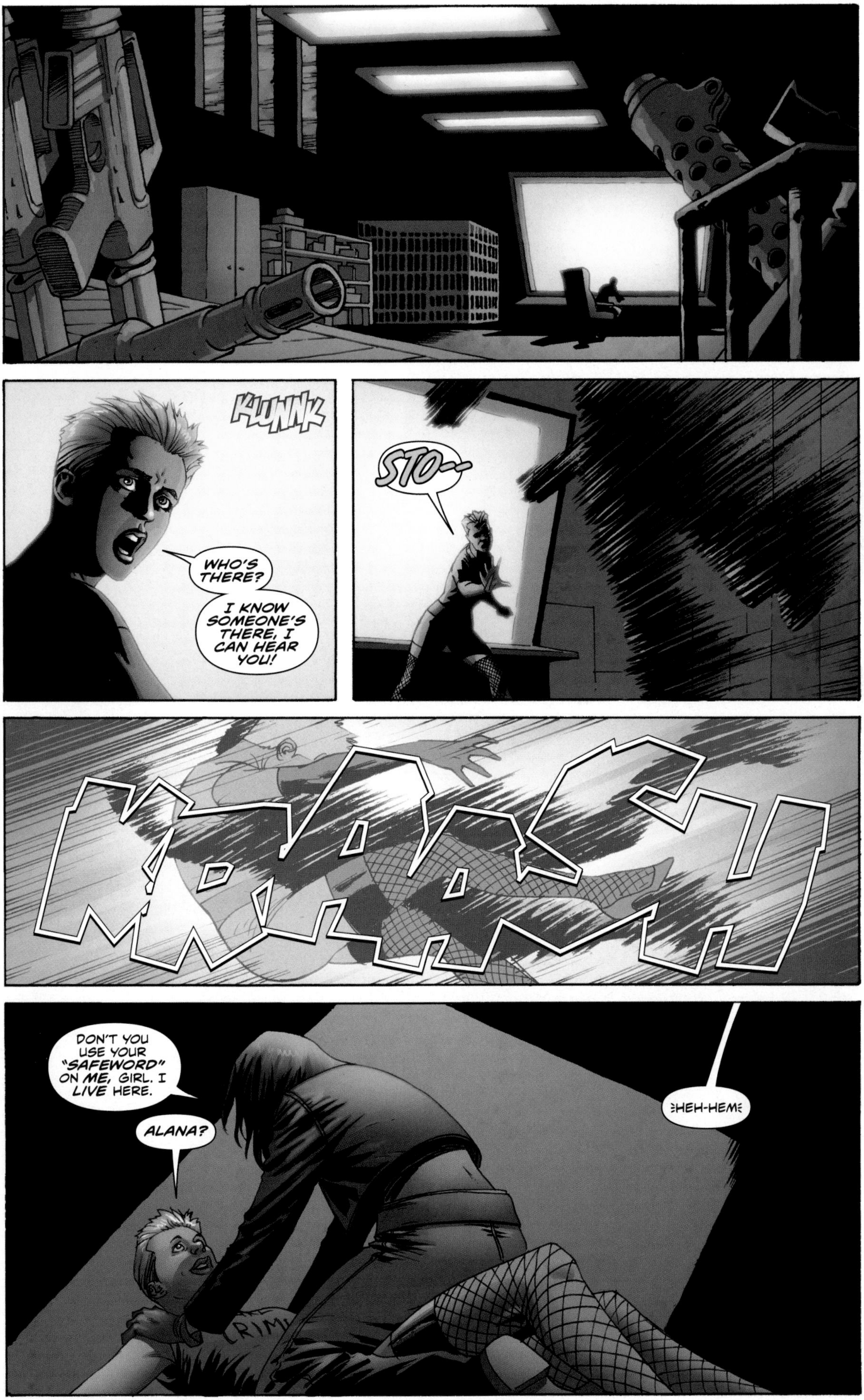

KLUNNK
WHO'S THERE?
I KNOW SOMEONE'S THERE, I CAN HEAR YOU!
STO--
KRAASCH
DON'T YOU USE YOUR "SAFEWORD" ON ME, GIRL. I LIVE HERE.
ALANA?
HEH-HEM

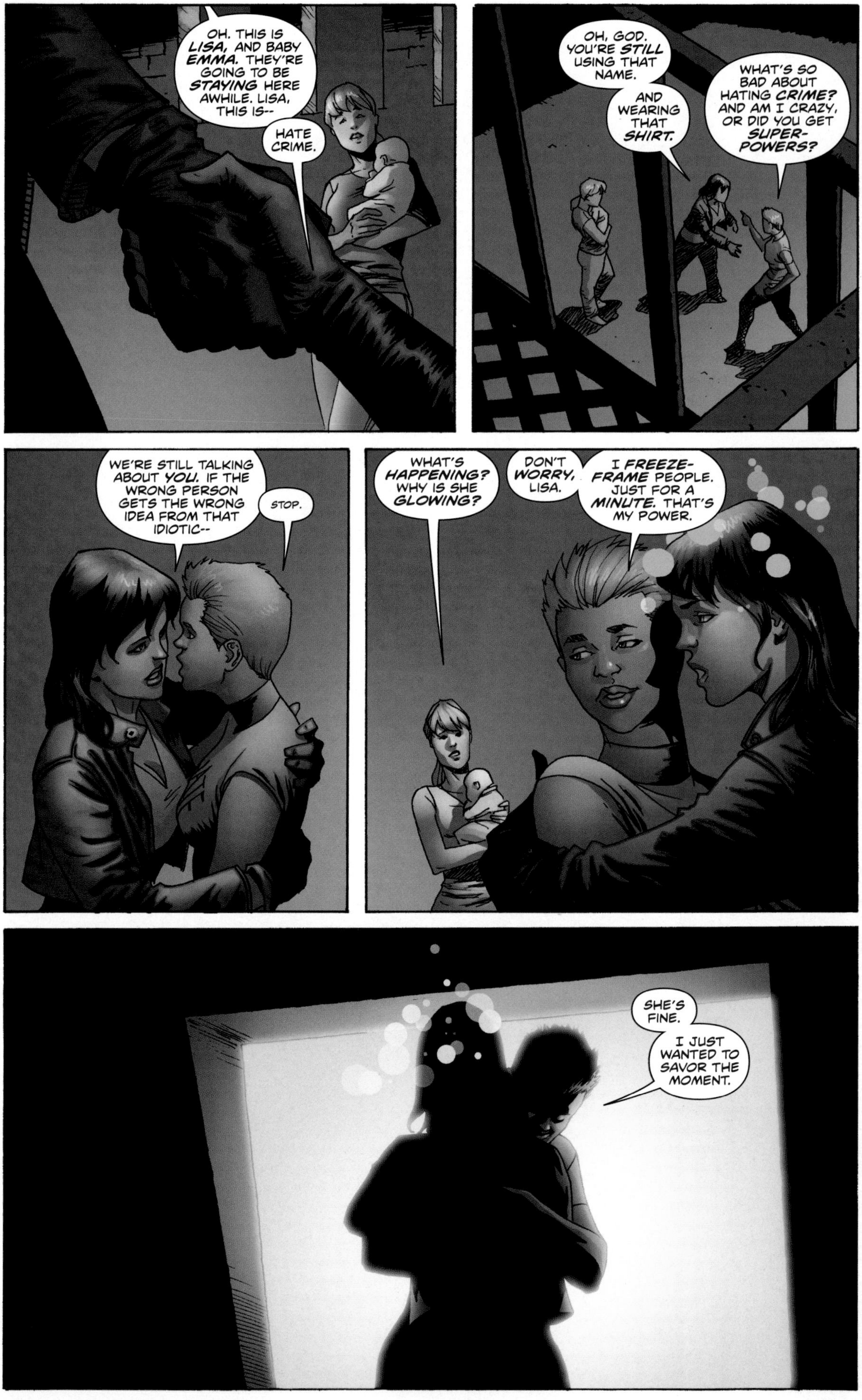

OH. THIS IS LISA, AND BABY EMMA. THEY'RE GOING TO BE STAYING HERE AWHILE. LISA, THIS IS--
HATE CRIME.
OH, GOD. YOU'RE STILL USING THAT NAME.
AND WEARING THAT SHIRT.
WHAT'S SO BAD ABOUT HATING CRIME? AND AM I CRAZY, OR DID YOU GET SUPER-POWERS?
WE'RE STILL TALKING ABOUT YOU. IF THE WRONG PERSON GETS THE WRONG IDEA FROM THAT IDIOTIC--
STOP.
WHAT'S HAPPENING? WHY IS SHE GLOWING?
DON'T WORRY, LISA.
I FREEZE-FRAME PEOPLE. JUST FOR A MINUTE. THAT'S MY POWER.
SHE'S FINE.
I JUST WANTED TO SAVOR THE MOMENT.

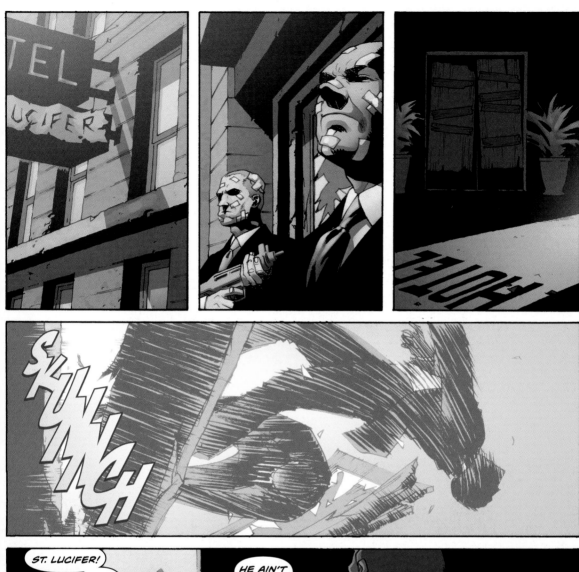

SKUNNNCH

ST. LUCIFER!

LET'S TALK!

HE AIN'T HERE!

THEN I'LL WAIT!

RATTATTATTATTATTA

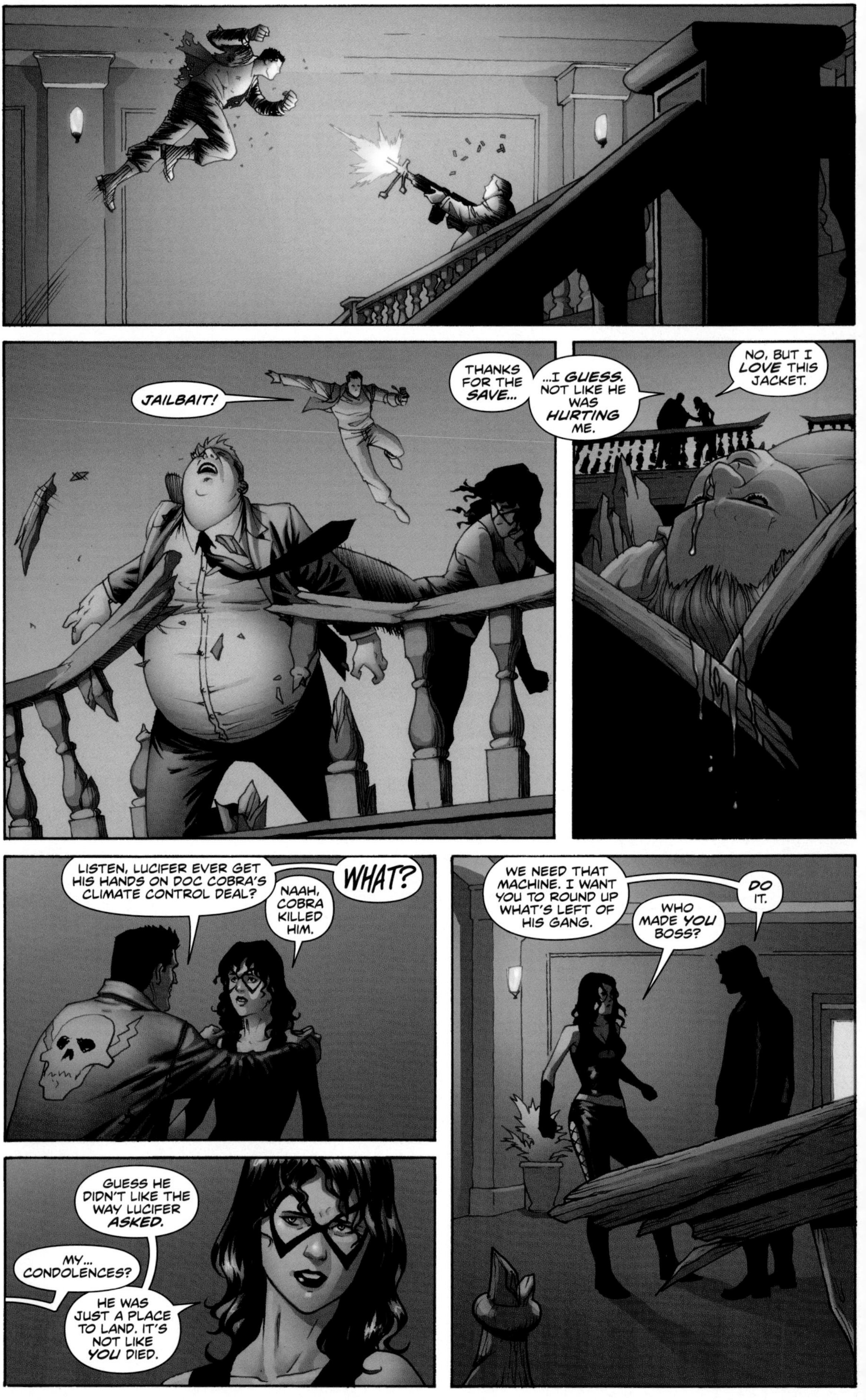
JAILBAIT!
THANKS FOR THE SAVE...
...I GUESS. NOT LIKE HE WAS HURTING ME.
NO, BUT I LOVE THIS JACKET.
LISTEN, LUCIFER EVER GET HIS HANDS ON DOC COBRA'S CLIMATE CONTROL DEAL?
WHAT?
NAAH, COBRA KILLED HIM.
GUESS HE DIDN'T LIKE THE WAY LUCIFER ASKED.
MY... CONDOLENCES?
HE WAS JUST A PLACE TO LAND. IT'S NOT LIKE YOU DIED.
WE NEED THAT MACHINE. I WANT YOU TO ROUND UP WHAT'S LEFT OF HIS GANG.
DO IT.
WHO MADE YOU BOSS?

MEET THE NEW BOSS. *DIFFERENT* THAN THE OLD BOSS.

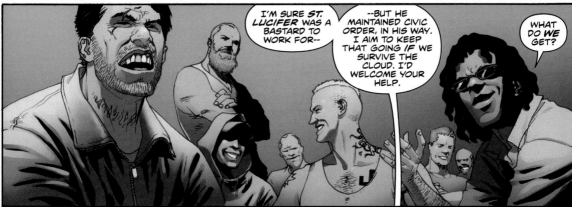

I'M SURE *ST. LUCIFER* WAS A BASTARD TO WORK FOR--

--BUT HE MAINTAINED CIVIC ORDER, IN HIS WAY. I AIM TO KEEP THAT GOING *IF* WE SURVIVE THE CLOUD. I'D WELCOME YOUR HELP.

WHAT DO *WE* GET?

MY APPROVAL. BELIEVE ME, IF WE LIVE THROUGH THIS, YOU'LL WANT IT.

NOW WHO RUNS TECH AROUND HERE?

YOU. SET MR. HENRIE UP WITH EVERYTHING HE NEEDS TO TRACK THE CLOUD.

THE REST OF YOU ARE GOING ON A RUN WITH ME. WE LEAVE IN THIRTY MINUTES TO GET THAT CLIMATE CONTROL DEVICE FROM DOC COBRA--

--AND SAVE COALVILLE.

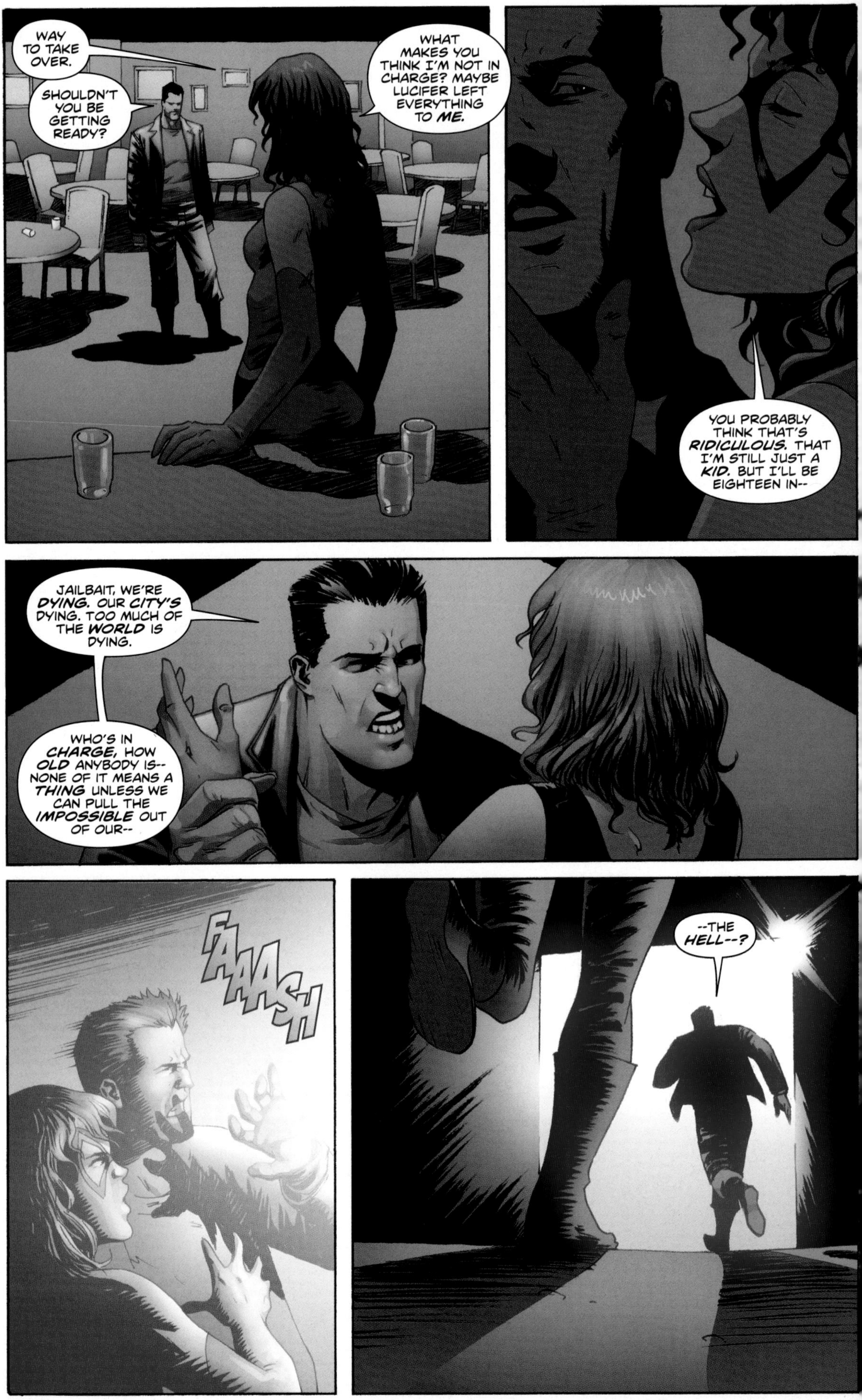
WAY TO TAKE OVER.
SHOULDN'T YOU BE GETTING READY?
WHAT MAKES YOU THINK I'M NOT IN CHARGE? MAYBE LUCIFER LEFT EVERYTHING TO ME.
YOU PROBABLY THINK THAT'S RIDICULOUS. THAT I'M STILL JUST A KID. BUT I'LL BE EIGHTEEN IN--
JAILBAIT, WE'RE DYING. OUR CITY'S DYING. TOO MUCH OF THE WORLD IS DYING.
WHO'S IN CHARGE, HOW OLD ANYBODY IS-- NONE OF IT MEANS A THING UNLESS WE CAN PULL THE IMPOSSIBLE OUT OF OUR--
FAAASH
--THE HELL--?

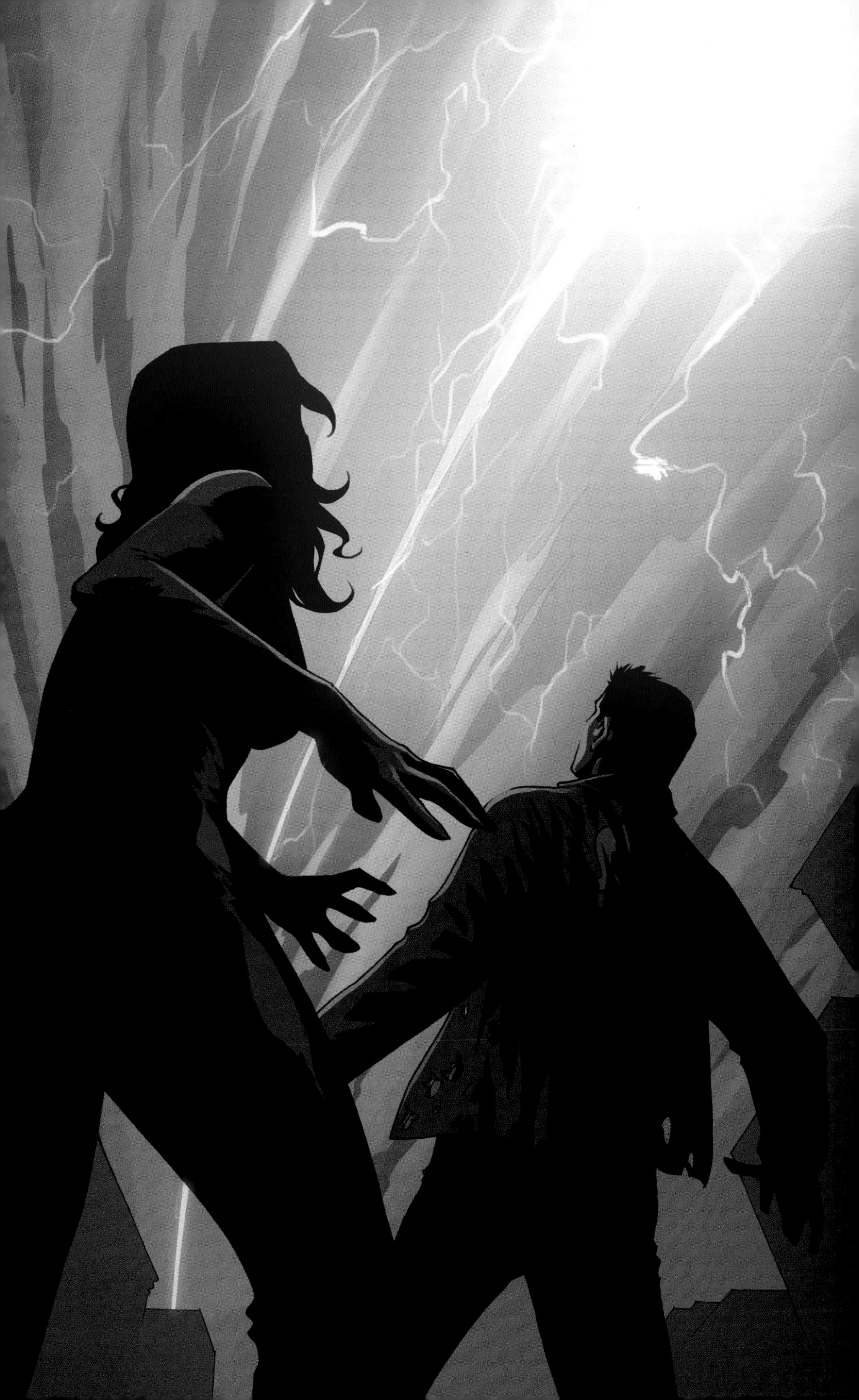

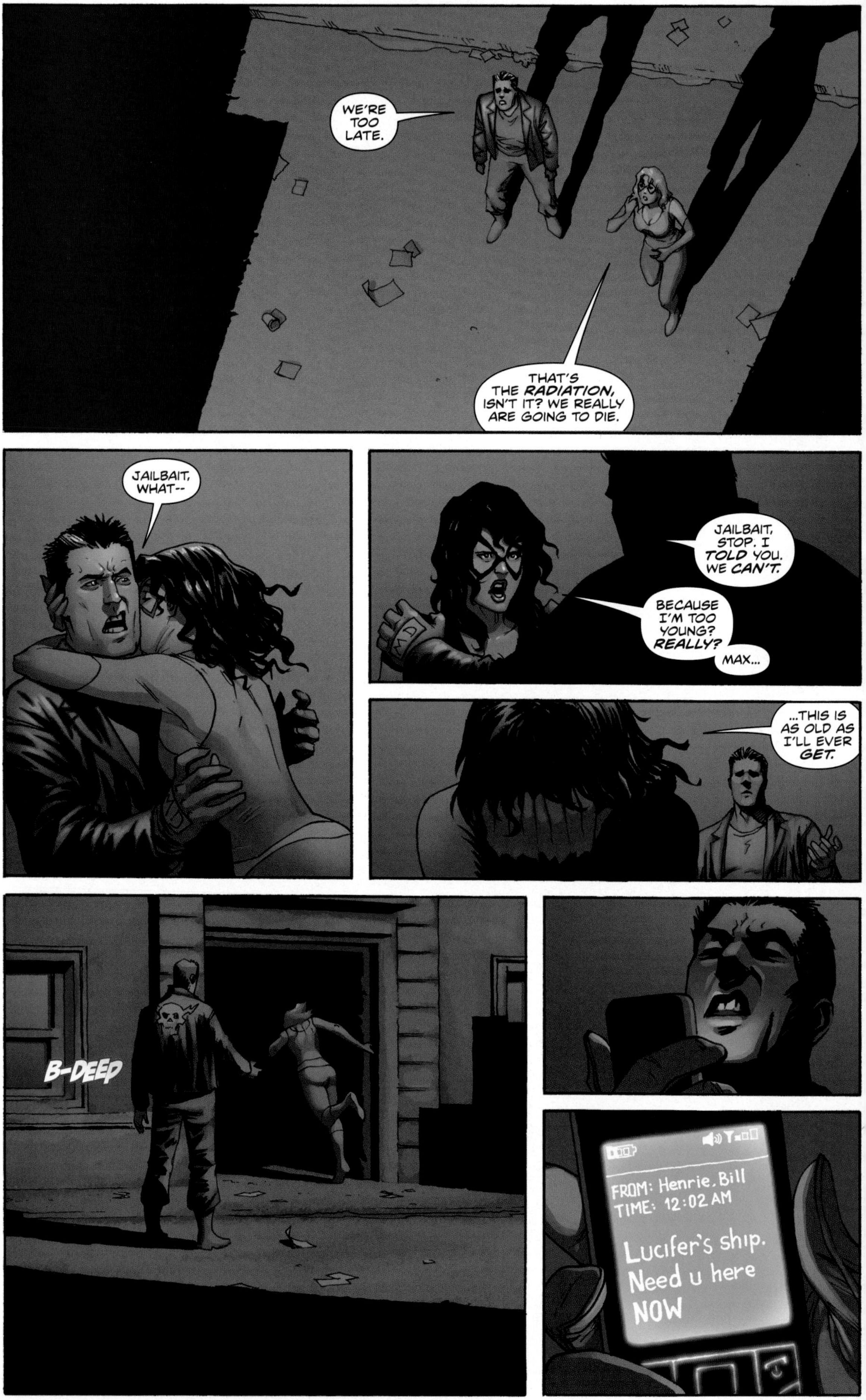
WE'RE TOO LATE.
THAT'S THE RADIATION, ISN'T IT? WE REALLY ARE GOING TO DIE.
JAILBAIT, WHAT--
JAILBAIT, STOP. I TOLD YOU. WE CAN'T.
BECAUSE I'M TOO YOUNG? REALLY?
MAX...
...THIS IS AS OLD AS I'LL EVER GET.
B-DEEP
FROM: Henrie, Bill
TIME: 12:02 AM
Lucifer's ship. Need u here NOW

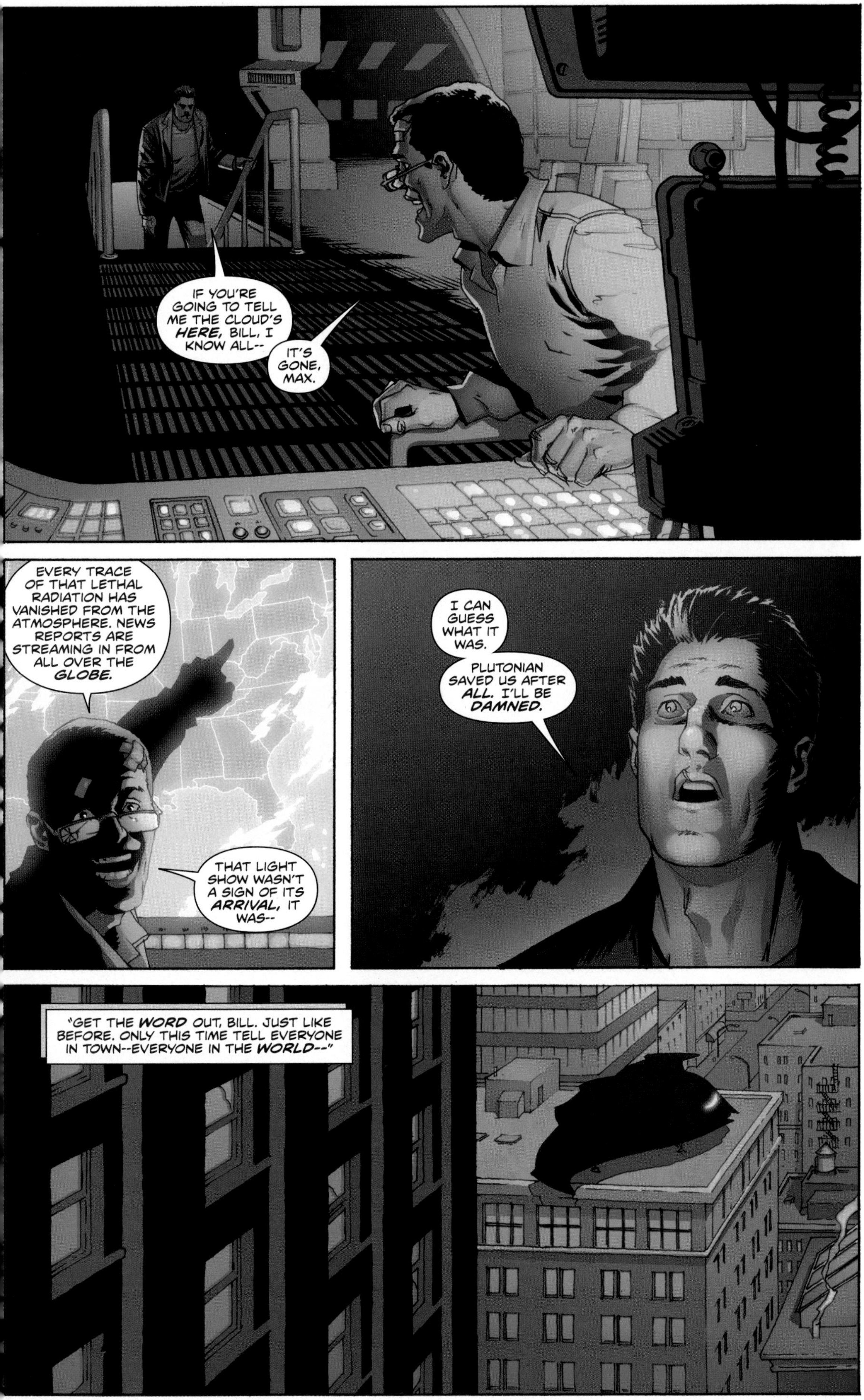

IF YOU'RE GOING TO TELL ME THE CLOUD'S *HERE,* BILL, I KNOW ALL--
IT'S GONE, MAX.
EVERY TRACE OF THAT LETHAL RADIATION HAS VANISHED FROM THE ATMOSPHERE. NEWS REPORTS ARE STREAMING IN FROM ALL OVER THE *GLOBE.*
THAT LIGHT SHOW WASN'T A SIGN OF ITS *ARRIVAL,* IT WAS--
I CAN GUESS WHAT IT WAS.
PLUTONIAN SAVED US AFTER *ALL.* I'LL BE *DAMNED.*
"GET THE *WORD* OUT, BILL. JUST LIKE BEFORE. ONLY THIS TIME TELL EVERYONE IN TOWN--EVERYONE IN THE *WORLD--*"

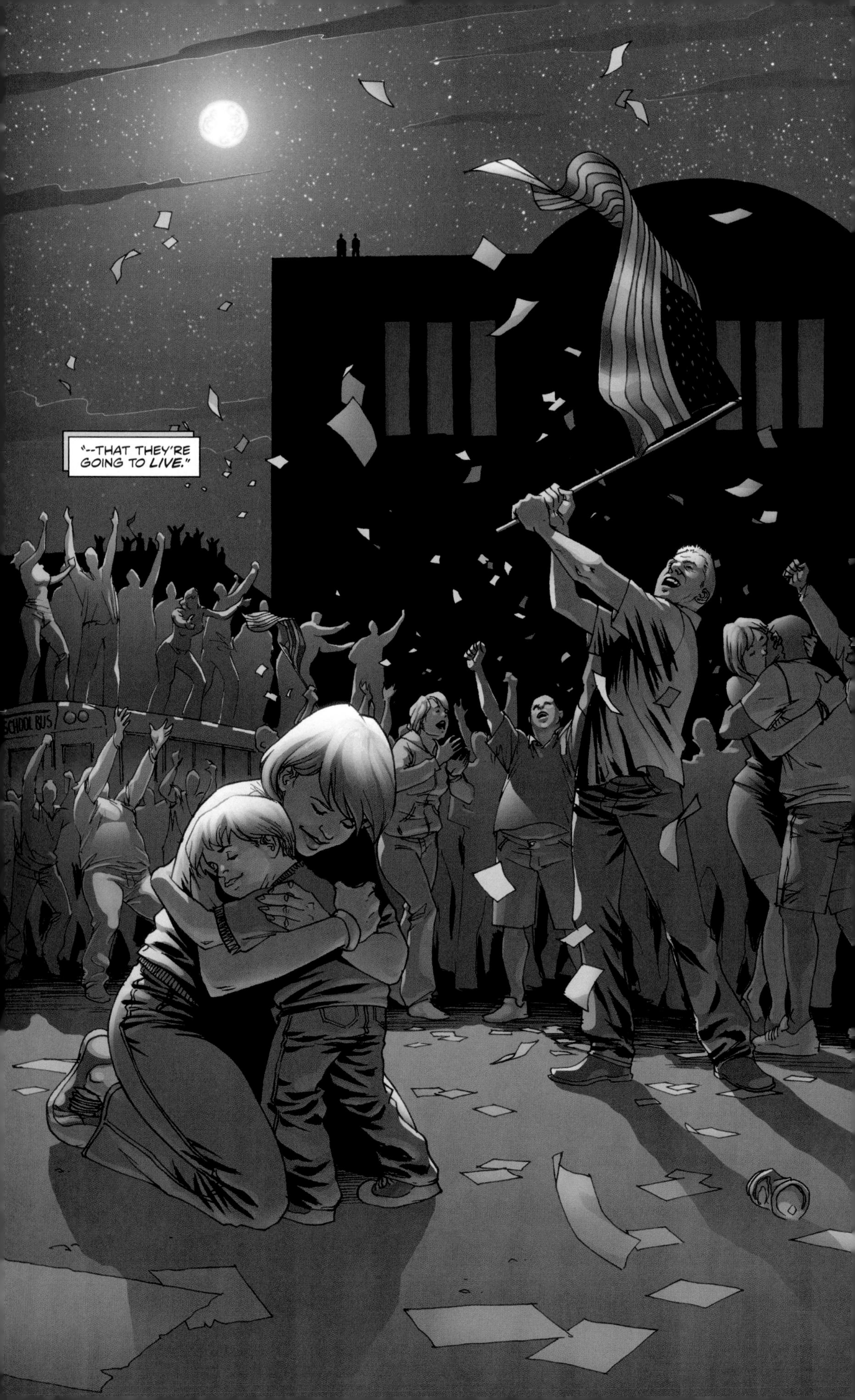
"--THAT THEY'RE GOING TO *LIVE*."
SCHOOL BUS

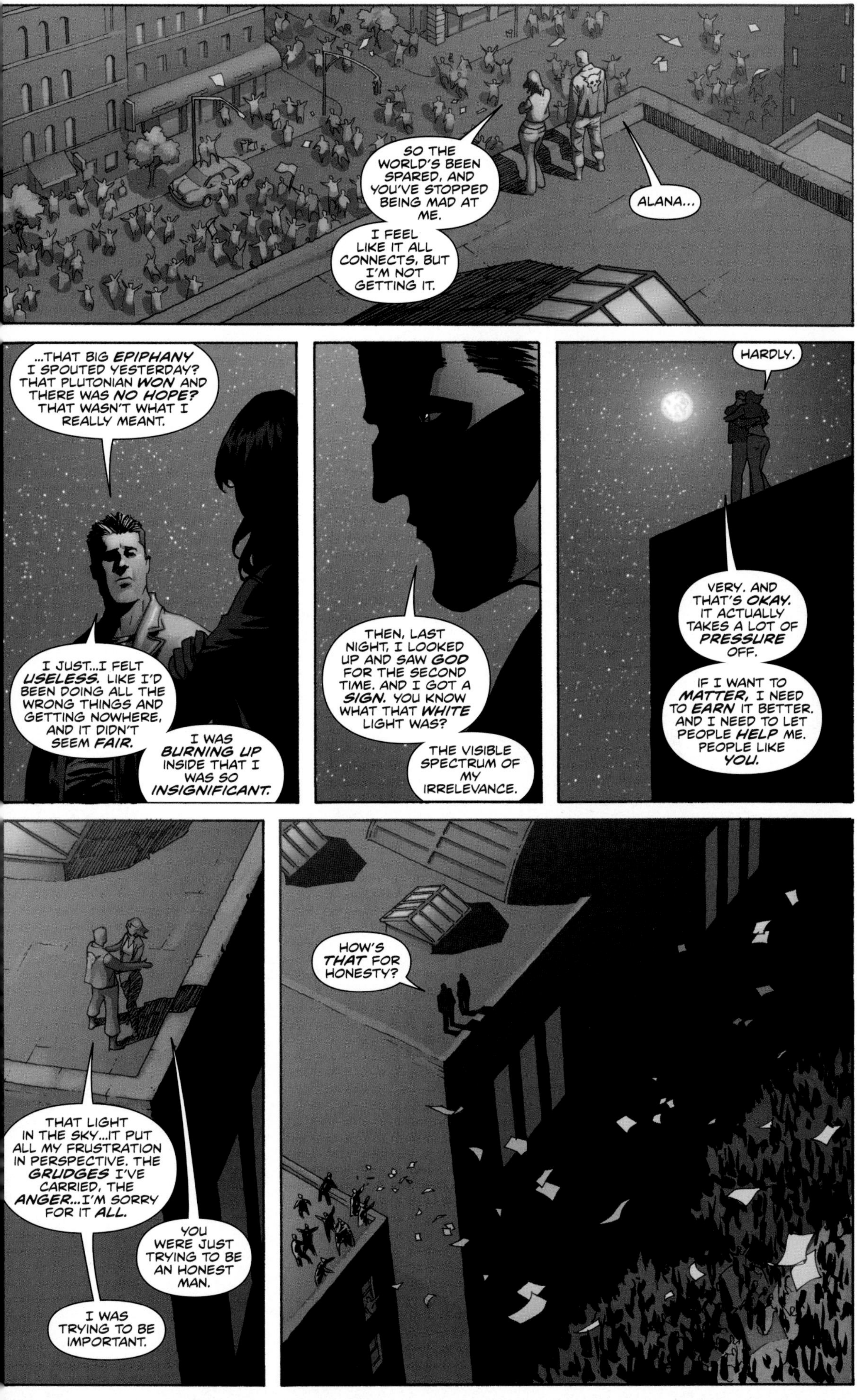
SO THE WORLD'S BEEN SPARED, AND YOU'VE STOPPED BEING MAD AT ME.
I FEEL LIKE IT ALL CONNECTS, BUT I'M NOT GETTING IT.
ALANA...
...THAT BIG EPIPHANY I SPOUTED YESTERDAY? THAT PLUTONIAN WON AND THERE WAS NO HOPE? THAT WASN'T WHAT I REALLY MEANT.
I JUST...I FELT USELESS. LIKE I'D BEEN DOING ALL THE WRONG THINGS AND GETTING NOWHERE, AND IT DIDN'T SEEM FAIR.
I WAS BURNING UP INSIDE THAT I WAS SO INSIGNIFICANT.
THEN, LAST NIGHT, I LOOKED UP AND SAW GOD FOR THE SECOND TIME. AND I GOT A SIGN. YOU KNOW WHAT THAT WHITE LIGHT WAS?
THE VISIBLE SPECTRUM OF MY IRRELEVANCE.
HARDLY.
VERY. AND THAT'S OKAY. IT ACTUALLY TAKES A LOT OF PRESSURE OFF.
IF I WANT TO MATTER, I NEED TO EARN IT BETTER. AND I NEED TO LET PEOPLE HELP ME. PEOPLE LIKE YOU.
THAT LIGHT IN THE SKY...IT PUT ALL MY FRUSTRATION IN PERSPECTIVE. THE GRUDGES I'VE CARRIED, THE ANGER...I'M SORRY FOR IT ALL.
YOU WERE JUST TRYING TO BE AN HONEST MAN.
I WAS TRYING TO BE IMPORTANT.
HOW'S THAT FOR HONESTY?

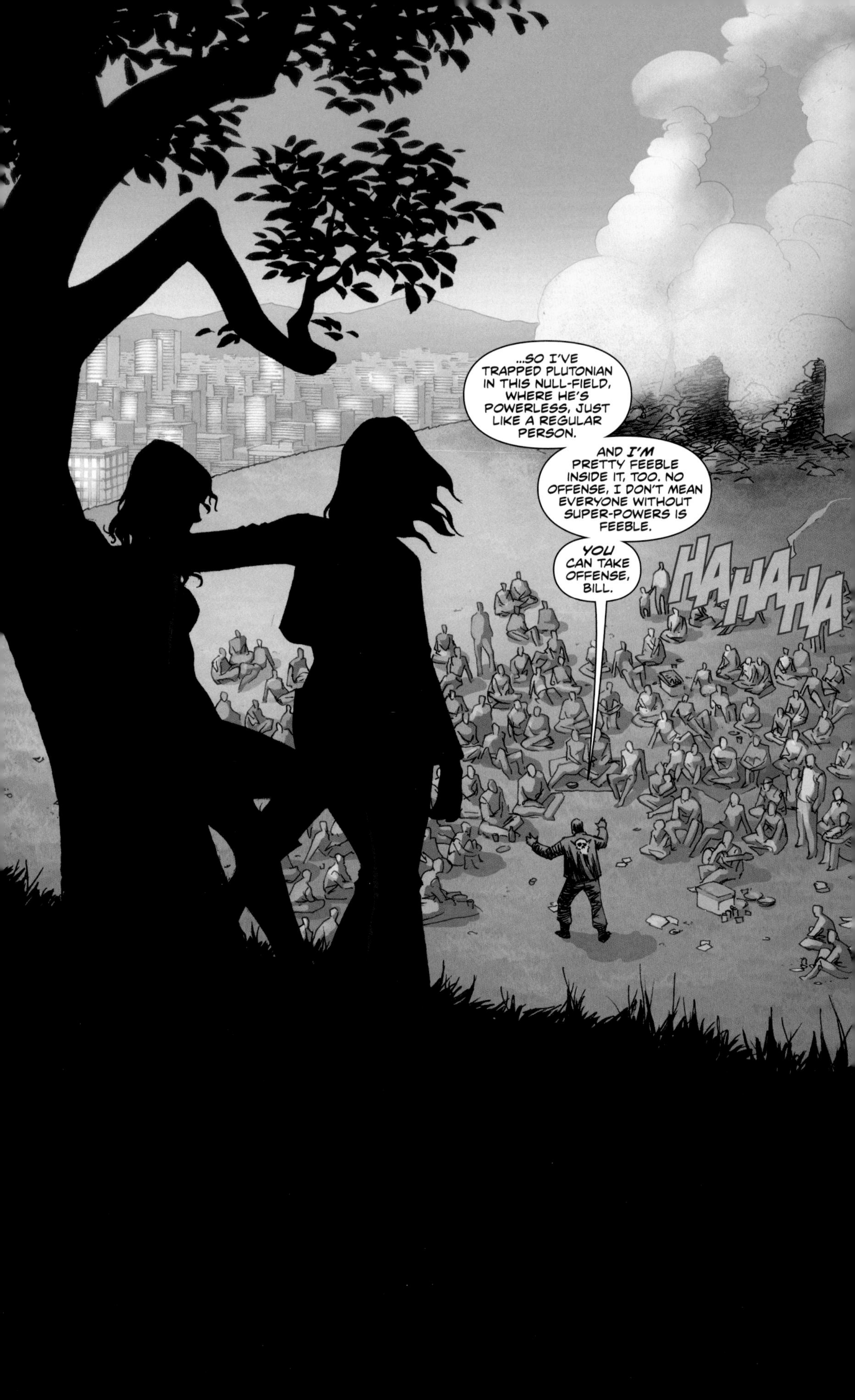

...SO I'VE TRAPPED PLUTONIAN IN THIS NULL-FIELD, WHERE HE'S POWERLESS, JUST LIKE A REGULAR PERSON.
AND I'M PRETTY FEEBLE INSIDE IT, TOO. NO OFFENSE, I DON'T MEAN EVERYONE WITHOUT SUPER-POWERS IS FEEBLE.
YOU CAN TAKE OFFENSE, BILL.
HAHAHA

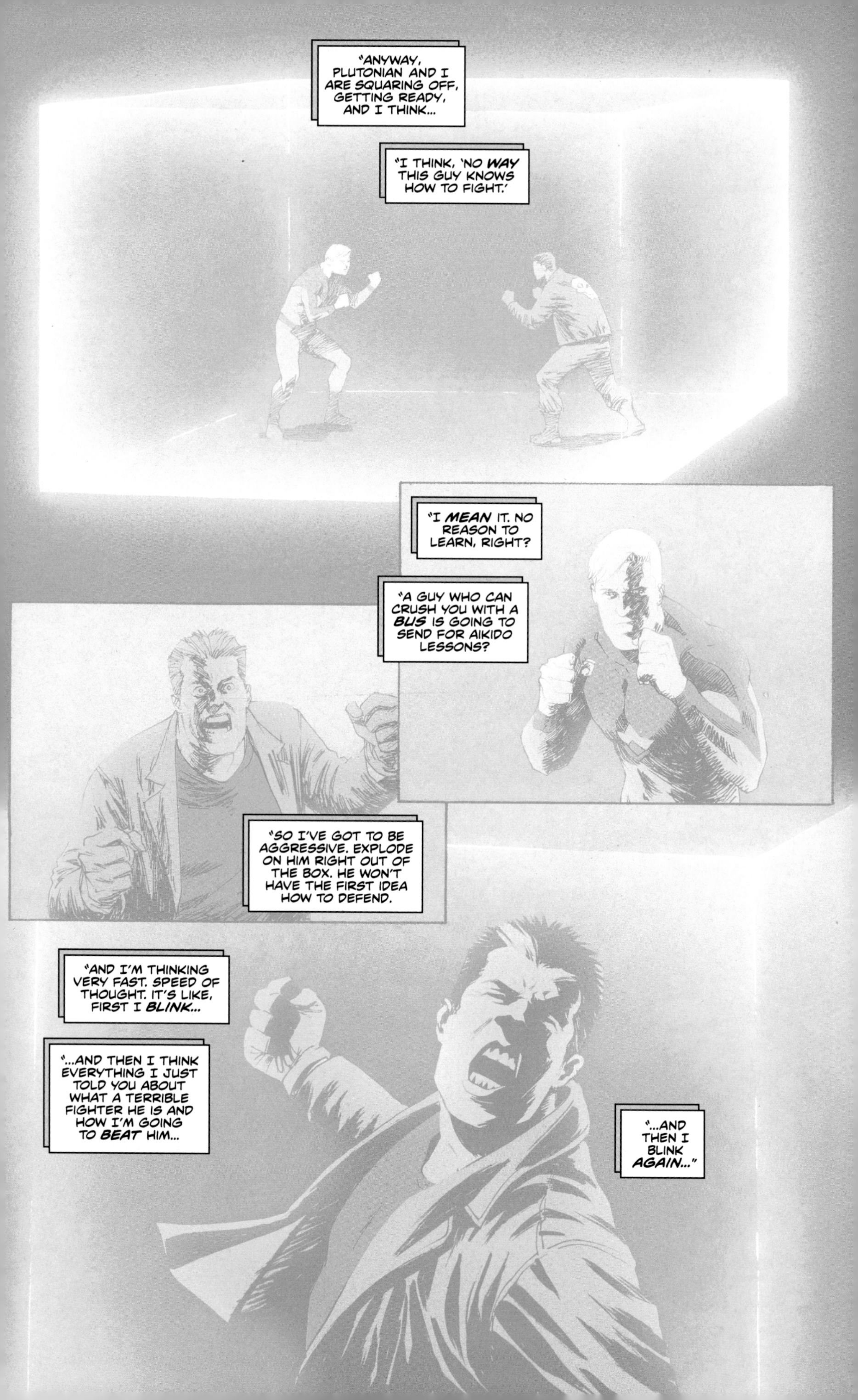
"ANYWAY, PLUTONIAN AND I ARE SQUARING OFF, GETTING READY, AND I THINK...
"I THINK, 'NO WAY THIS GUY KNOWS HOW TO FIGHT.'
"I MEAN IT. NO REASON TO LEARN, RIGHT?
"A GUY WHO CAN CRUSH YOU WITH A BUS IS GOING TO SEND FOR AIKIDO LESSONS?
"SO I'VE GOT TO BE AGGRESSIVE. EXPLODE ON HIM RIGHT OUT OF THE BOX. HE WON'T HAVE THE FIRST IDEA HOW TO DEFEND.
"AND I'M THINKING VERY FAST. SPEED OF THOUGHT. IT'S LIKE, FIRST I BLINK...
"...AND THEN I THINK EVERYTHING I JUST TOLD YOU ABOUT WHAT A TERRIBLE FIGHTER HE IS AND HOW I'M GOING TO BEAT HIM...
"...AND THEN I BLINK AGAIN..."

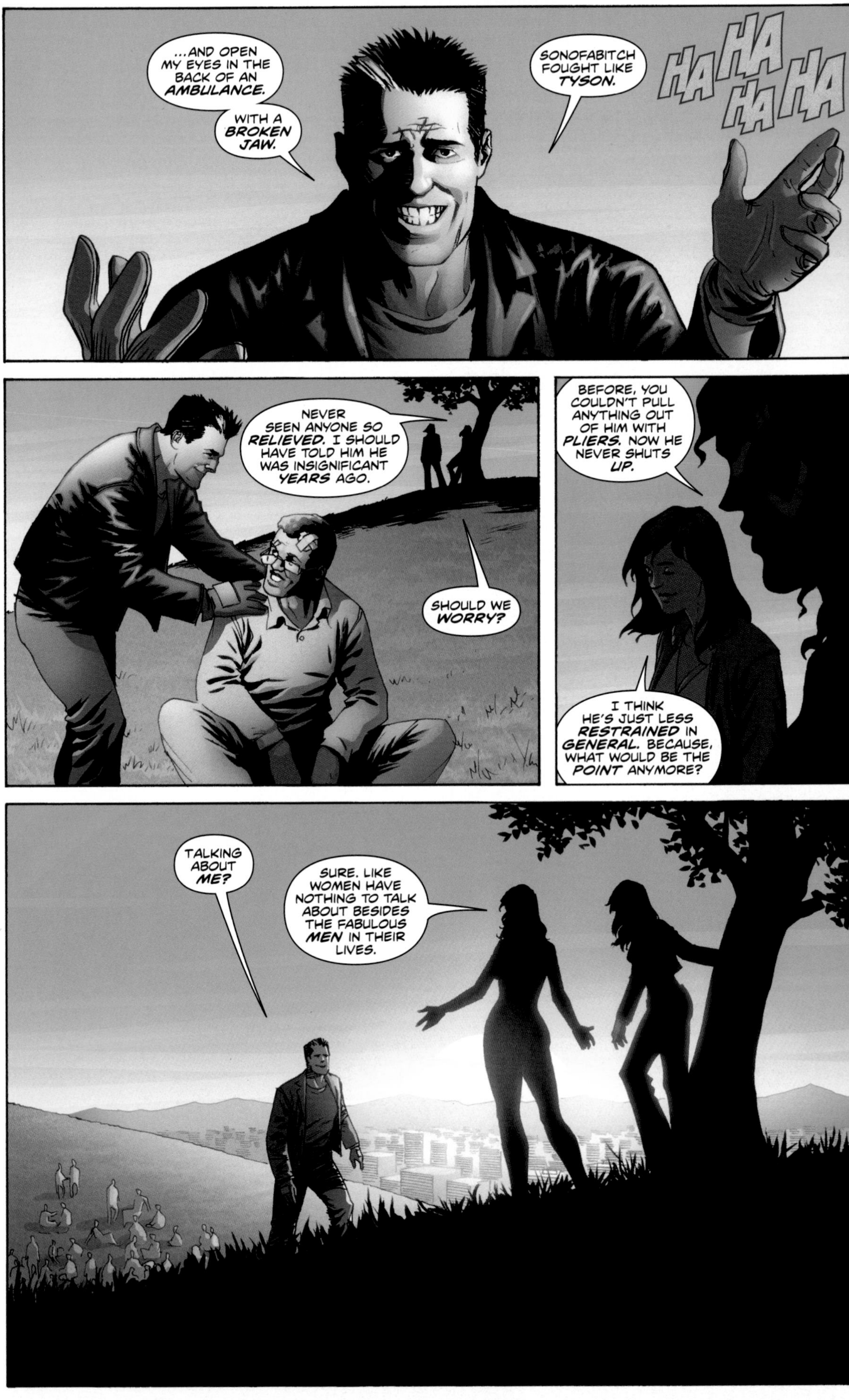
...AND OPEN MY EYES IN THE BACK OF AN AMBULANCE.
WITH A BROKEN JAW.
SONOFABITCH FOUGHT LIKE TYSON.
HA HA HA HA HA
NEVER SEEN ANYONE SO RELIEVED. I SHOULD HAVE TOLD HIM HE WAS INSIGNIFICANT YEARS AGO.
SHOULD WE WORRY?
BEFORE, YOU COULDN'T PULL ANYTHING OUT OF HIM WITH PLIERS. NOW HE NEVER SHUTS UP.
I THINK HE'S JUST LESS RESTRAINED IN GENERAL. BECAUSE, WHAT WOULD BE THE POINT ANYMORE?
TALKING ABOUT ME?
SURE. LIKE WOMEN HAVE NOTHING TO TALK ABOUT BESIDES THE FABULOUS MEN IN THEIR LIVES.

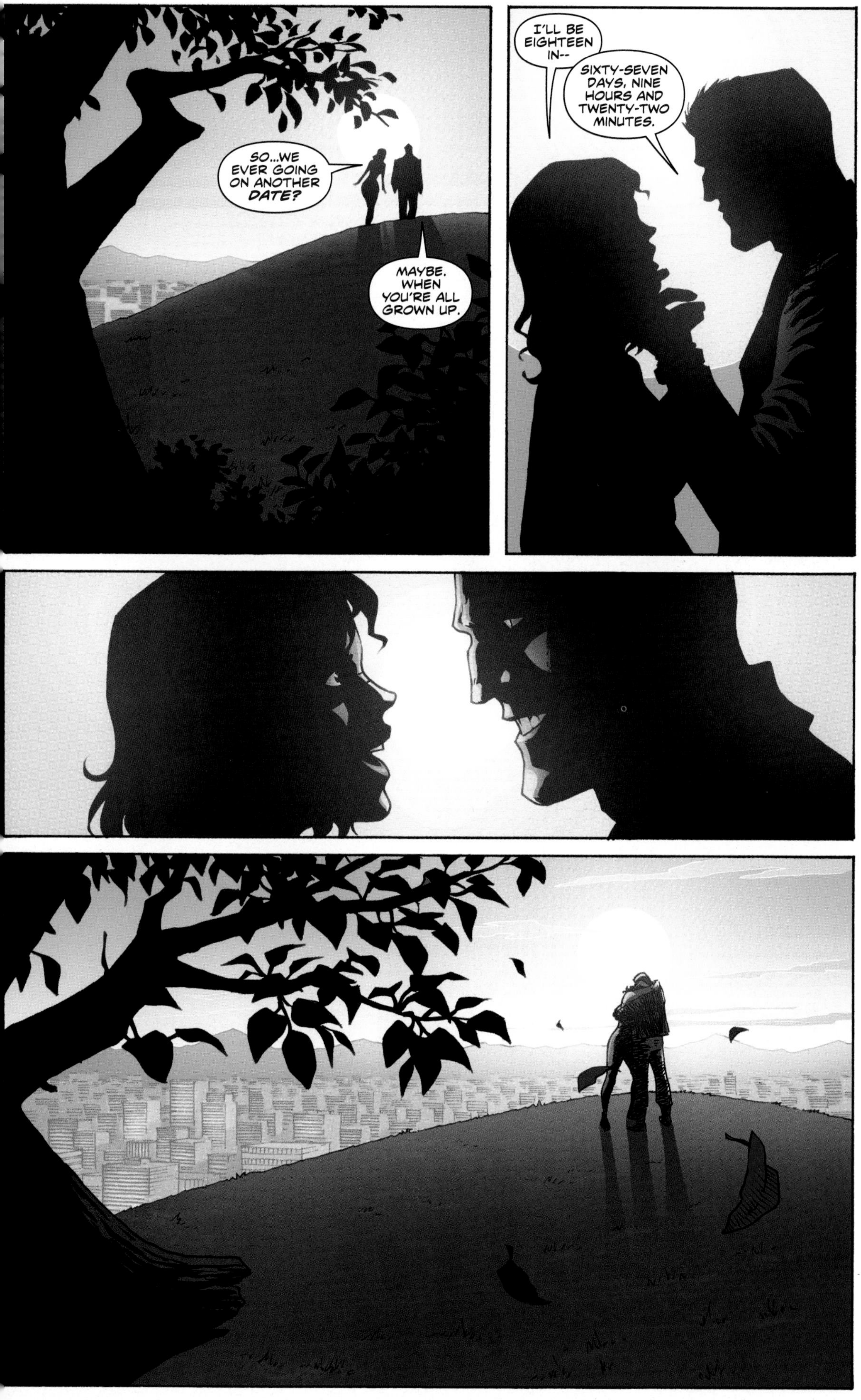
SO...WE EVER GOING ON ANOTHER DATE?
MAYBE. WHEN YOU'RE ALL GROWN UP.
I'LL BE EIGHTEEN IN--
SIXTY-SEVEN DAYS, NINE HOURS AND TWENTY-TWO MINUTES.

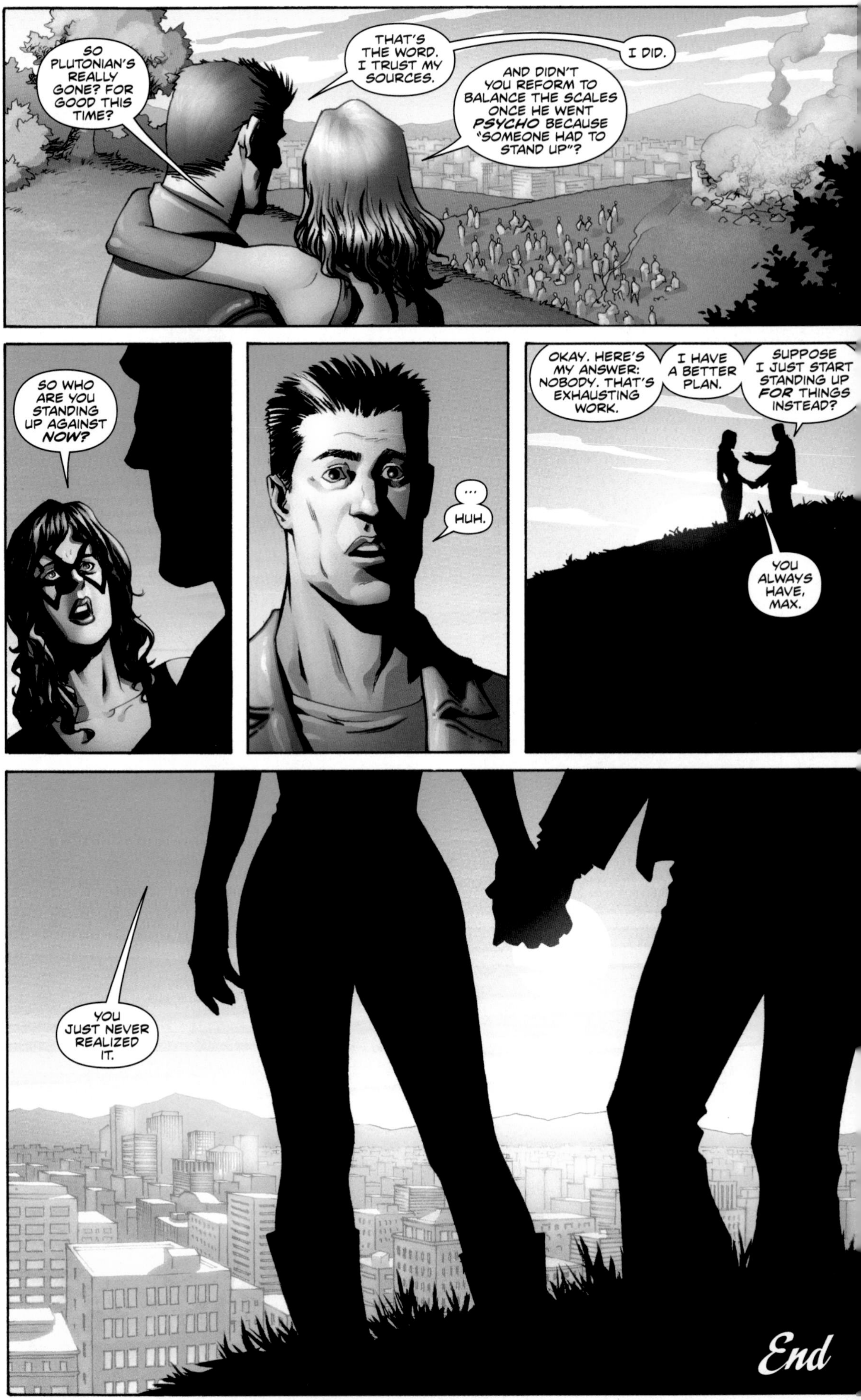

SO PLUTONIAN'S REALLY GONE? FOR GOOD THIS TIME?
THAT'S THE WORD. I TRUST MY SOURCES.
I DID.
AND DIDN'T YOU REFORM TO BALANCE THE SCALES ONCE HE WENT PSYCHO BECAUSE "SOMEONE HAD TO STAND UP"?
SO WHO ARE YOU STANDING UP AGAINST NOW?
...
HUH.
OKAY. HERE'S MY ANSWER: NOBODY. THAT'S EXHAUSTING WORK.
I HAVE A BETTER PLAN.
SUPPOSE I JUST START STANDING UP FOR THINGS INSTEAD?
YOU ALWAYS HAVE, MAX.
YOU JUST NEVER REALIZED IT.
End

COVER GALLERY

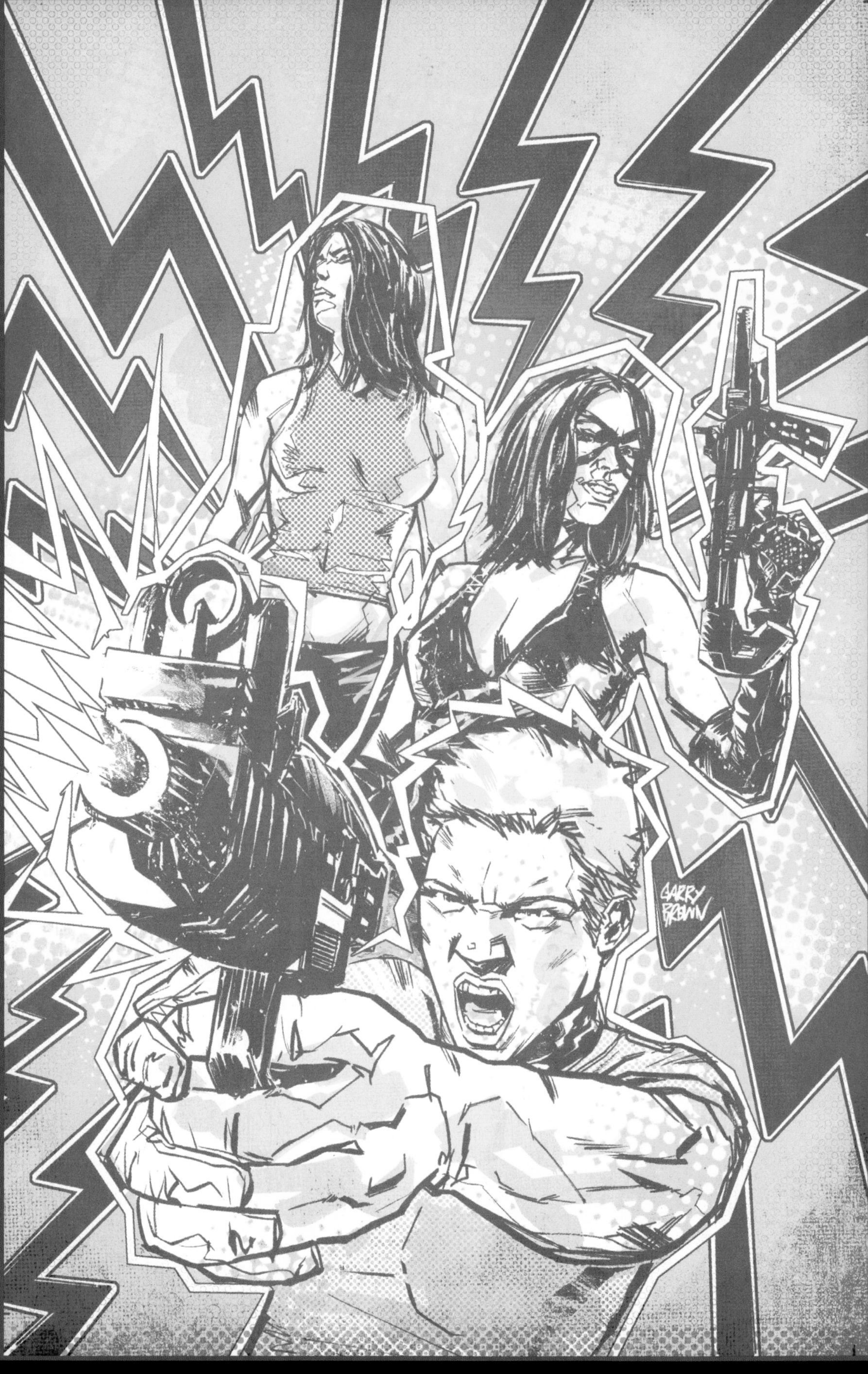
GARRY BROWN

COVER 27A: GARRY BROWN

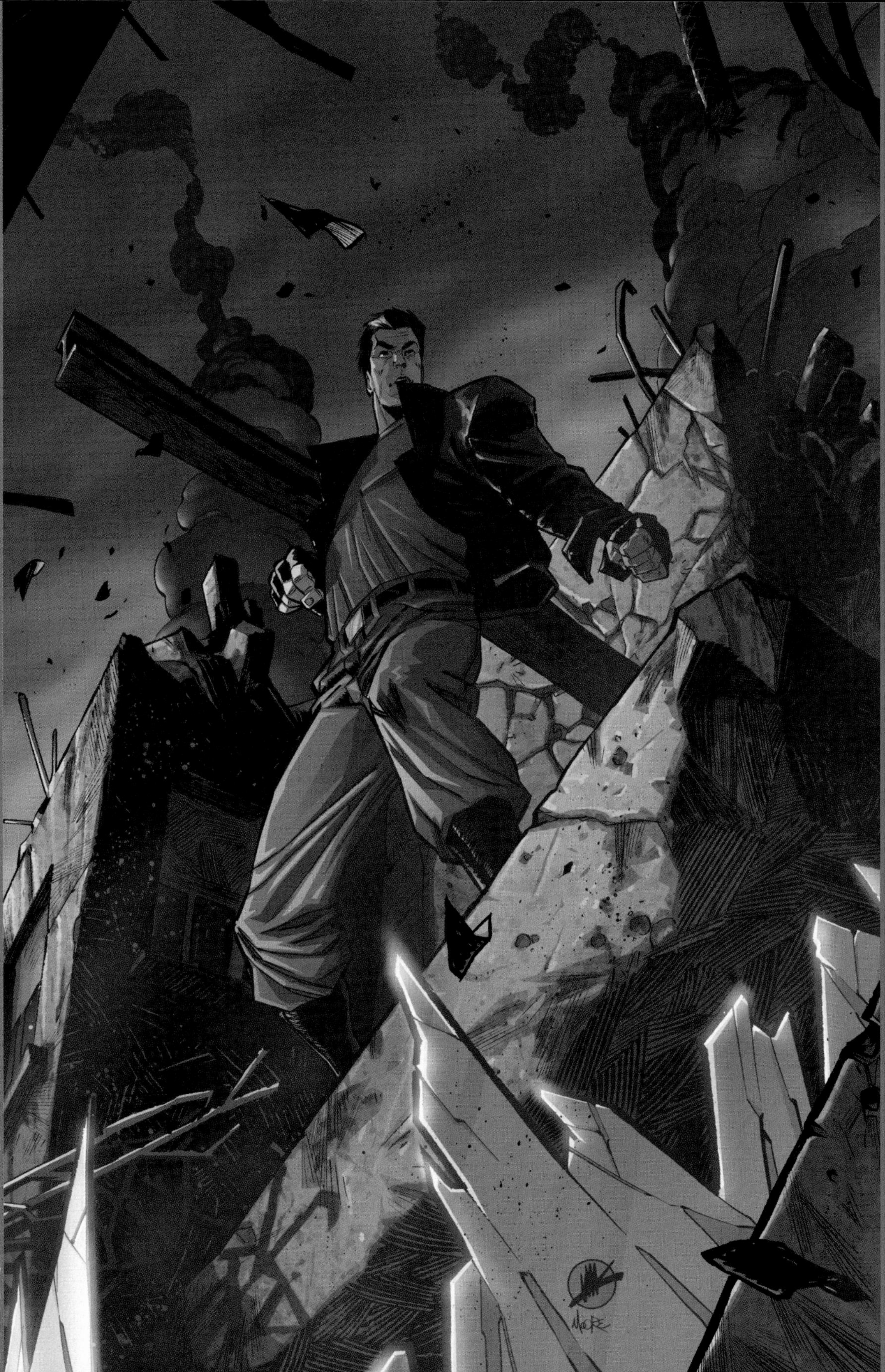

COVER 27B: MATTEO SCALERA
COLORIST: DARRIN MOORE

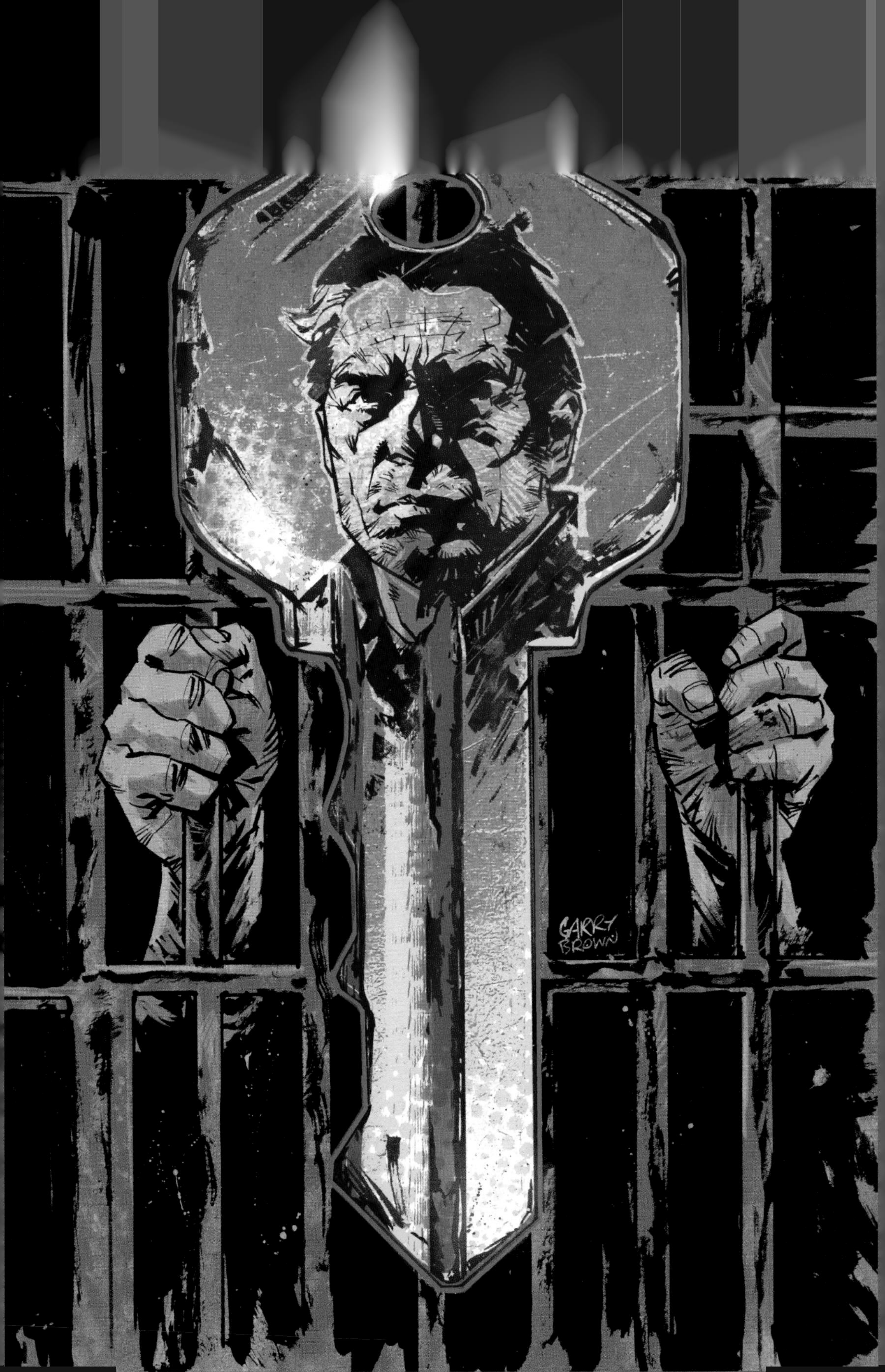
GARRY
BROWN

BA: GARR

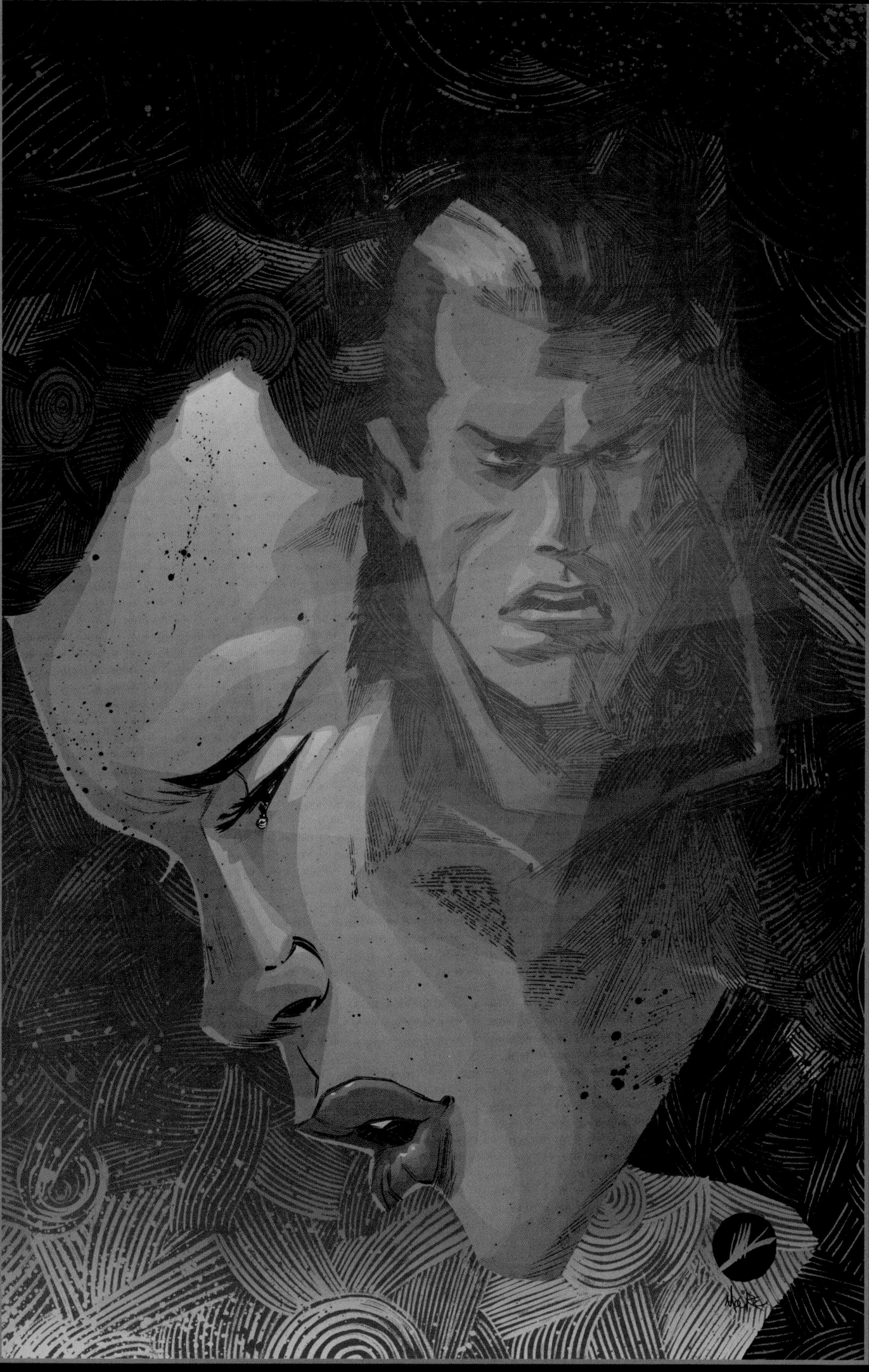

COVER 28B: MATTEO SCALERA
COLORIST: NOLAN WOODARD

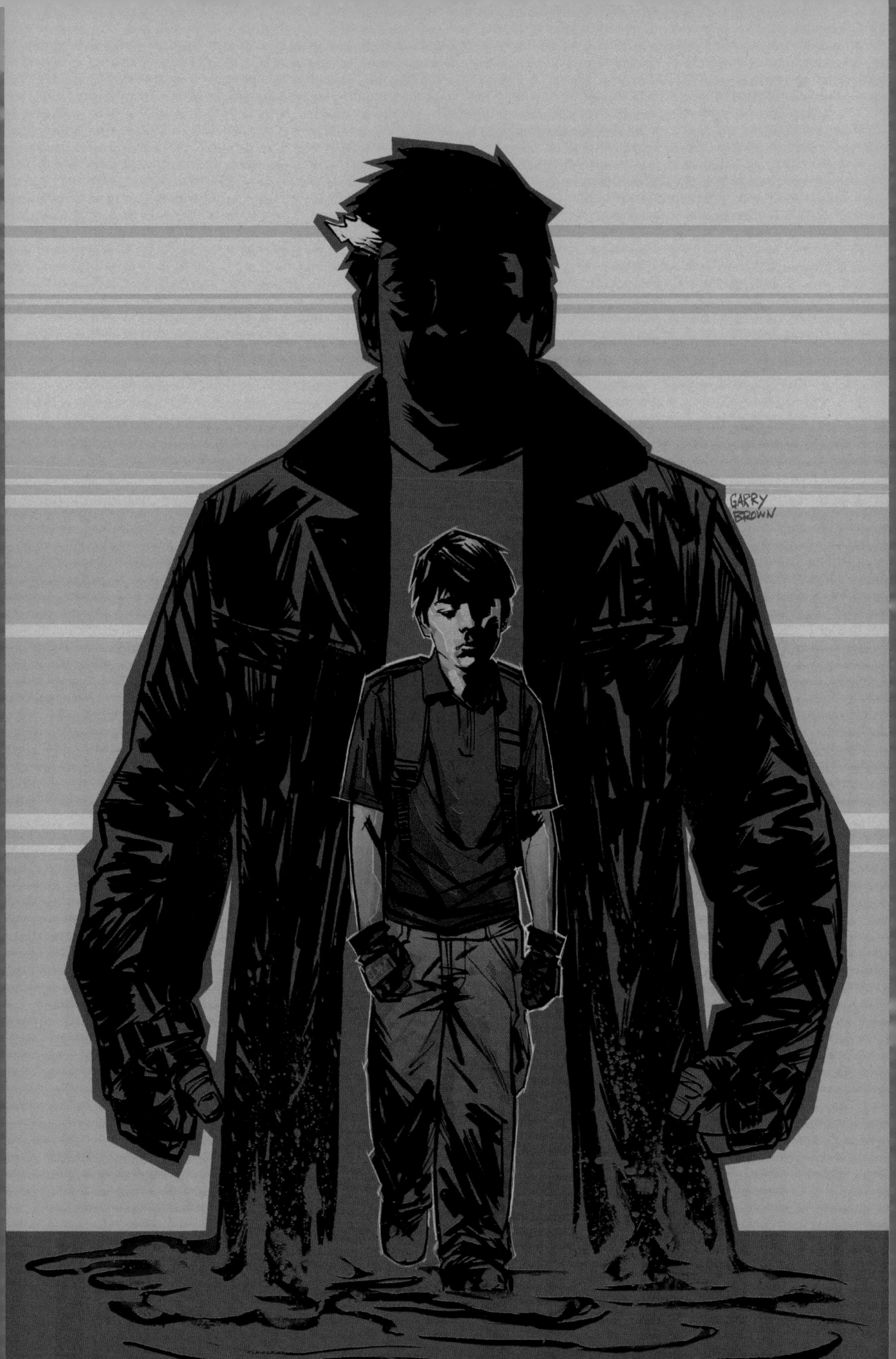
GARRY
BROWN

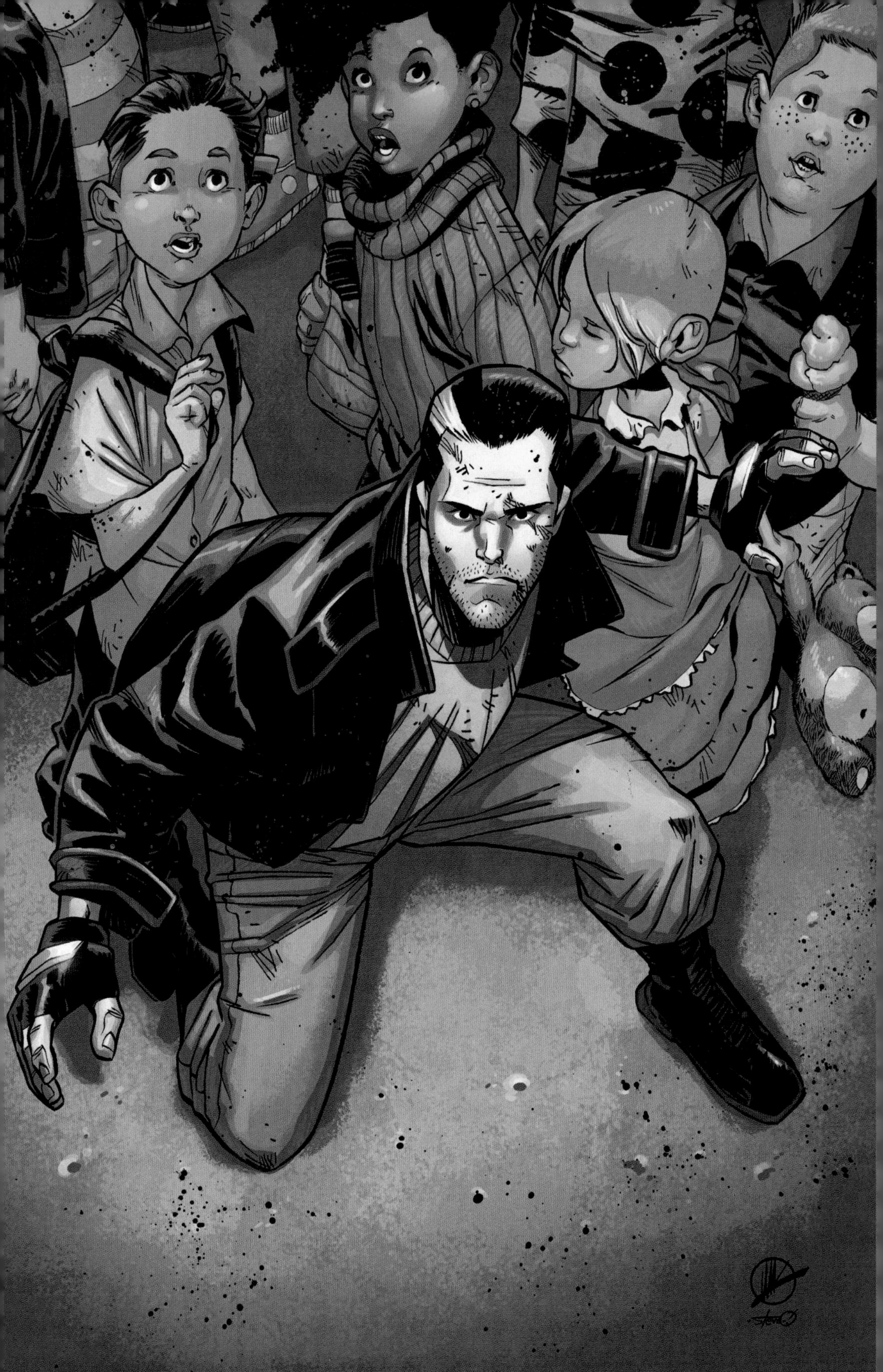

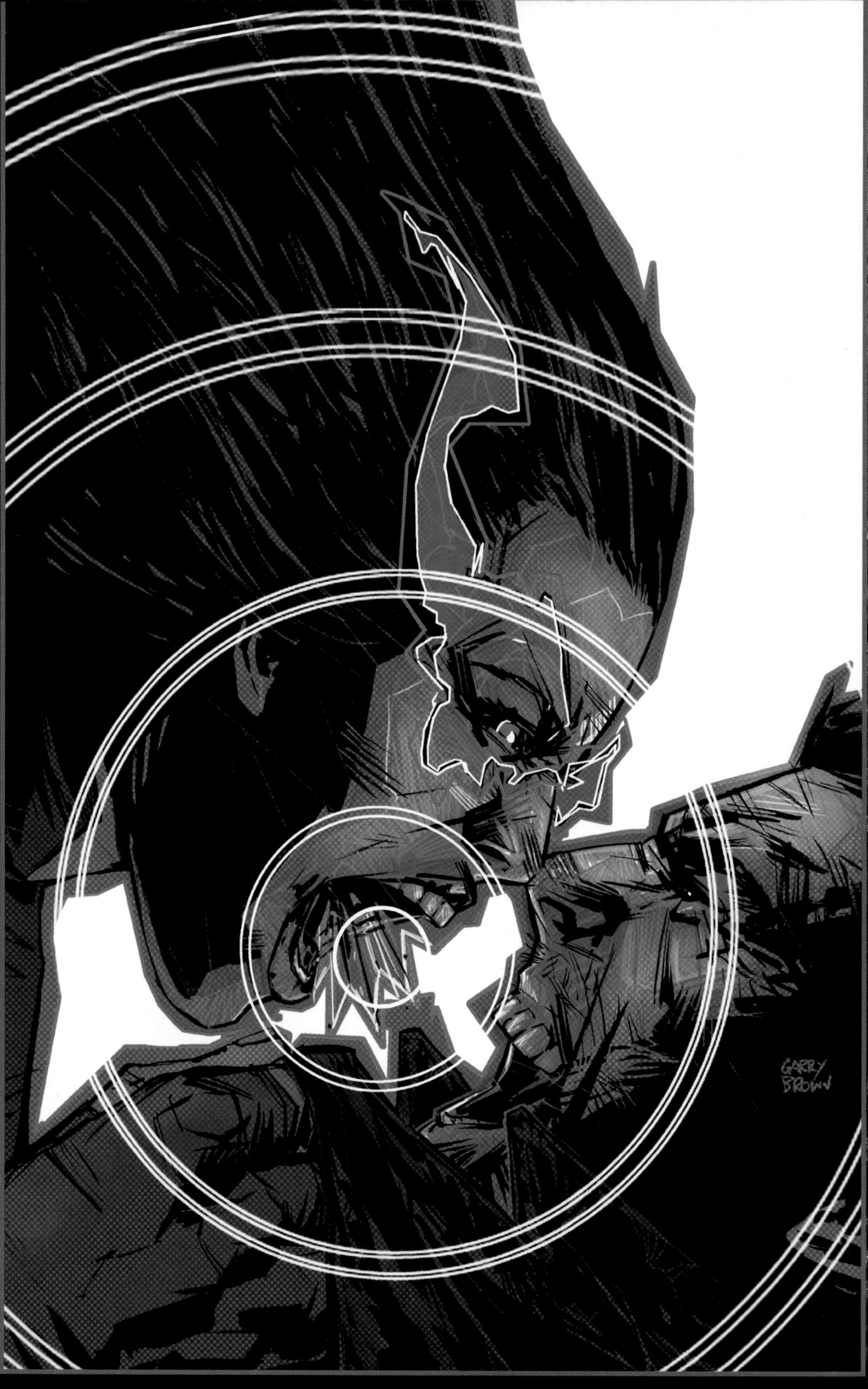
GARRY BROWN

COVER 30A: GARRY BROWN

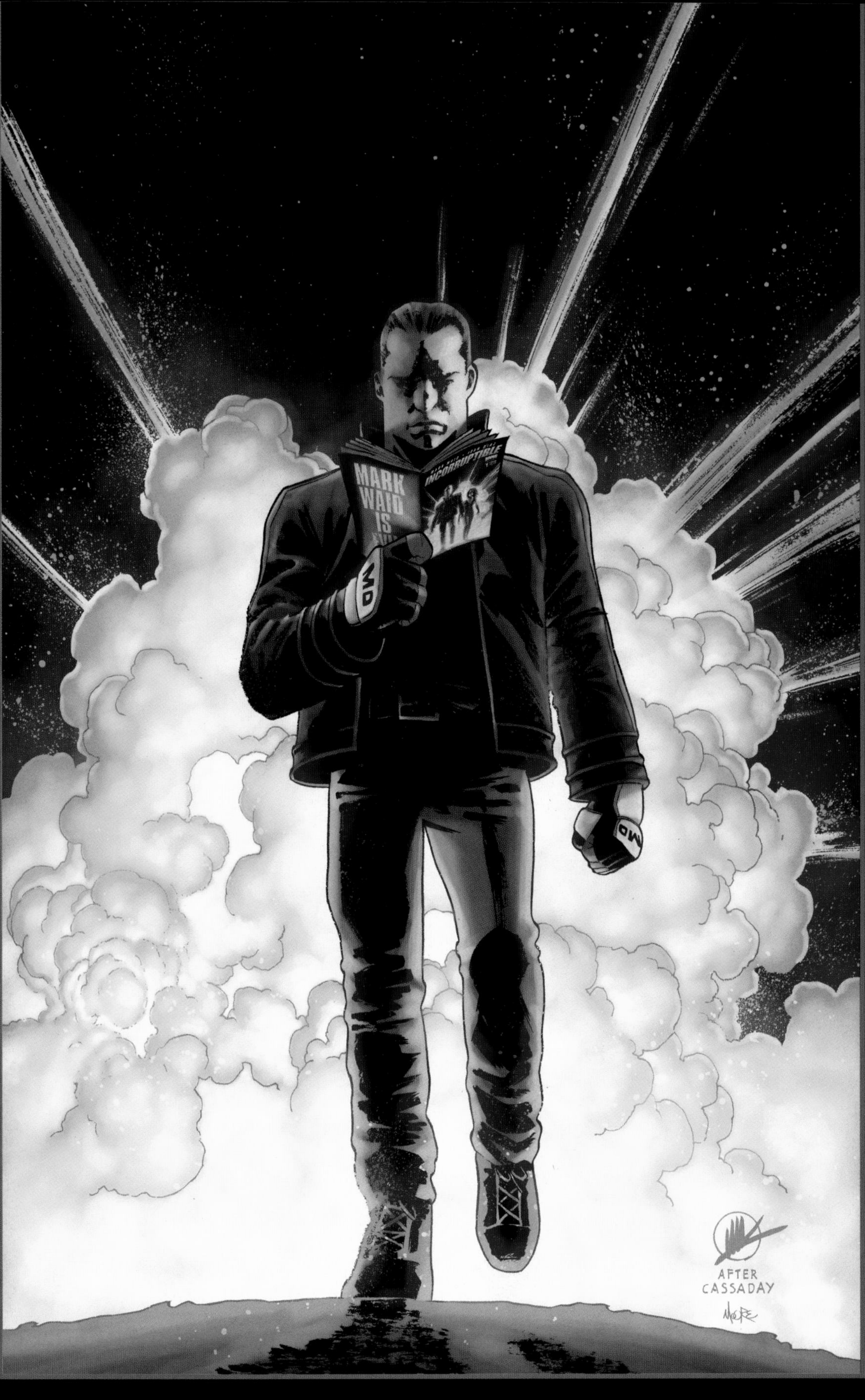
MARK WAID IS EVIL
INCORRUPTIBLE
MD
MD
AFTER CASSADAY
MOORE

COVER 30B: MATTEO SCALERA
COLORIST: DARRIN MOORE

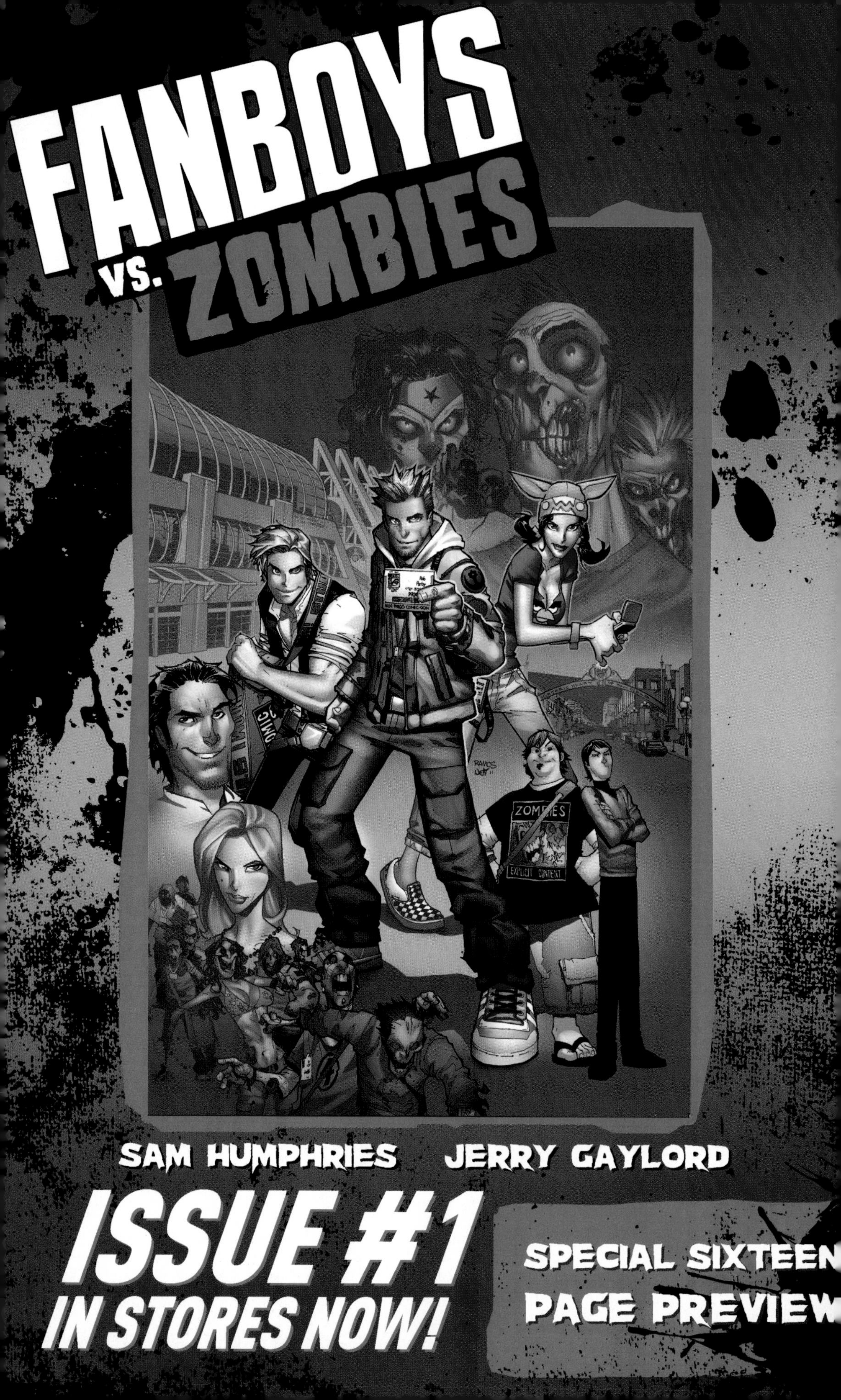
FANBOYS
VS.
ZOMBIES
ZOMBIES
EXPLICIT CONTENT
SAM HUMPHRIES
JERRY GAYLORD
ISSUE #1
IN STORES NOW!
SPECIAL SIXTEEN
PAGE PREVIEW

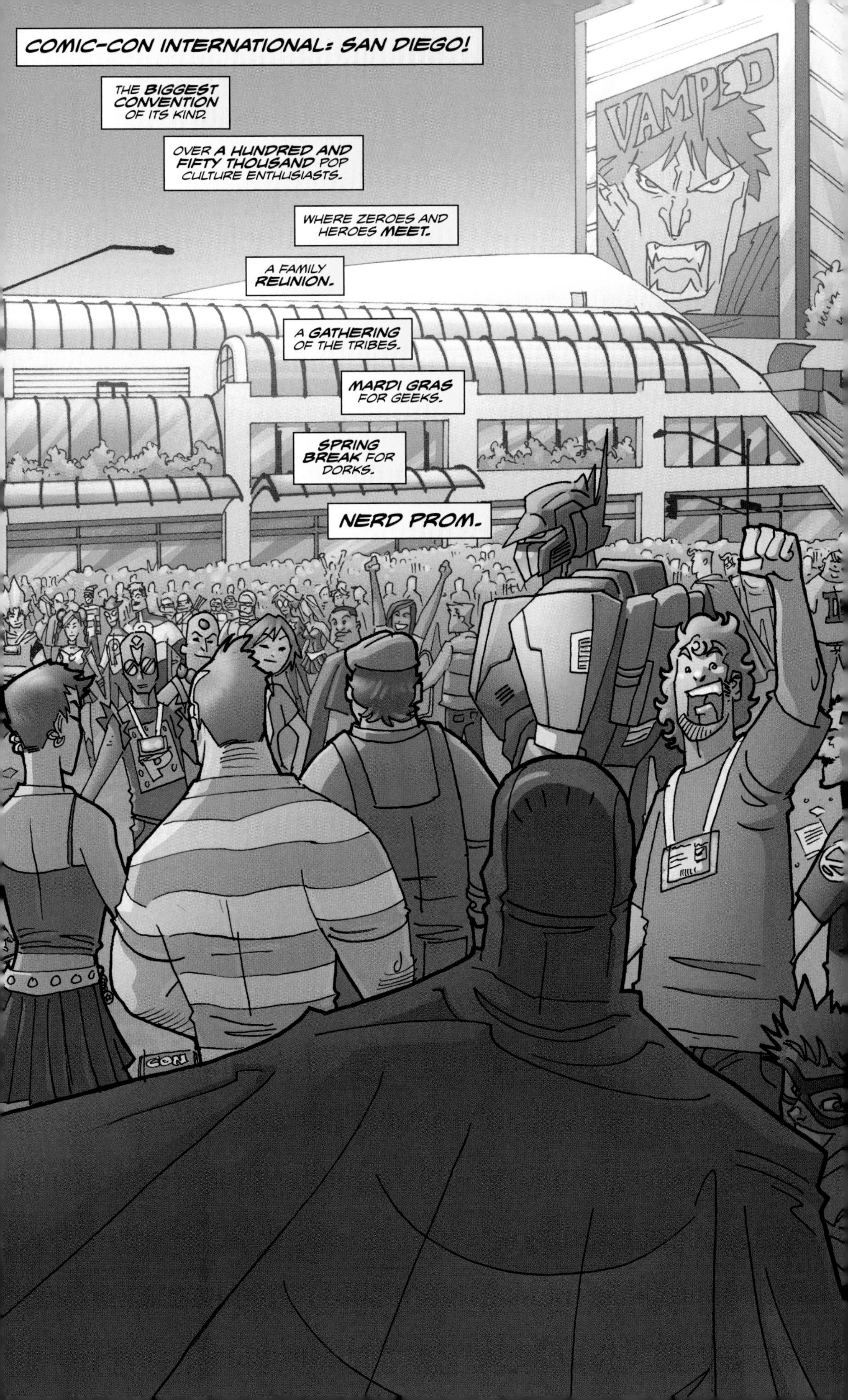
COMIC-CON INTERNATIONAL: SAN DIEGO!
THE BIGGEST CONVENTION OF ITS KIND.
OVER A HUNDRED AND FIFTY THOUSAND POP CULTURE ENTHUSIASTS.
WHERE ZEROES AND HEROES MEET.
A FAMILY REUNION.
A GATHERING OF THE TRIBES.
MARDI GRAS FOR GEEKS.
SPRING BREAK FOR DORKS.
NERD PROM.
VAMPED
CON

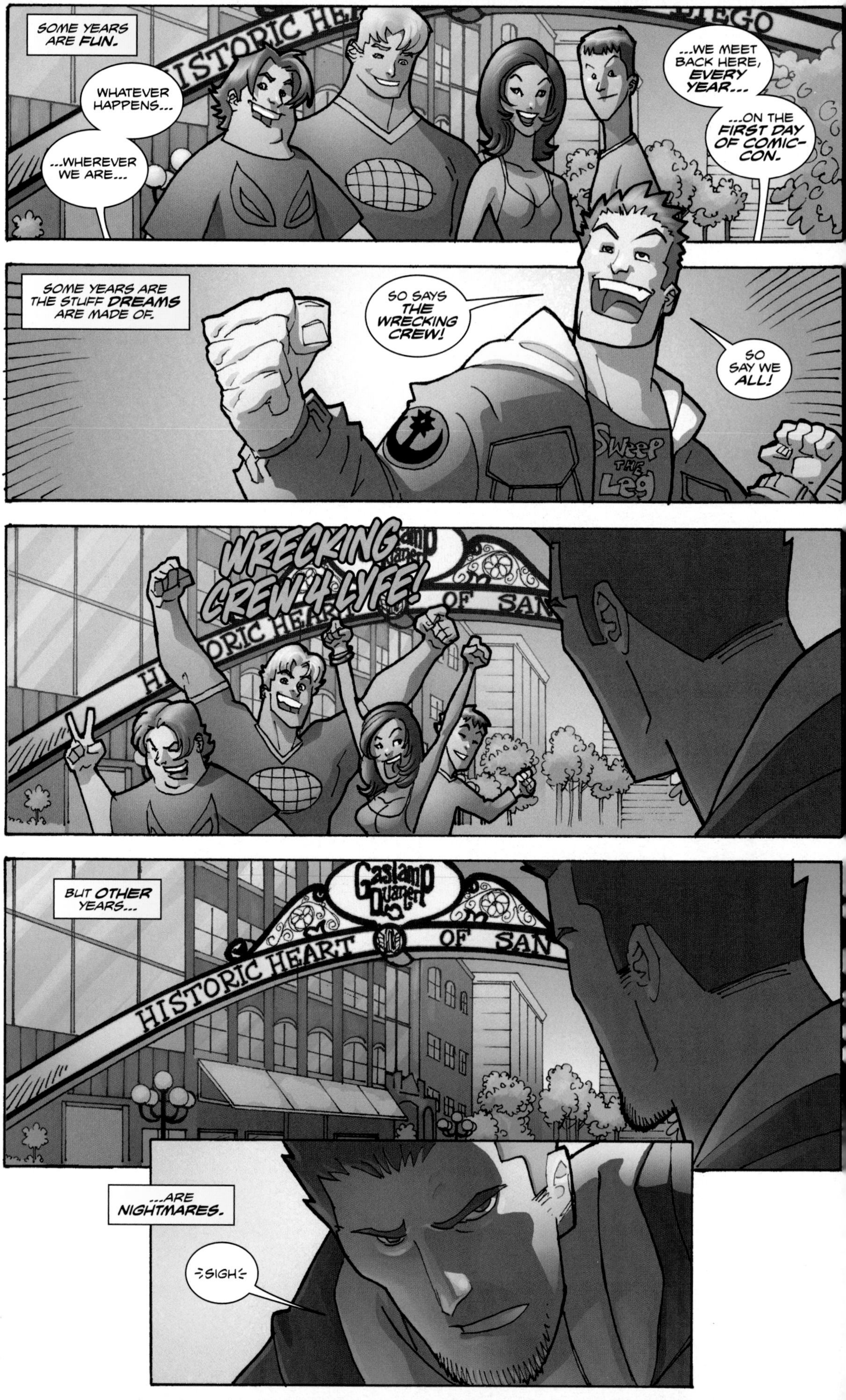
SOME YEARS ARE FUN.
WHATEVER HAPPENS...
...WHEREVER WE ARE...
...WE MEET BACK HERE, EVERY YEAR...
...ON THE FIRST DAY OF COMIC-CON.
SOME YEARS ARE THE STUFF DREAMS ARE MADE OF.
SO SAYS THE WRECKING CREW!
SO SAY WE ALL!
Sweep THE Leg
WRECKING CREW 4 LYFE!
BUT OTHER YEARS...
Gaslamp Quarter
HISTORIC HEART OF SAN
...ARE NIGHTMARES.
SIGH

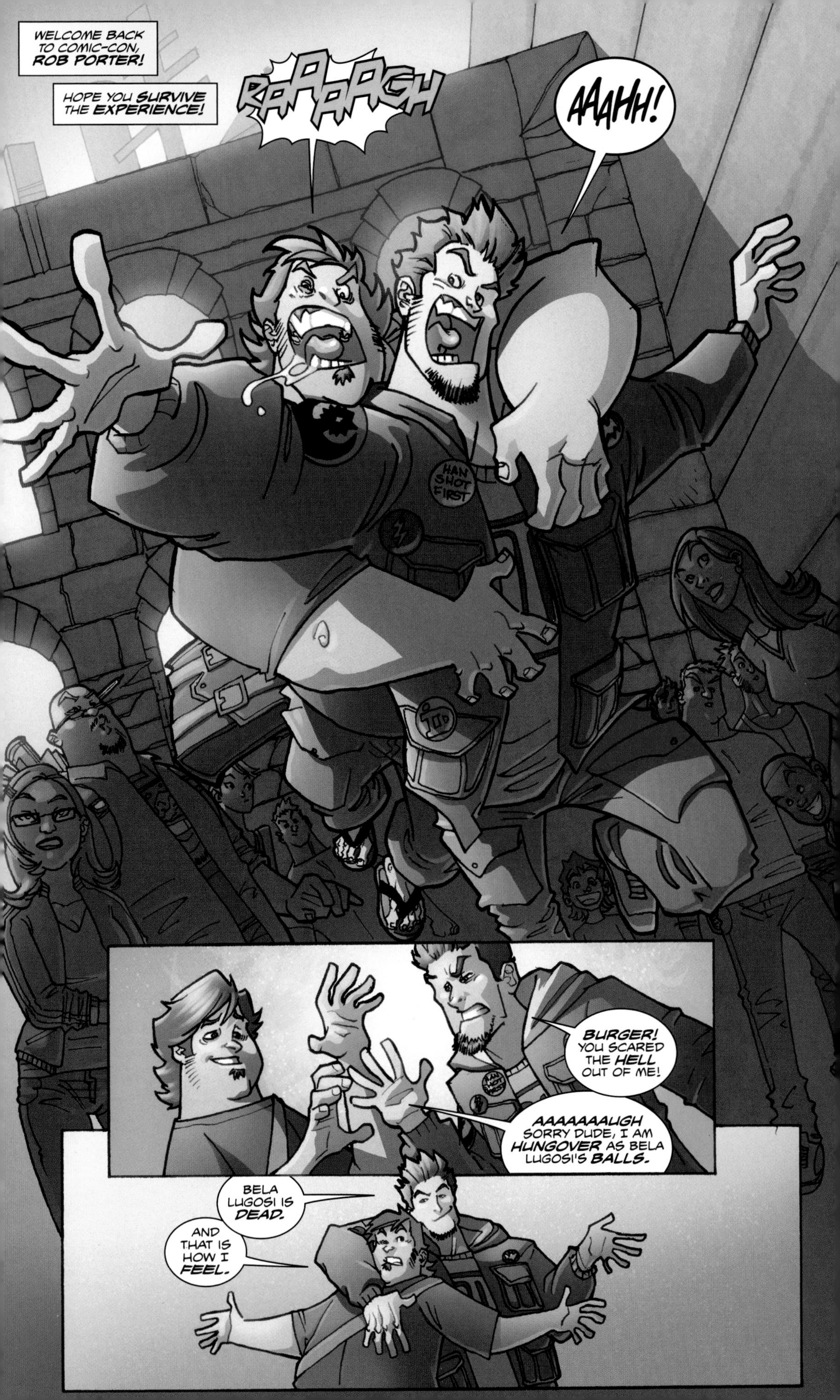
WELCOME BACK TO COMIC-CON, ROB PORTER!
HOPE YOU SURVIVE THE EXPERIENCE!
RAAARGH
AAAHH!
HAN SHOT FIRST
BURGER! YOU SCARED THE HELL OUT OF ME!
AAAAAAAUGH SORRY DUDE, I AM HUNGOVER AS BELA LUGOSI'S BALLS.
BELA LUGOSI IS DEAD.
AND THAT IS HOW I FEEL.

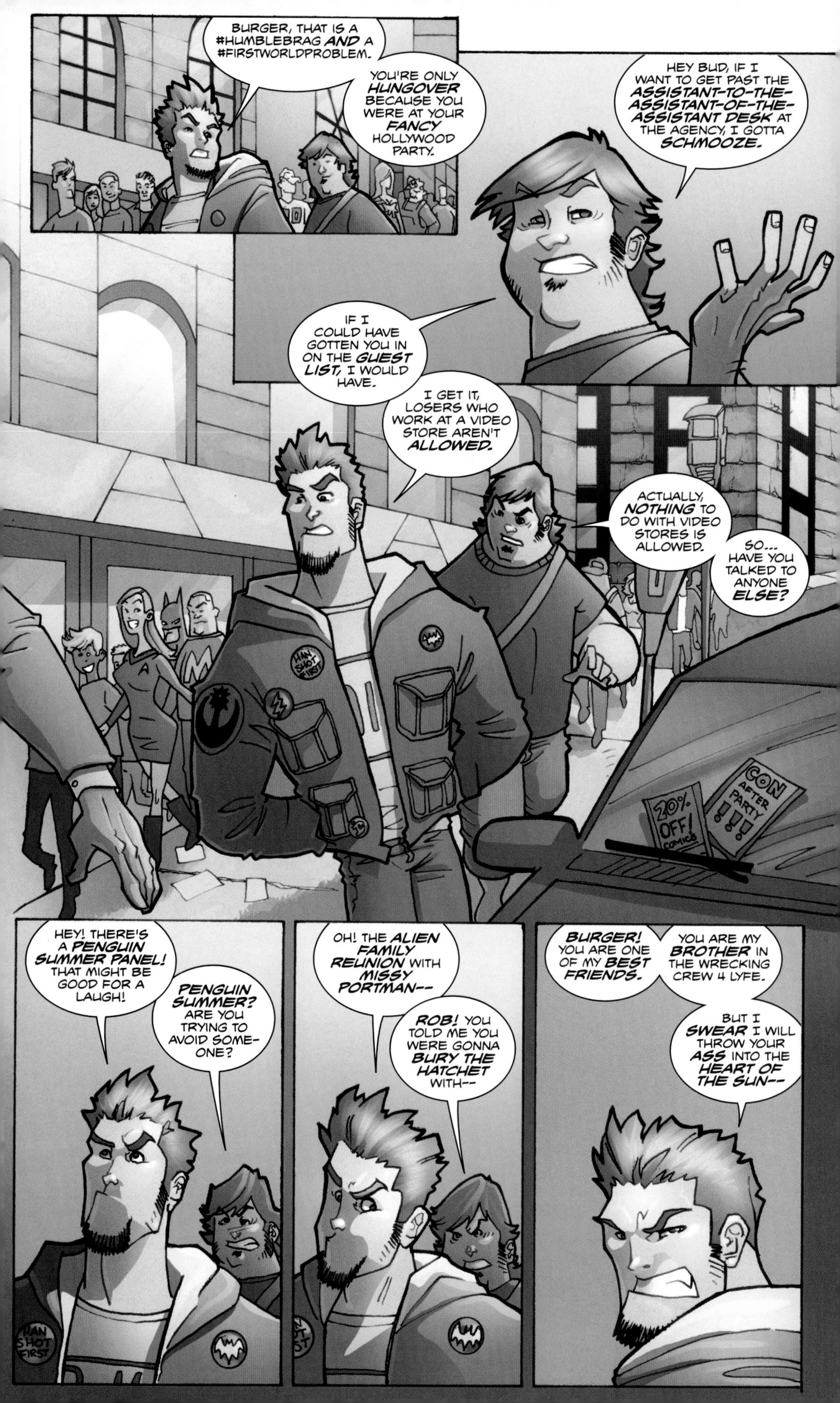
BURGER, THAT IS A #HUMBLEBRAG AND A #FIRSTWORLDPROBLEM.
YOU'RE ONLY HUNGOVER BECAUSE YOU WERE AT YOUR FANCY HOLLYWOOD PARTY.
HEY BUD, IF I WANT TO GET PAST THE ASSISTANT-TO-THE-ASSISTANT-OF-THE-ASSISTANT DESK AT THE AGENCY, I GOTTA SCHMOOZE.
IF I COULD HAVE GOTTEN YOU IN ON THE GUEST LIST, I WOULD HAVE.
I GET IT, LOSERS WHO WORK AT A VIDEO STORE AREN'T ALLOWED.
ACTUALLY, NOTHING TO DO WITH VIDEO STORES IS ALLOWED.
SO... HAVE YOU TALKED TO ANYONE ELSE?
HAN SHOT FIRST
20% OFF! COMICS
CON AFTER PARTY !!!
HEY! THERE'S A PENGUIN SUMMER PANEL! THAT MIGHT BE GOOD FOR A LAUGH!
PENGUIN SUMMER? ARE YOU TRYING TO AVOID SOME-ONE?
OH! THE ALIEN FAMILY REUNION WITH MISSY PORTMAN--
ROB! YOU TOLD ME YOU WERE GONNA BURY THE HATCHET WITH--
BURGER! YOU ARE ONE OF MY BEST FRIENDS.
YOU ARE MY BROTHER IN THE WRECKING CREW 4 LYFE.
BUT I SWEAR I WILL THROW YOUR ASS INTO THE HEART OF THE SUN--

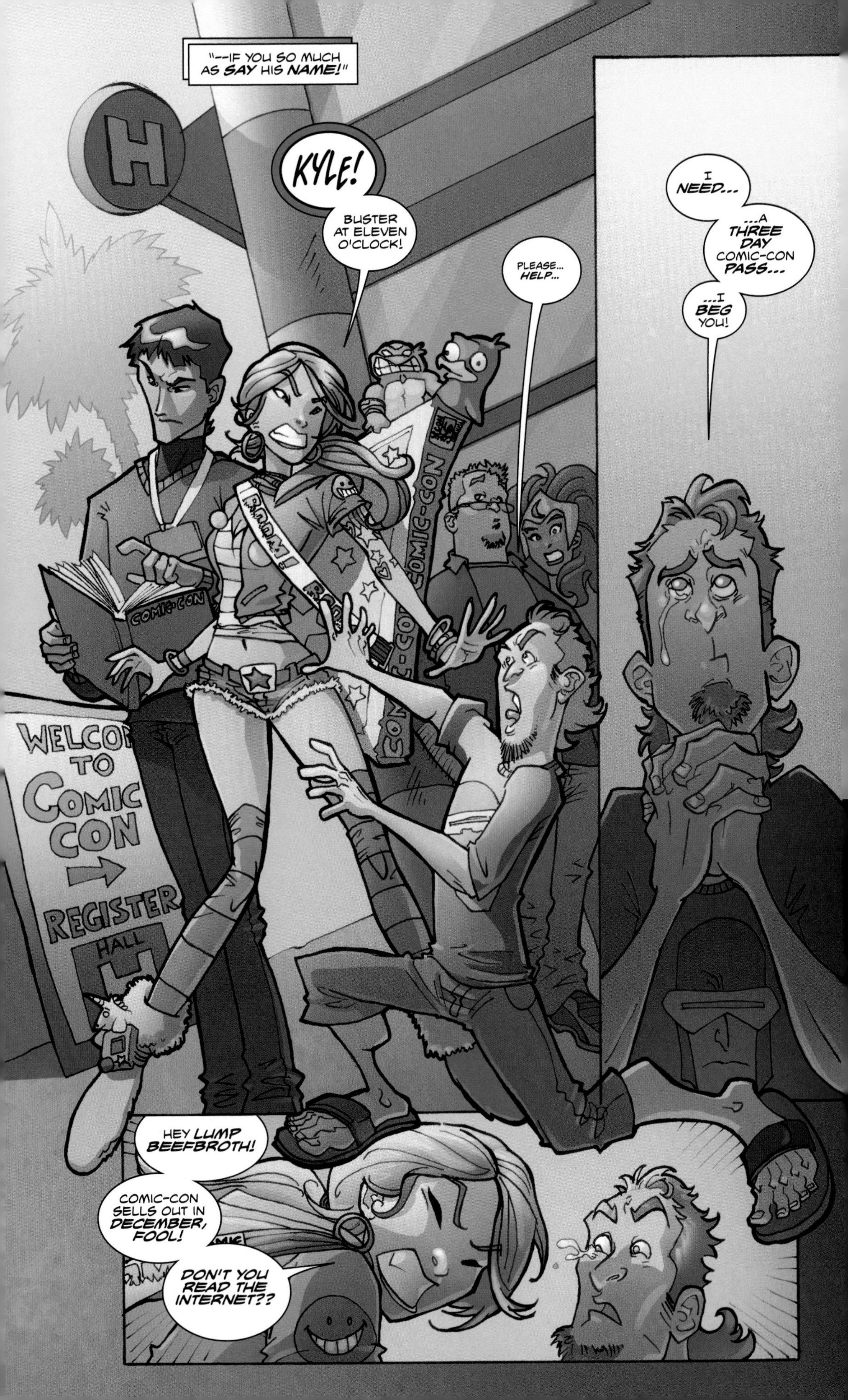
"--IF YOU SO MUCH AS SAY HIS NAME!"
KYLE!
BUSTER AT ELEVEN O'CLOCK!
PLEASE... HELP...
I NEED...
...A THREE DAY COMIC-CON PASS...
...I BEG YOU!
WELCOME TO COMIC CON
REGISTER HALL H
COMIC-CON
HEY LUMP BEEFBROTH!
COMIC-CON SELLS OUT IN DECEMBER, FOOL!
DON'T YOU READ THE INTERNET??

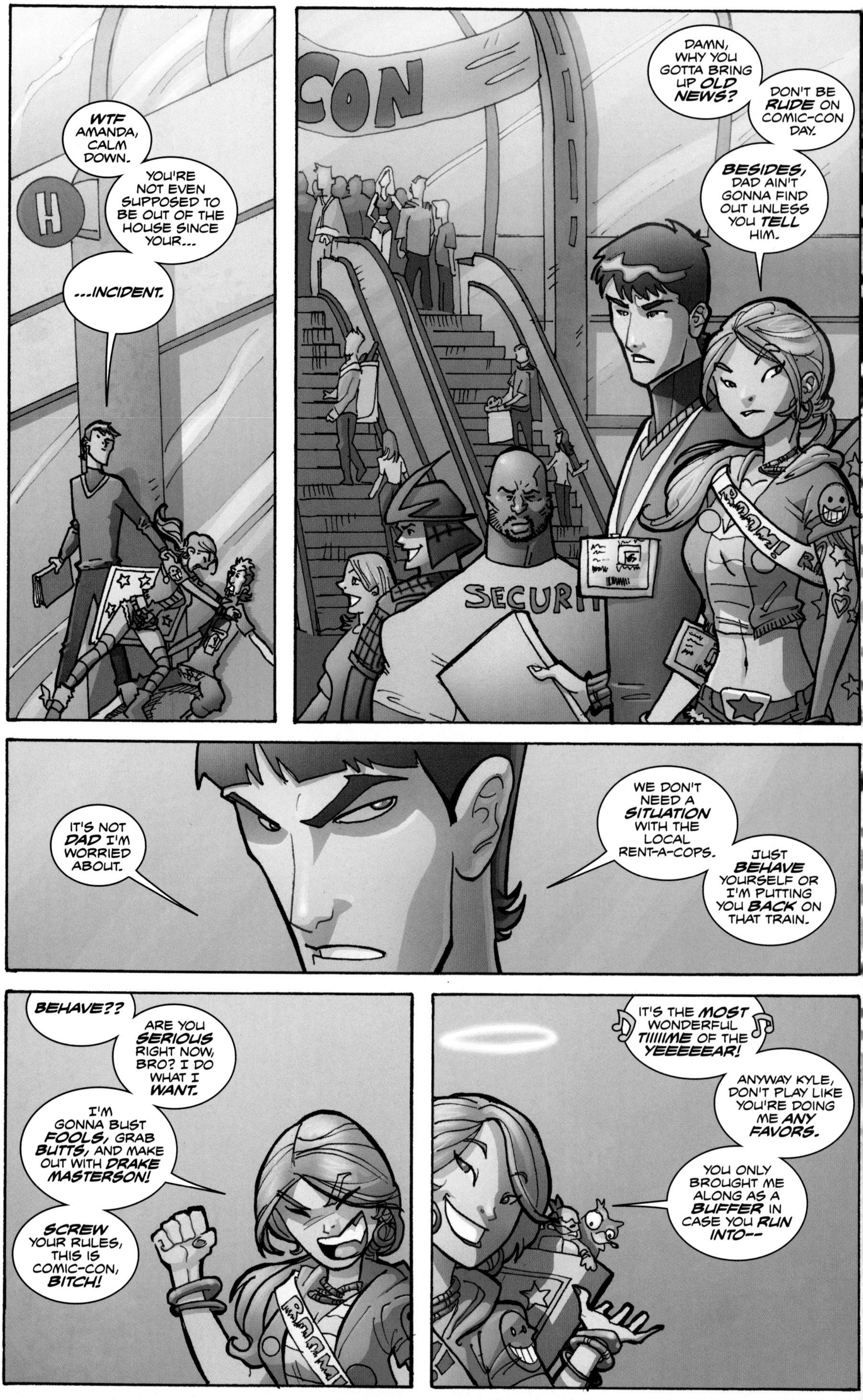
WTF AMANDA, CALM DOWN.
YOU'RE NOT EVEN SUPPOSED TO BE OUT OF THE HOUSE SINCE YOUR...
...INCIDENT.
CON
DAMN, WHY YOU GOTTA BRING UP OLD NEWS?
DON'T BE RUDE ON COMIC-CON DAY.
BESIDES, DAD AIN'T GONNA FIND OUT UNLESS YOU TELL HIM.
SECURIT
IT'S NOT DAD I'M WORRIED ABOUT.
WE DON'T NEED A SITUATION WITH THE LOCAL RENT-A-COPS.
JUST BEHAVE YOURSELF OR I'M PUTTING YOU BACK ON THAT TRAIN.
BEHAVE??
ARE YOU SERIOUS RIGHT NOW, BRO? I DO WHAT I WANT.
I'M GONNA BUST FOOLS, GRAB BUTTS, AND MAKE OUT WITH DRAKE MASTERSON!
SCREW YOUR RULES, THIS IS COMIC-CON, BITCH!
IT'S THE MOST WONDERFUL TIIIIIME OF THE YEEEEEAR!
ANYWAY KYLE, DON'T PLAY LIKE YOU'RE DOING ME ANY FAVORS.
YOU ONLY BROUGHT ME ALONG AS A BUFFER IN CASE YOU RUN INTO--

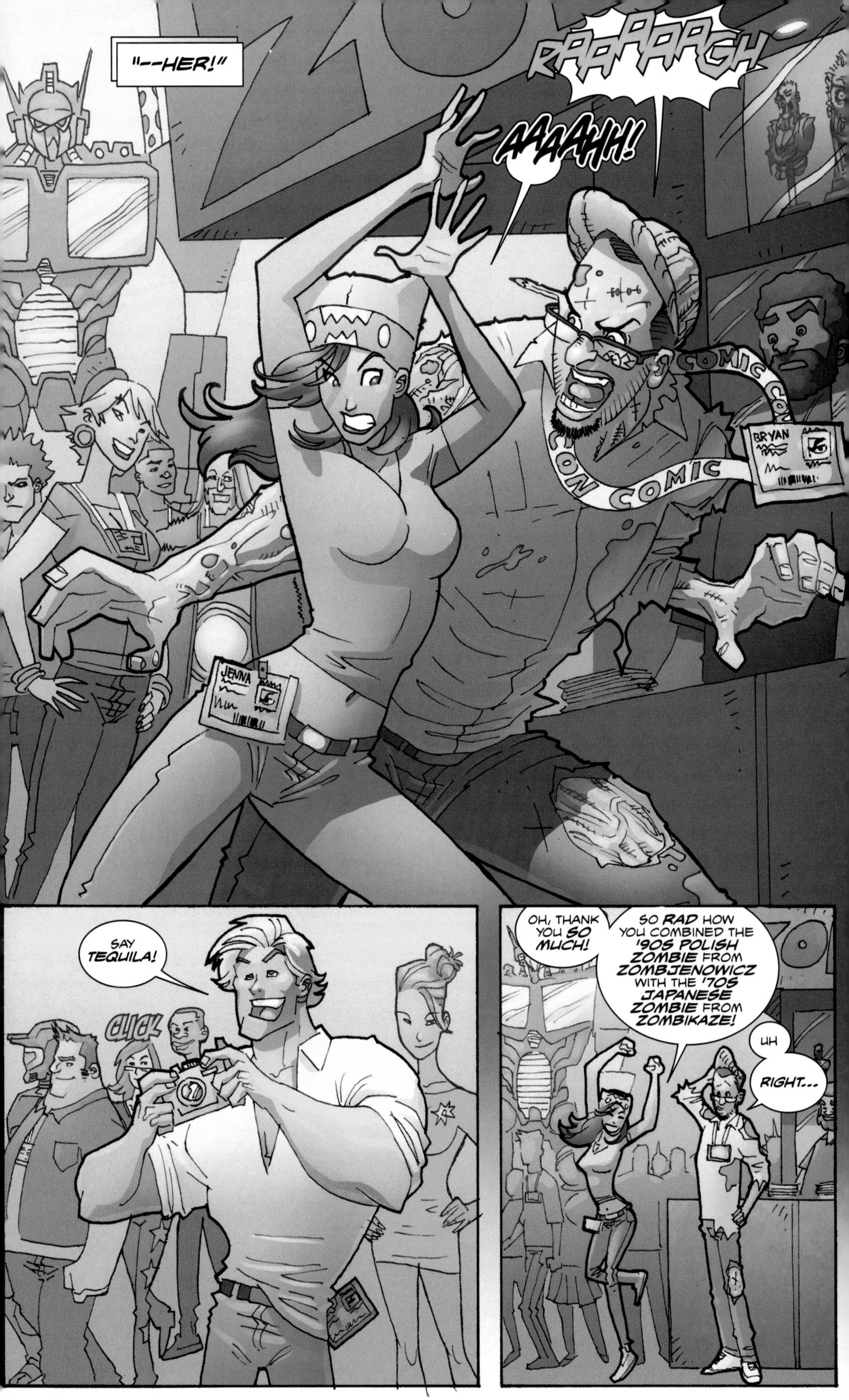
"--HER!"
RAAAAARGH
AAAAHH!
JENNA
BRYAN
COMIC CON
SAY TEQUILA!
CLICK
OH, THANK YOU SO MUCH!
SO RAD HOW YOU COMBINED THE '90S POLISH ZOMBIE FROM ZOMBJENOWICZ WITH THE '70S JAPANESE ZOMBIE FROM ZOMBIKAZE!
UH
RIGHT...

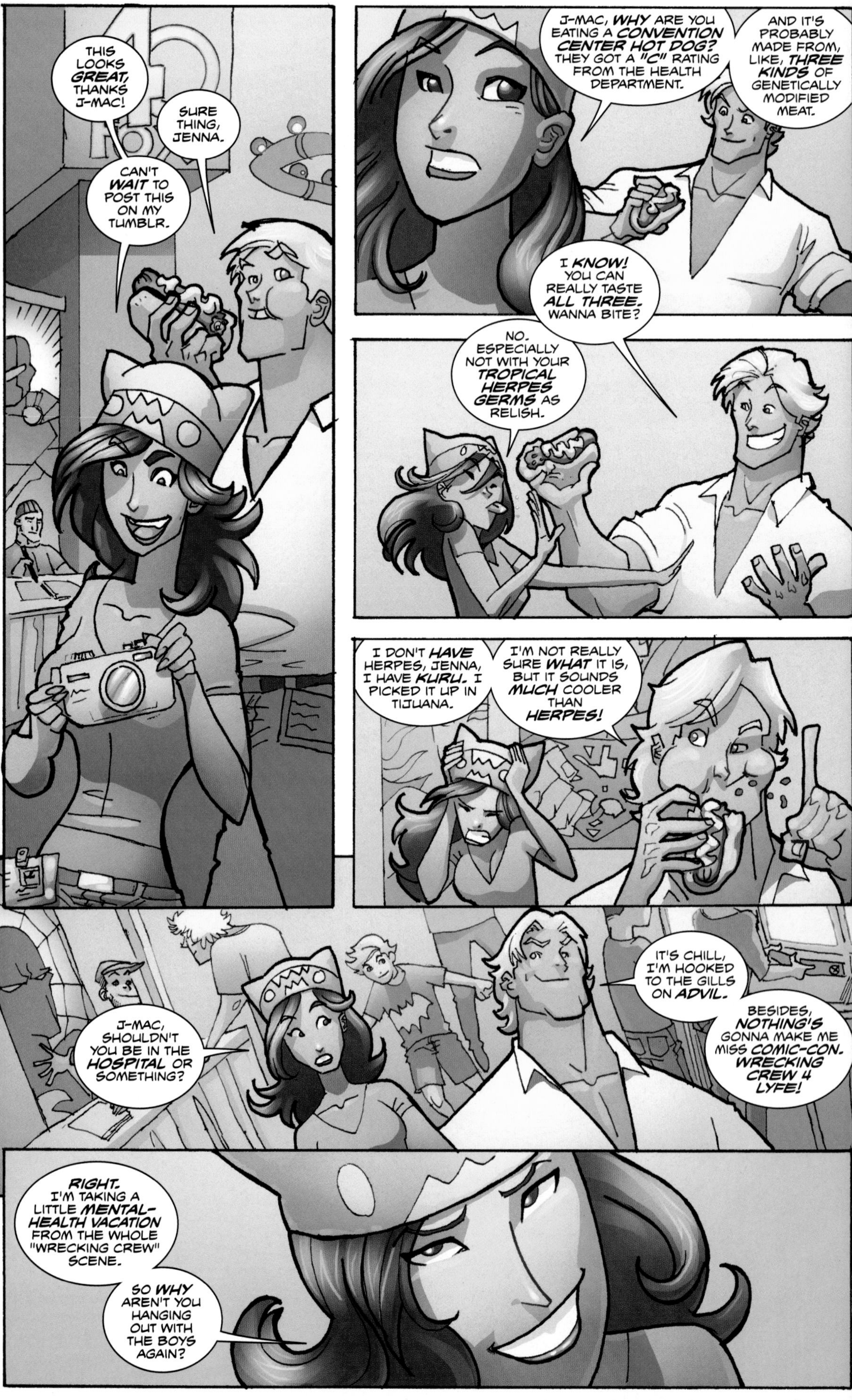
THIS LOOKS GREAT, THANKS J-MAC!
SURE THING, JENNA.
CAN'T WAIT TO POST THIS ON MY TUMBLR.
J-MAC, WHY ARE YOU EATING A CONVENTION CENTER HOT DOG? THEY GOT A "C" RATING FROM THE HEALTH DEPARTMENT.
AND IT'S PROBABLY MADE FROM, LIKE, THREE KINDS OF GENETICALLY MODIFIED MEAT.
I KNOW! YOU CAN REALLY TASTE ALL THREE. WANNA BITE?
NO. ESPECIALLY NOT WITH YOUR TROPICAL HERPES GERMS AS RELISH.
I DON'T HAVE HERPES, JENNA, I HAVE KURU. I PICKED IT UP IN TIJUANA.
I'M NOT REALLY SURE WHAT IT IS, BUT IT SOUNDS MUCH COOLER THAN HERPES!
J-MAC, SHOULDN'T YOU BE IN THE HOSPITAL OR SOMETHING?
IT'S CHILL, I'M HOOKED TO THE GILLS ON ADVIL.
BESIDES, NOTHING'S GONNA MAKE ME MISS COMIC-CON. WRECKING CREW 4 LYFE!
RIGHT. I'M TAKING A LITTLE MENTAL-HEALTH VACATION FROM THE WHOLE "WRECKING CREW" SCENE.
SO WHY AREN'T YOU HANGING OUT WITH THE BOYS AGAIN?

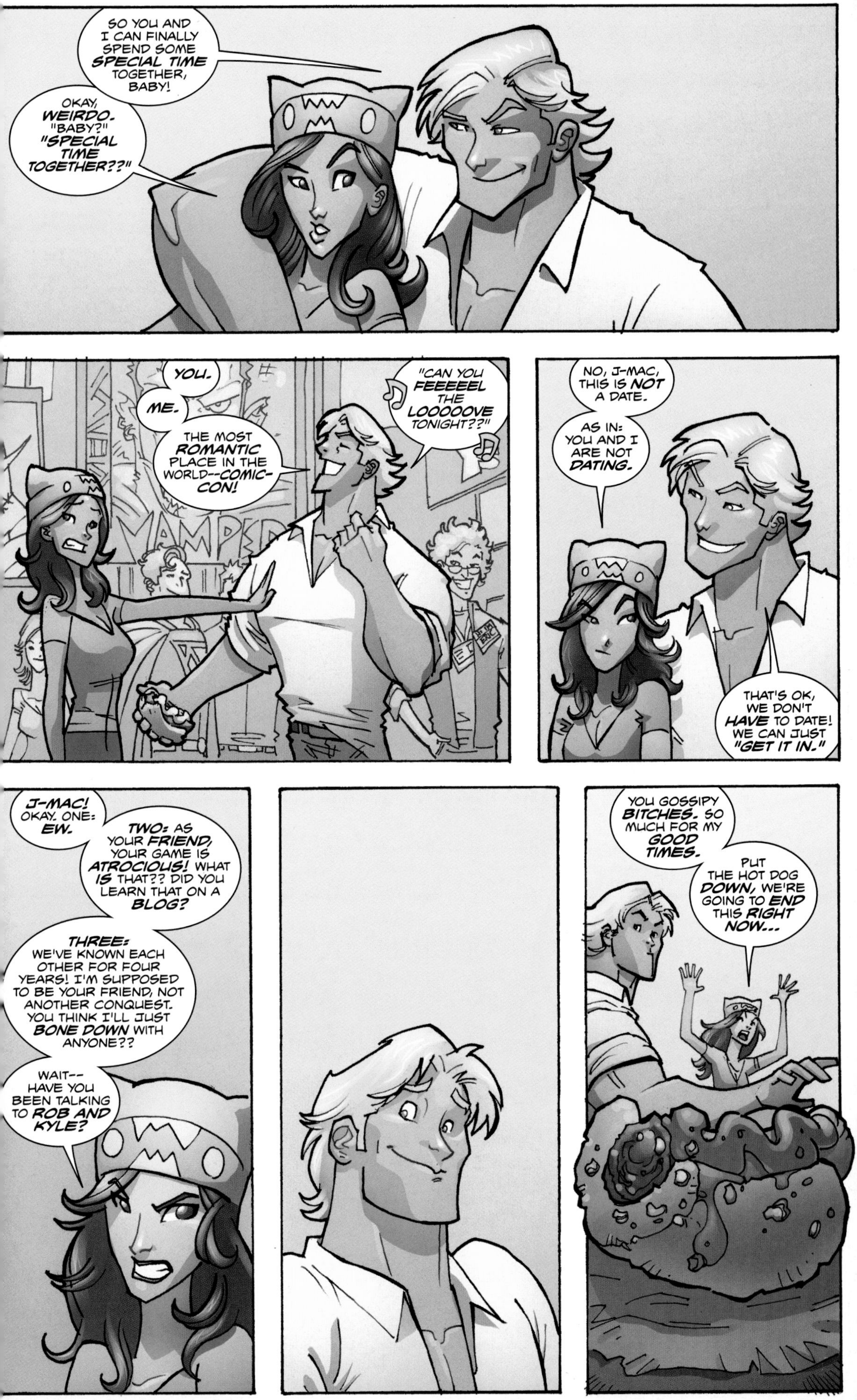
SO YOU AND I CAN FINALLY SPEND SOME SPECIAL TIME TOGETHER, BABY!
OKAY, WEIRDO. "BABY?" "SPECIAL TIME TOGETHER??"
YOU.
ME.
THE MOST ROMANTIC PLACE IN THE WORLD--COMIC-CON!
"CAN YOU FEEEEEL THE LOOOOOVE TONIGHT??"
NO, J-MAC, THIS IS NOT A DATE.
AS IN: YOU AND I ARE NOT DATING.
THAT'S OK, WE DON'T HAVE TO DATE! WE CAN JUST "GET IT IN."
J-MAC! OKAY. ONE: EW.
TWO: AS YOUR FRIEND, YOUR GAME IS ATROCIOUS! WHAT IS THAT?? DID YOU LEARN THAT ON A BLOG?
THREE: WE'VE KNOWN EACH OTHER FOR FOUR YEARS! I'M SUPPOSED TO BE YOUR FRIEND, NOT ANOTHER CONQUEST. YOU THINK I'LL JUST BONE DOWN WITH ANYONE??
WAIT-- HAVE YOU BEEN TALKING TO ROB AND KYLE?
YOU GOSSIPY BITCHES. SO MUCH FOR MY GOOD TIMES.
PUT THE HOT DOG DOWN, WE'RE GOING TO END THIS RIGHT NOW...

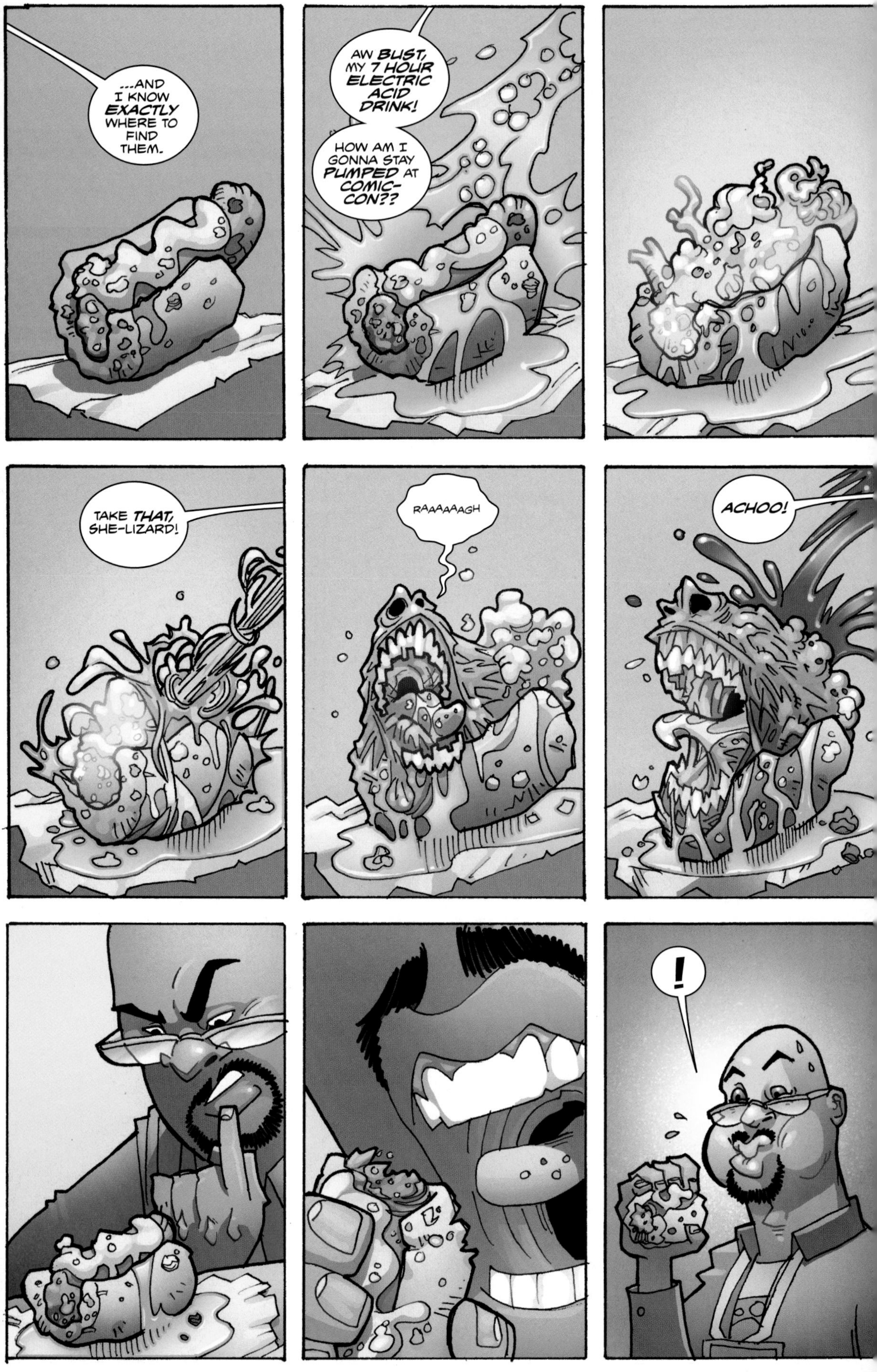
...AND I KNOW EXACTLY WHERE TO FIND THEM.
AW BUST, MY 7 HOUR ELECTRIC ACID DRINK!
HOW AM I GONNA STAY PUMPED AT COMIC-CON??
TAKE THAT, SHE-LIZARD!
RAAAAAAGH
ACHOO!
!

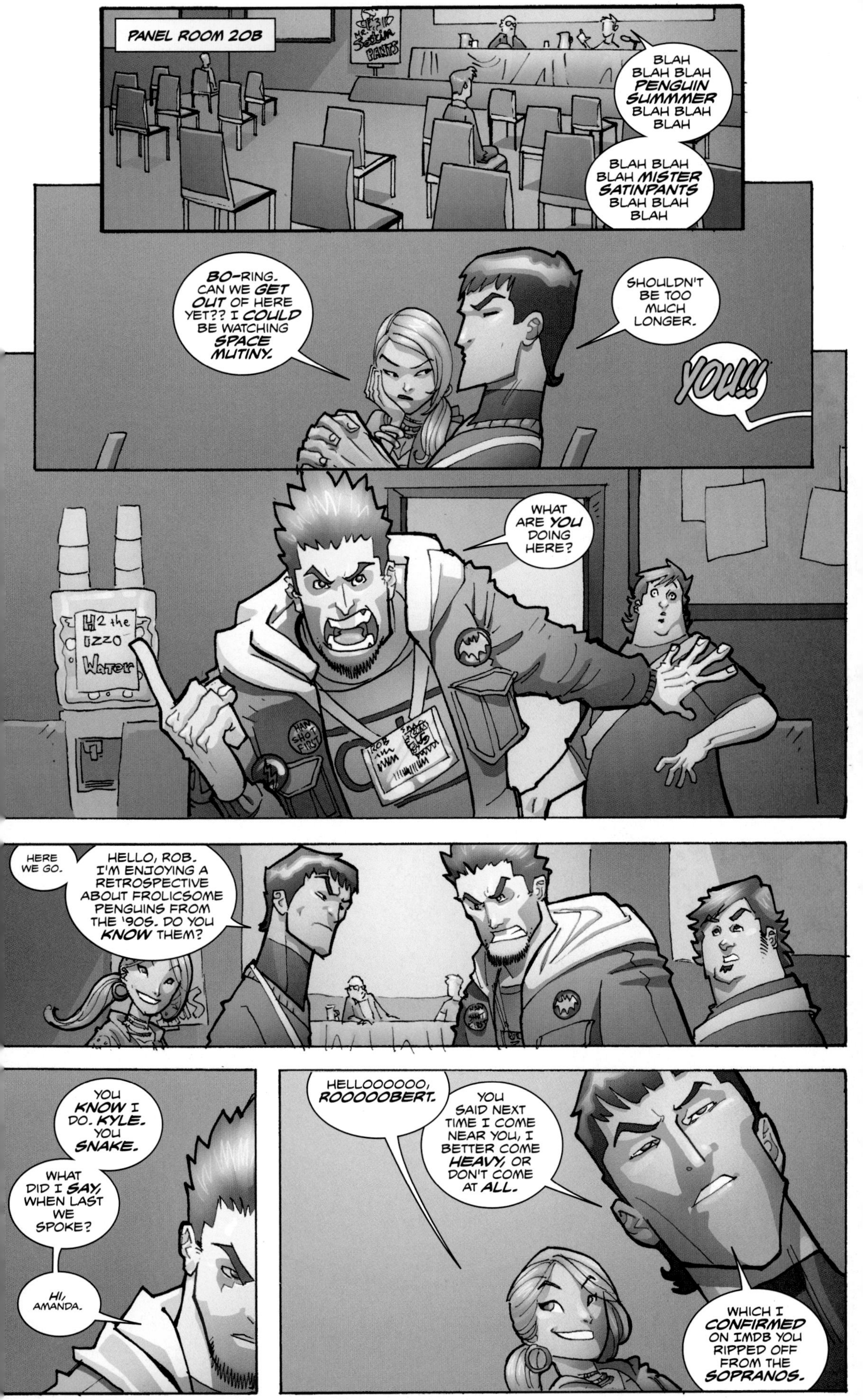
PANEL ROOM 208
MR. SATIN PANTS
BLAH BLAH BLAH PENGUIN SUMMMER BLAH BLAH BLAH
BLAH BLAH BLAH MISTER SATINPANTS BLAH BLAH BLAH
BO-RING. CAN WE GET OUT OF HERE YET?? I COULD BE WATCHING SPACE MUTINY.
SHOULDN'T BE TOO MUCH LONGER.
YOU!!
WHAT ARE YOU DOING HERE?
H2 the IZZO Water
HAN SHOT FIRST
ROB
HERE WE GO.
HELLO, ROB. I'M ENJOYING A RETROSPECTIVE ABOUT FROLICSOME PENGUINS FROM THE '90S. DO YOU KNOW THEM?
YOU KNOW I DO. KYLE. YOU SNAKE.
WHAT DID I SAY, WHEN LAST WE SPOKE?
HI, AMANDA.
HELLOOOOOO, ROOOOOBERT.
YOU SAID NEXT TIME I COME NEAR YOU, I BETTER COME HEAVY, OR DON'T COME AT ALL.
WHICH I CONFIRMED ON IMDB YOU RIPPED OFF FROM THE SOPRANOS.

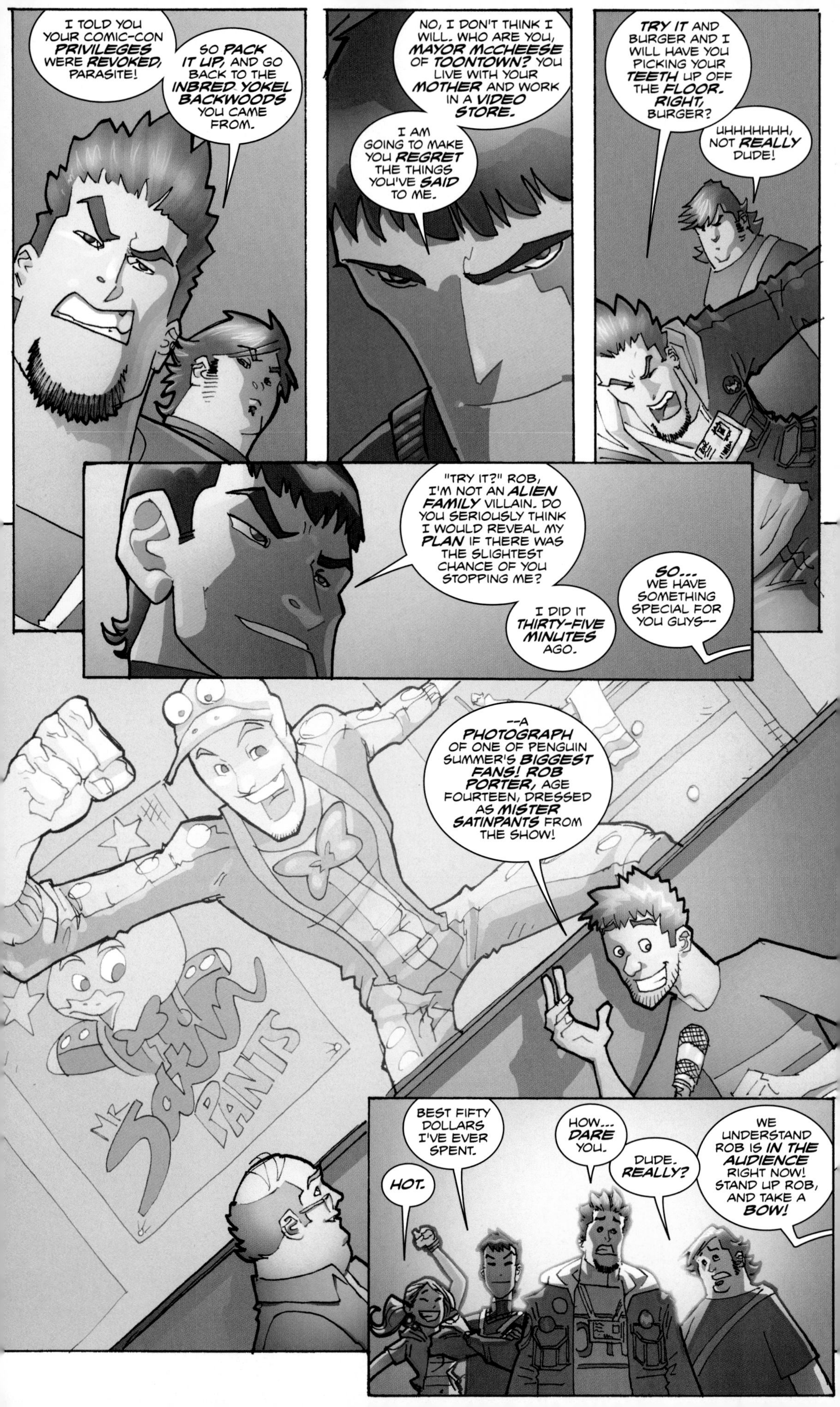
I TOLD YOU YOUR COMIC-CON PRIVILEGES WERE REVOKED, PARASITE!
SO PACK IT UP, AND GO BACK TO THE INBRED YOKEL BACKWOODS YOU CAME FROM.
NO, I DON'T THINK I WILL. WHO ARE YOU, MAYOR McCHEESE OF TOONTOWN? YOU LIVE WITH YOUR MOTHER AND WORK IN A VIDEO STORE.
I AM GOING TO MAKE YOU REGRET THE THINGS YOU'VE SAID TO ME.
TRY IT AND BURGER AND I WILL HAVE YOU PICKING YOUR TEETH UP OFF THE FLOOR. RIGHT, BURGER?
UHHHHHHH, NOT REALLY DUDE!
"TRY IT?" ROB, I'M NOT AN ALIEN FAMILY VILLAIN. DO YOU SERIOUSLY THINK I WOULD REVEAL MY PLAN IF THERE WAS THE SLIGHTEST CHANCE OF YOU STOPPING ME?
I DID IT THIRTY-FIVE MINUTES AGO.
SO... WE HAVE SOMETHING SPECIAL FOR YOU GUYS--
--A PHOTOGRAPH OF ONE OF PENGUIN SUMMER'S BIGGEST FANS! ROB PORTER, AGE FOURTEEN, DRESSED AS MISTER SATINPANTS FROM THE SHOW!
MR. SATIN PANTS
BEST FIFTY DOLLARS I'VE EVER SPENT.
HOT.
HOW... DARE YOU.
DUDE. REALLY?
WE UNDERSTAND ROB IS IN THE AUDIENCE RIGHT NOW! STAND UP ROB, AND TAKE A BOW!

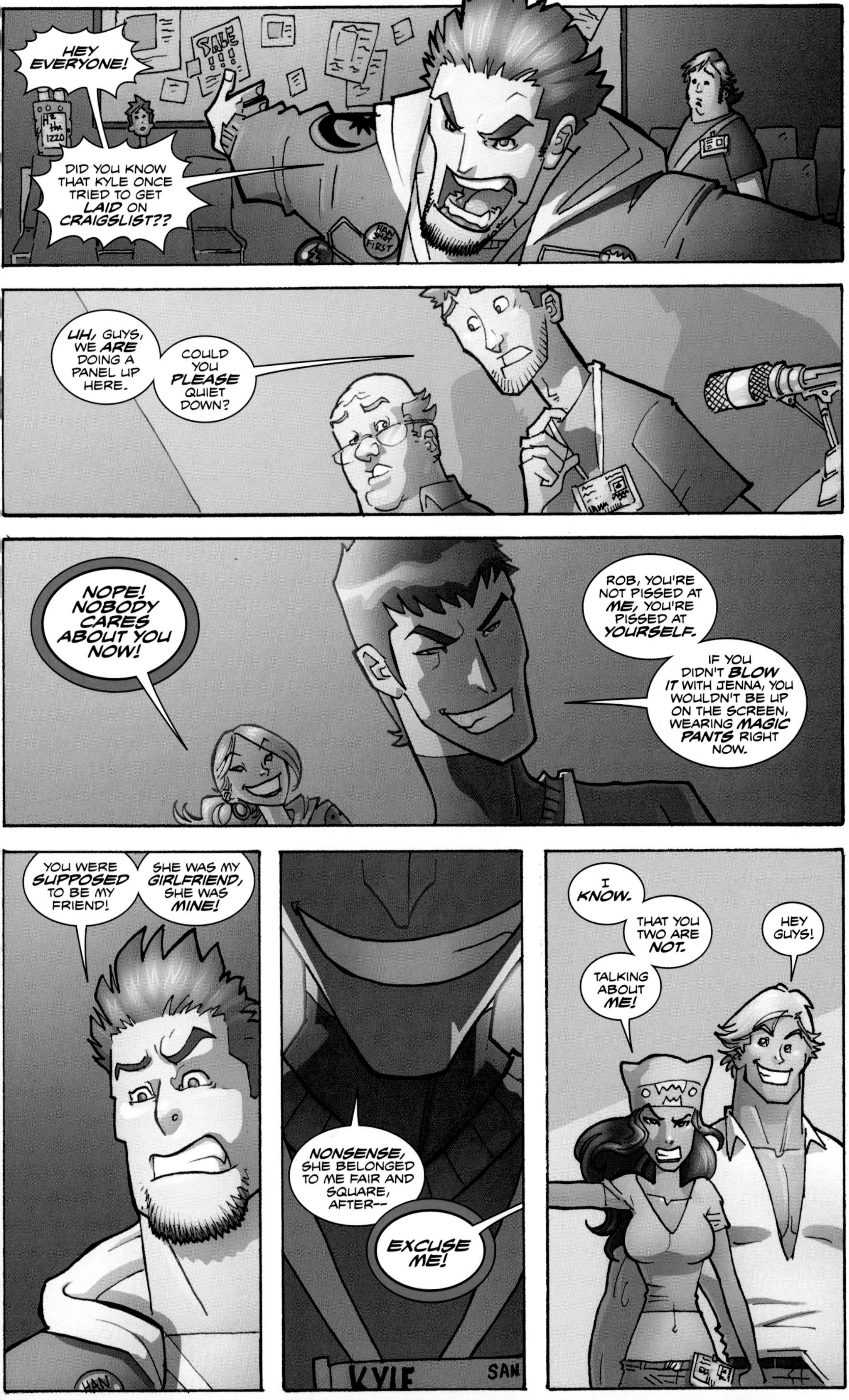
HEY EVERYONE!
DID YOU KNOW THAT KYLE ONCE TRIED TO GET LAID ON CRAIGSLIST??
SALE
HAN SHOT FIRST
UH, GUYS, WE ARE DOING A PANEL UP HERE.
COULD YOU PLEASE QUIET DOWN?
NOPE! NOBODY CARES ABOUT YOU NOW!
ROB, YOU'RE NOT PISSED AT ME, YOU'RE PISSED AT YOURSELF.
IF YOU DIDN'T BLOW IT WITH JENNA, YOU WOULDN'T BE UP ON THE SCREEN, WEARING MAGIC PANTS RIGHT NOW.
YOU WERE SUPPOSED TO BE MY FRIEND!
SHE WAS MY GIRLFRIEND, SHE WAS MINE!
NONSENSE, SHE BELONGED TO ME FAIR AND SQUARE, AFTER--
EXCUSE ME!
KYLE
SAN
I KNOW.
THAT YOU TWO ARE NOT.
TALKING ABOUT ME!
HEY GUYS!

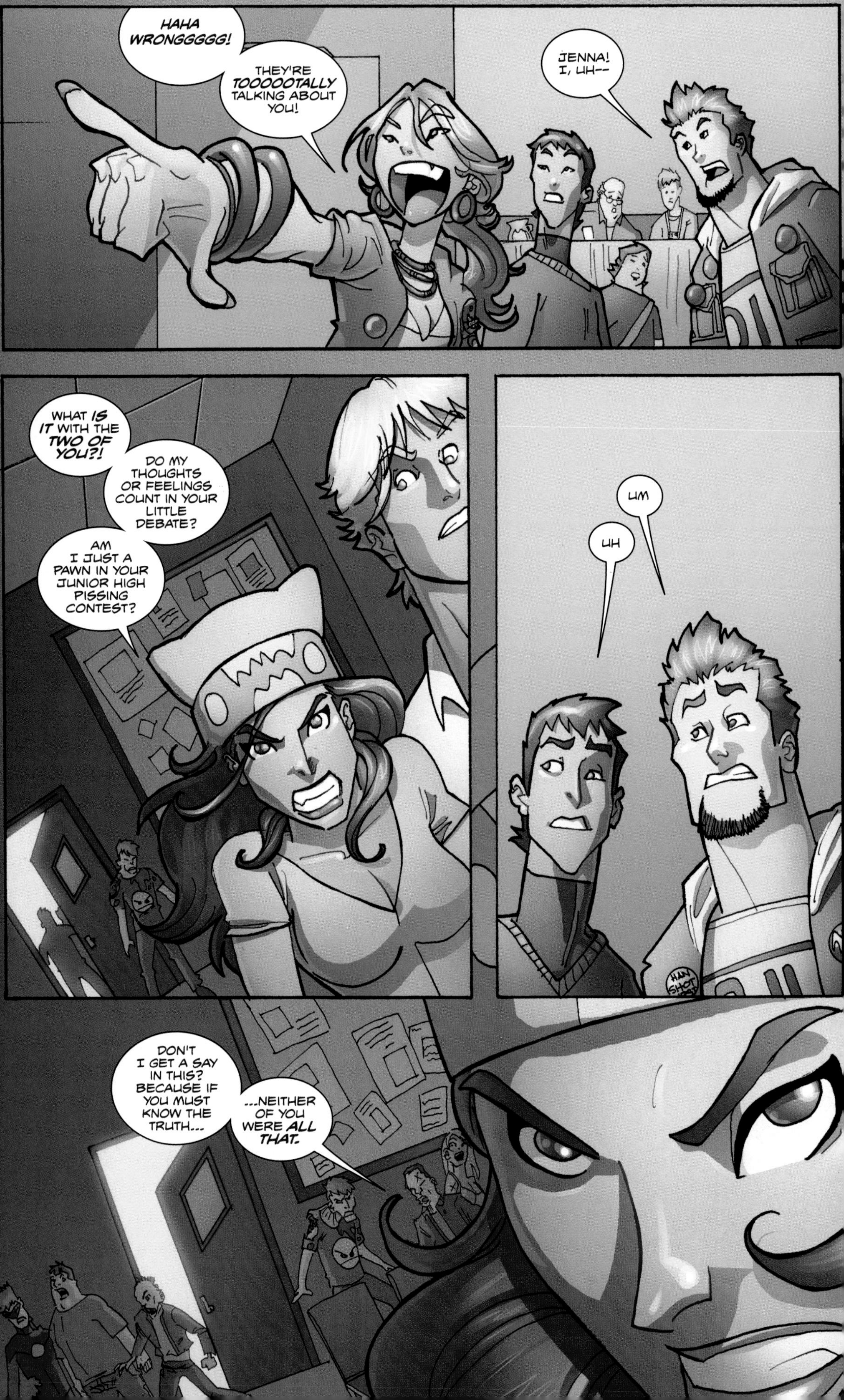
HAHA WRONGGGGG!
THEY'RE TOOOOOTALLY TALKING ABOUT YOU!
JENNA! I, UH--
WHAT IS IT WITH THE TWO OF YOU?!
DO MY THOUGHTS OR FEELINGS COUNT IN YOUR LITTLE DEBATE?
AM I JUST A PAWN IN YOUR JUNIOR HIGH PISSING CONTEST?
UM
UH
DON'T I GET A SAY IN THIS? BECAUSE IF YOU MUST KNOW THE TRUTH...
...NEITHER OF YOU WERE ALL THAT.

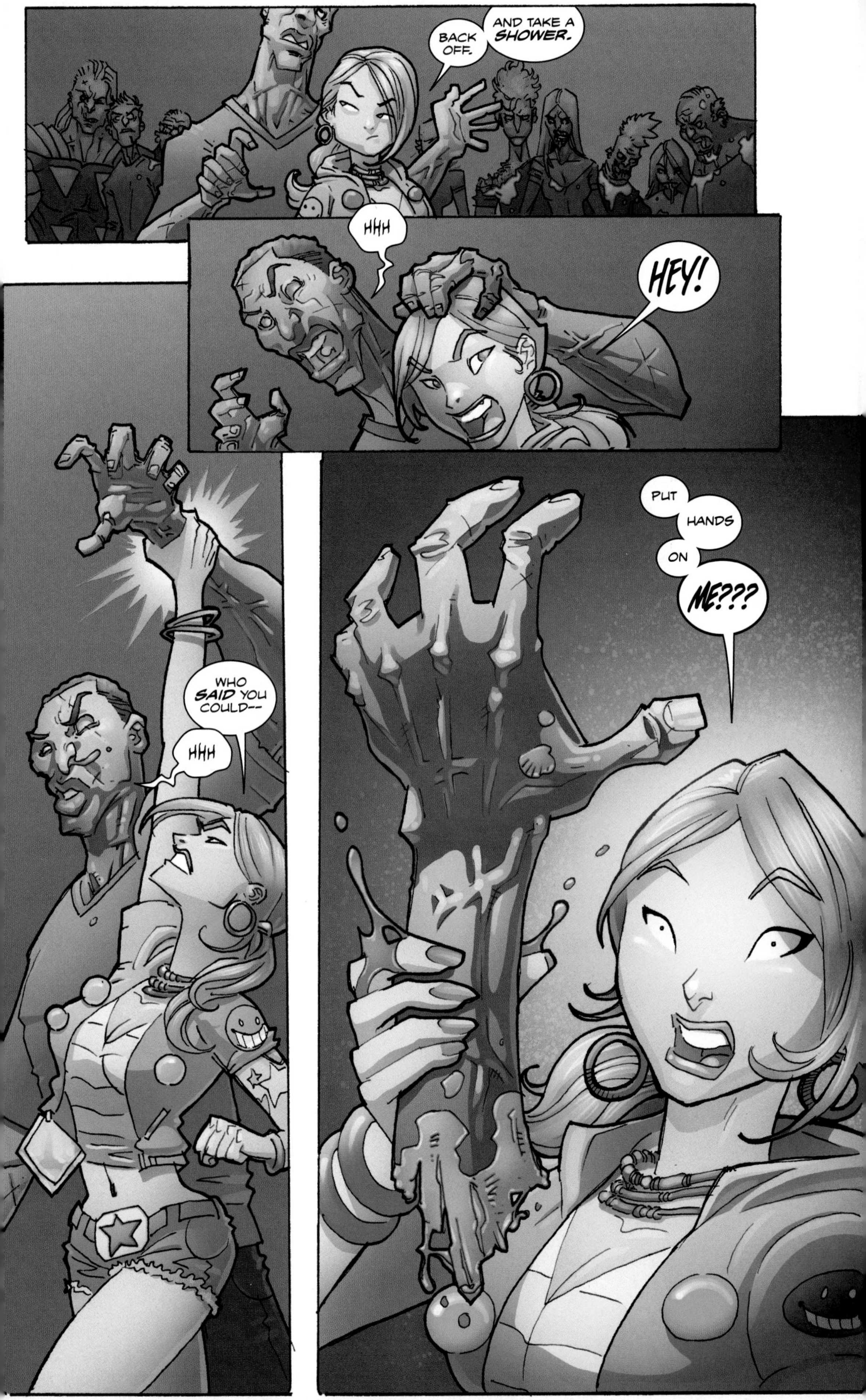
BACK OFF.
AND TAKE A SHOWER.
HHH
HEY!
WHO SAID YOU COULD--
HHH
PUT HANDS ON ME???

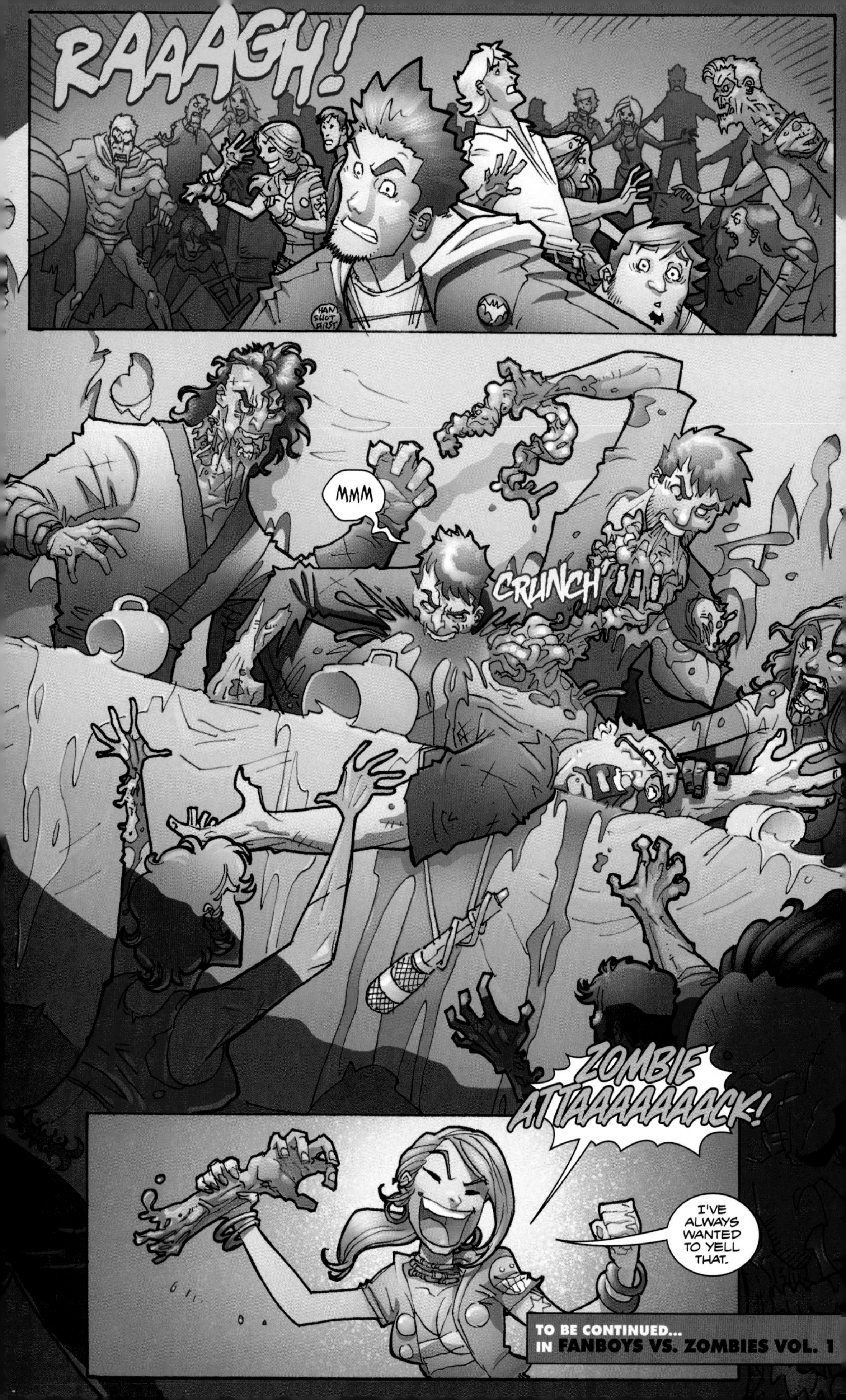
RAAAGH!
HAN SHOT FIRST
MMM
CRUNCH
ZOMBIE ATTAAAAAAACK!
I'VE ALWAYS WANTED TO YELL THAT.
TO BE CONTINUED... IN FANBOYS VS. ZOMBIES VOL. 1

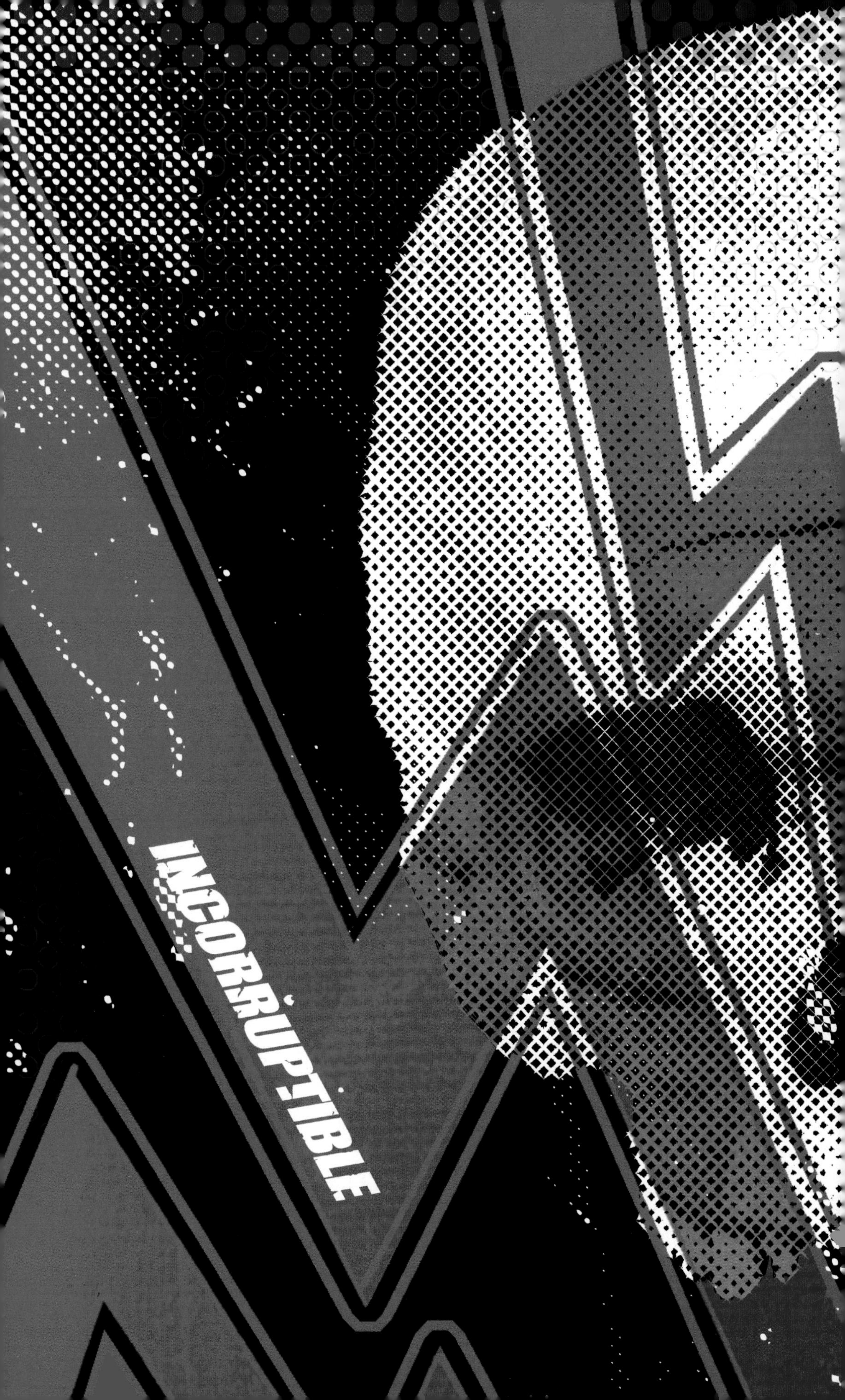
INCORRUPTIBLE

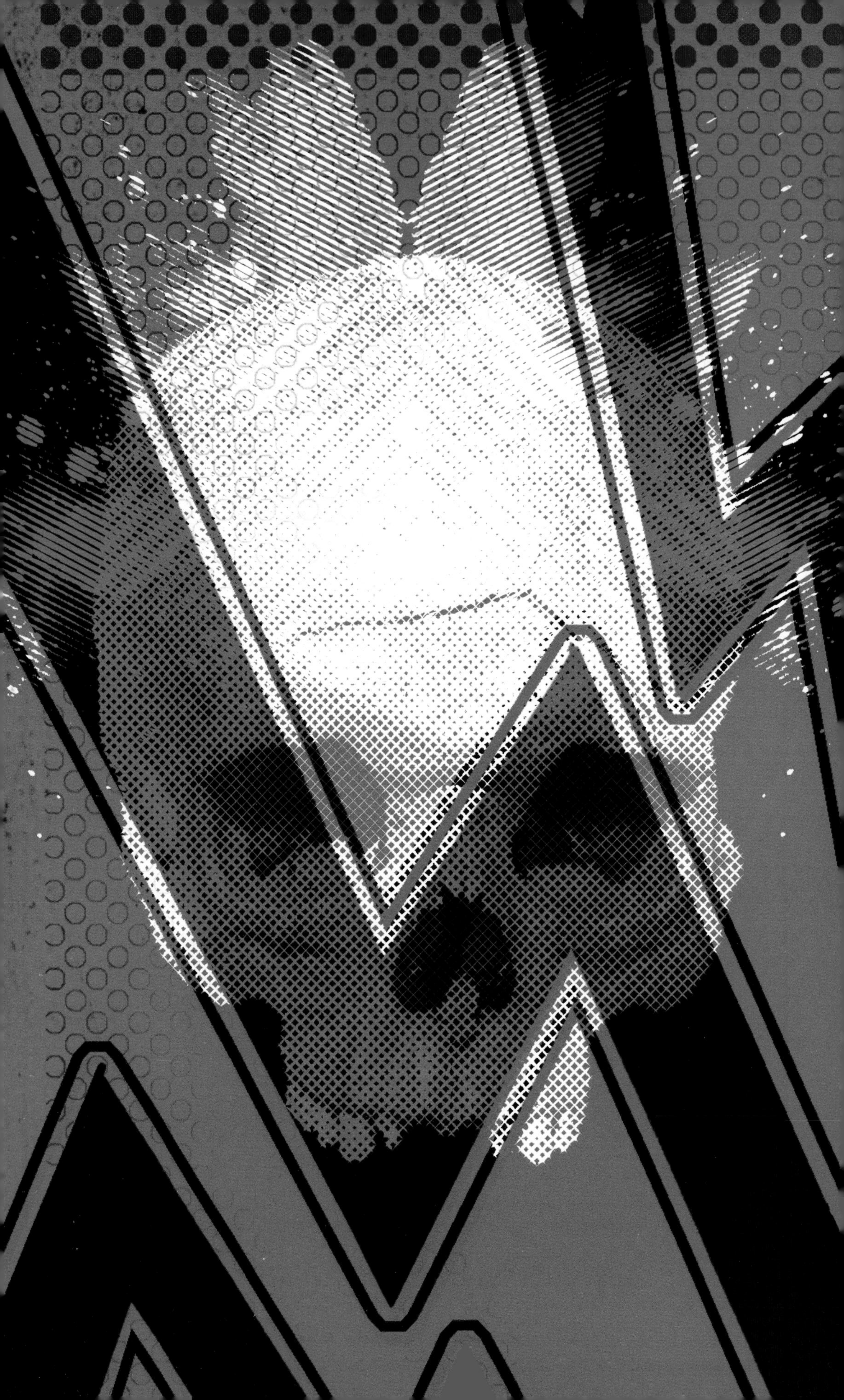

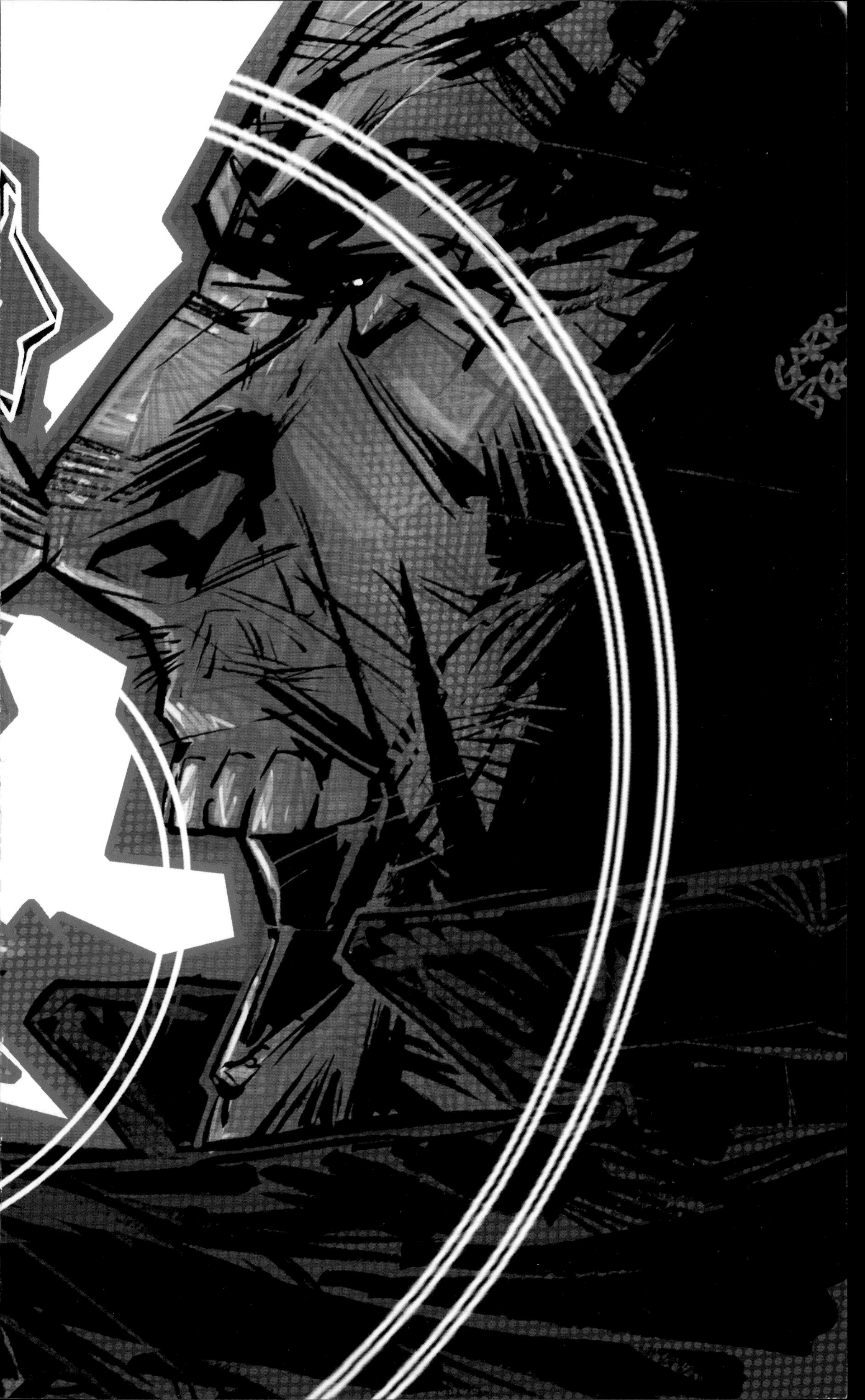

"Mark Waid is a master storyteller and this book serves as his testament." – Player Affinity

THE EXPLOSIVE FINALE TO MARK WAID'S SUPERVILLAIN REDEMPTION TALE!

Max Damage, formerly the world's most notorious super-powered criminal, now stands as a last hope against the world's savior turned ruthless villain — the Plutonian.

Max Damage sits at the edge of the end of the world. Coalville is in chaos, transformed into a fiefdom ruled by a supervillain. A desperate plot to stop the Plutonian has failed, resulting in a cloud of deadly radiation spreading slowly across the planet. But although he's lost both friends and allies, Max is not alone...and he has one last trick up his sleeve...

An explosive conclusion to the flip-side of the multiple Eisner & Harvey Award-nominated hit series IRREDEEMABLE, by the author of Eisner Award winner KINGDOM COME and EMPIRE.

STUDIOS

$16.99 US • WWW.BOOM-STUDIOS.COM
ISBN 978-1-60886-085-2

"...a hugely entertaining series, from a writer in full command of his voice and his genre."

— The Onion A.V. Club

"Everything seems to go right with this book: great writing and art come together to form a brilliant read...be sure to get on-board now...5 Stars"

— Major Spoilers

"I love this book...if you haven't been reading...get caught up...4.5/5"

— Comic Vine